GENESIS AND GROWTH OF NEHRUISM

GENESIS AND GROWTH OF NEHRUISM

Volume I

Commitment to Communism

SITA RAM GOEL

VOICE OF INDIA
New Delhi

First published, 1993
First reprint, 2018

ISBN 978-81-85990-11-8

website: www.voiceofin.com

Published by Voice of India, 2/18, Ansari Road, New Delhi – 110 002.
Printed at D.K. Fine Arts Press (Pvt.) Ltd., Delhi – 110 052.

CONTENTS

SECOND PREFACE

This book is a reprint with minor changes, mostly in language, of an old one published from New Delhi in December 1963 under the title *'In Defence of Comrade Krishna Menon'*. That book, in turn, was compilation of a series of my articles which appeared under the same general title in the New Delhi weekly, *Organiser*, from October 1961 to October 1962. The book carried a Foreword and a Preface as well. The Foreword was written by Mr. Philip Spratt.[1] In the Preface I detailed the activities of the Society for Defence of Freedom in Asia (SDFA) which our group had organised in 1952 for informing the people of Asia in general and India in particular about the character of Communism as a far more formidable imperialism than that which the Asian people had fought in the recent past.

The title of the series in the *Organiser* had been suggested by the public opinion prevailing at that time vis-a-vis Pandit Nehru's foreign policy, particularly with regard to Red China. Communist atrocities in Tibet and intrusions into India's own territory had created widespread disillusionment with that policy. But few people were prepared to hold Pandit Nehru responsible for the fiasco. Most people believed that he had been misled by V.K. Krishna Menon, his close confidant for many years and the Minister of Defence in his Cabinet at that time. I did not share this popular belief which, I thought, was prompted by the psychology of finding a scapegoat for the sins of a national hero. It was, however, sponsored and spread by some sycophants of Pandit Nehru who disliked Krishna Menon for one reason or the other. Having studied Pandit Nehru's writings, speeches, and doings over the years, I could see quite clearly that it was his own infatuation for Communism which had made him blind towards communist designs at home and abroad, and at last trapped him in the cul-de-sac from which he was trying to find a way out with the help of the Soviet Union. Krishna Menon had no standing of his own, either in the

---

[1] Philip Spratt was an Englishman who came to India as a top Comintern agent in 1926. He organised the first communist party in this country. Arrested in 1929 by the British Government of India, he became the chief accused in the Meerut Conspiracy Case, and served a term in prison. His ideas underwent a change after reading Mahatma Gandhi, and subsequently he became a great critic of Communism. He married an Indian lady and lived in India till his death. I published his book, *Blowing Up India: Reminiscences of a Comintern Agent*, from Calcutta in 1955. It was a forecast of the tragic events to which Pandit Nehru's policies were leading the country.

Congress Party or in the country at large. He was no more than Pandit Nehru's minion for saying and doing what his master could not or did not want to say or do himself. Justice demanded that the blame for policy blunders be laid where it really belonged. I thought that Krishna Menon deserved a defence against an accusation which had no legs to stand upon.

My defence of Krishna Menon, however, did not go beyond the first article of the series. The rest of it was devoted to the real culprit — Pandit Nehru. I had traced his career as a committed communist ever since he visited the Soviet Union in November 1927. The book which comprised the series was, therefore, subtitled as *A Political Biography of Pandit Nehru.*

The subtitle was apt. But the exercise, as it looks now, was far from complete. I had not realized at that time that the ideological orientation which had vitiated Pandit Nehru's vision vis-a-vis world affairs and the Communist Party of India, had done the same when it came to viewing matters at home — at first when he emerged as a front rank leader of the Freedom Movement against British imperialism, and later on when he functioned as the first prime minister of India for eighteen long years. It was only when I started examining what passes for Secularism in this country that I became aware of the widespread mischief he had fathered in many other fields. I discovered that he was the author or patron of all anti-national attitudes, elements, and forces with which we stand faced at present.

In a way, it was well that I did not undertake a comprehensive study of Pandit Nehru at that time. I would have suffered from a serious disadvantage. The source material which has become available in recent years would have remained untapped by me, particularly the *Selected Works of Jawaharlal Nehru* which started coming out in 1970.[2] Even in the matter of his being a committed

[2] The first 15 volumes of *Selected Works of Jawaharlal Nehru* were published by Orient Longman Limited, from 1970 to 1982. They were not named as comprising the First Series but may be regarded as such in view of next set of volumes being named as the Second Series. Starting in 1984, the Oxford University Press has published 16 volumes so far (upto Volume 16, Part I, Volume 14 having two Parts). Many more volumes may be expected because the latest volume takes us only upto September 1950 when Pandit Nehru was still in the midst of a struggle for supremacy which he attained in the Congress Party and the country at large only after the death of Sardar Patel in December 1950. But we need not wait for further volumes because the main ideas which he implemented when he was secure in power had become formed in his mind long before 1950. Professor Sarvepalli Gopal, the General Editor of both the Series and a dedicated Nehruvian, can be depended upon to highlight those ideas.

communist I have come across plenty of new evidence, particularly his letters to Krishna Menon, Lady Mountbatten, Padmja Naidu, and sundry other communists and fellow-travellers.

Mr. Spratt had observed that after reading my series he had realised that Pandit Nehru was a much more faithful communist than he (Spratt) had thought. Having waded through the *Selected Works of Jawaharlal Nehru*, I can say with full sense of responsibility that he was far more committed a communist than Mr. Spratt had suspected.

I can now see quite clearly that Pandit Nehru had learnt studiously to look through communist glasses on every problem that arose in pre- and post-independence India. The solutions he sought for various problems were also suggested by what he eulogised as the Great Soviet Experiment. He did not prevail every time because there were other forces in the field. But he tried his utmost and to the end of his days to steer the Freedom Movement, the Indian National Congress, and the country at large in a decisively communist direction. Had not Mao Tse-tung spoiled his game at the very time when he was at the peak of his power and prestige, at home and abroad, he would have handed over the country to the communist mafia.

It was inevitable that, in the process of pressing forward communist patterns of thought and action, he became more and more alienated from India's indigenous society and culture. At the same time, he became more and more friendly towards every factor and force which was out to disintegrate this country, uproot its people, and destroy its cultural heritage. He ended by becoming a combined embodiment of all the imperialist ideologies that have flooded this country in the wake of foreign invasions or interventions — Islam, Christianity, White Man's Burden, and Communism. The results are there for all of us to see.

It is a truism that every Indian who converts to Christianity or Islam becomes hostile to India's indegenous society and culture. Swami Vivekananda had observed long ago that every member of India's ancient society who converts to Christianity or Islam is not only one member less but one enemy more. He would have said the same, had he seen the latter-day converts to Communism. The hostility which a communist harbours towards everything authentically Indian has to be seen in order to be believed.

The fact is that Islam and Christianity and Communism are basically projections of the same poison in the human psyche which produces permanent enmity between a people's past and its present, between one section of that people and another, and between different peoples of the world. It is only the verbiage which they use for presenting their dogmas which sounds different.[3] Christianity and Islam have snapped the ties which linked many people in Asia, Africa, Europe, and the Americas to their cultural past. They have created civil strife in every society they have visited. And they have led many imperialist onslaughts from the lands of the believers to those of the unbelievers. Communism did the same wherever it came to prevail. India under Pandit Nehru and his dynasty could not be an exception.

II

It was my intention to summarise, in this Second Preface, Pandit Nehru's pronouncements on many subjects other than Communism and communist causes. There was not a subject under the sun on which he did not write or speak in *ex cathedra* tones. In fact, he claimed a monopoly of wisdom in all fields, and quite often laid down the line to be followed by everyone, everywhere. He was intolerant of all dissent, and dismissed those who had the courage to differ with him as living in the past or serving vested interests.

But as I survey the notes which I have taken from his voluminous verbiage, I feel that if I were to do justice to all the themes under his purview this Second Preface will grow into another volume as big as the one under reprint. So I have decided to present the know-all Pandit Nehru in another volume which I hope to complete before long. For the present, I am confining my comments to the great damage he did to democracy and the freedom of debate in India.

It was natural for him as a communist to frown upon every attempt at having a close look at Communism, communist countries, communist parties, and communist causes. But as Communism in India was in active alliance with all anti-national forces, his frown extended to many other subjects, with the result that those subjects also became closed to public debate. One could discuss those subjects only if one was prepared to become a pariah in the

[3] I have dealt in some detail with this fundamental similarity of Christianity, Islam, and Communism in my *Perversion of India's Political Parlance*, Voice of India, 1984.

eyes of the dominant intelligentsia which he had spawned, and which he patronized. One invited the attention of the Intelligence Bureau as well if one persisted in defying the ban. India, like many communist countries, came to have a thought-police.

Pandit Nehru failed to hand over the Indian establishment to the communist mafia because of the set-back he suffered at the hands of Red China. That operation was completed by his daughter, Mrs. Indira Gandhi, to a very large extent. She had no ideology except unbridled power for herself and her family. So she was prone to use and be used by those who could support her single-minded pursuit. By the time she split the Congress Party in 1969, the communist mafia had perfected the Kumaramangalam plan of supporting her as the rope supports the hanged man. And she walked into the trap, prompted by the apparatus she had inherited from her father.

She surrounded herself with Moscow's men and women, recruited directly from the Communist Party of India and its fronts. The "progressive" flock from all over the country rushed to her "rescue" in her confrontation with patriots of long standing in her own party. They helped her to the hilt in retaining power. But, in exchange, they made her push her father's policies farther afield, and monopolized all positions of power and prestige in the truncated Congress Party, in the Government at the Centre as well as in the States, in the media and the academia, in the viable voluntary agencies, and in all other strategic institutions. A Jawaharlal Nehru University (JNU) was created and financed on a fabulous scale for collecting communist "professors" from all over the country, and making them pontificate on all subjects with puffed up authority and arrogance.

In the next few years, the "progressive" flock multiplied fast and several fold. All sorts of sycophants and time-servers also jumped on the bandwagon. Moscow's hatchet men, notably P.N. Haksar, Mrs. Indira Gandhi's Principal Private Secretary, had a field day. They fixed members of the communist mafia in many political positions that mattered. Next, they raised a chorus for a committed party cadre, a committed parliament, a committed press, a committed judiciary, a committed bureaucracy, a committed police, and a committed armed force. Nehruism had come out in its true colours. The country was soon reduced to a private fief of the Nehru dynasty, to be controlled and manipulated by Moscow.

The Emergency that followed in June 1975 was by no means an ad hoc idea accepted for meeting an abrupt situation. The idea of imposing an authoritarian regime on the country had been maturing for a long time in the minds of the communist mafia that Pandit Nehru had promoted. The situation, too, was being shaped in the same direction by the self-righteousness and consequent high-handedness which accompanied the idea. The seeds sown by Pandit Nehru were bearing fruits. All those who stood up against Mrs. Indira Gandhi's guiles and greed were denounced as agents of the CIA. The "progressive" flock was one again in the forefront of the "fight against forces of fascism". And by the time Mrs. Indira Gandhi realized what was happening, much mischief had been done.

The regimes that followed the Emergency did nothing to free the establishment from the stranglehold of the communist mafia. Members of the mafia have continued to occupy seats in the nation's parliament and state legislatures, and man many other prestigious institutions. It retains control of two strategic states on the borders with Bangladesh. In recent years, it has been leading the fight against what it has named as "Hindu fundamentalism". And its near monopoly in the media and the academia continues to control the ground rules for public discourse and discussion.

Nobody seems to remember that this is the same mafia which had been organized for the first time in Tashkent by M.N. Roy, who had brought to that place in 1919-20 a trainload of arms and ammunitions from Moscow in order to equip the Pathan tribals in the North-West, and let them loose on the Punjab as a preliminary to the rest of the country.

Nobody seems to remember that this is the same mafia which had waged a relentless war on the nation's fight for freedom during the twenties and early thirties, and named the Indian National Congress as a conspiracy of India's capitalists and landlords in league with world imperialism.

Nobody seems to remember that this is the same mafia which had joined hands with British imperialism in 1942, received British patronage as well as largesses, and spied on the patriots who were locked in battle with the British police during 1942-45.

Nobody seems to remember that this is the same mafia which had supported the demand for Pakistan from 1942 to 1947, supplied the Muslim League with a formidable array of arguments and statistics for fortifying its case, and advocated the balkanization of India into a score of sovereign states.

Nobody seems to remember that this is the same mafia which had risen in armed rebellion in 1948 against the newly born republic of India, joined hands with the Nizam of Hyderabad and his Razakar hoodlums, and murdered in cold blood many poor and innocent peasants in Telengana from 1948 to 1953 in the name of a proletarian revolution.

Nobody seems to remember that this is the same mafia which had denounced in 1948 Sri Ramakrishna as a homosexual pervert, Swami Vivekananda as a Hindu imperialist, Sri Aurobindo as a dirty war-monger, Rabindranath Tagore as a pimp, and stalwarts of the freedom movement such as Sardar Patel as the progeny of pigs and bastards of Birla and Tata.

Nobody seems to remember that this is the same mafia which had come out openly in support of Red China when that country occupied Tibet in 1950, drove out the Dalai Lama along with thousands of his followers in 1959, and finally invaded India herself in 1962 for inflicting on her a humiliation from which she has yet to recover.

Nobody seems to remember that this is the same mafia which had hailed, all through 1967-69, Mao Tse-tung as its Chairman, let loose a reign of terror and assassinations in West Bengal and elsewhere, and played football with the heads of policemen it had decapitated.

And, what is much worse, nobody seems to care as to how and by whom this communist mafia is being financed and used after the collapse of the Soviet Union, and whether it has been hired by the oil-rich Islamic imperialism for working in collaboration with the fifth-column of Pakistan in this country.

What we are witnessing instead is that the communist mafia has expanded its base, and recruited in its ranks most of those others who swear by Nehruvian Secularism. The disciples of M.N. Roy have always been in the forefront of Hindu-baiting which is all that Secularism has ever meant to them. The Socialists have shed, after the collapse of the Soviet Union, whatever differences they had with the communists on the subject of Stalinism, and have joined the united Secularist front. The followers of Rammanohar Lohia who function from various Janata factions stand blinded by anti-brahmanism, and are hand in glove with the communist mafia which now raises the same casteist slogans. The Sangh *parivar* is finding it difficult to disgorge the heavy doses of Nehruism which it had swallowed under Atal Bihari Vajpayi's stewardship, is praising the communist mafia as misguided patriots, and inviting the mafia's spokesmen to pontificate from its own platforms.

Small wonder that the political establishment in India continues to grind in the old Nehruvian grooves, and functions as if nothing has happened in this country and the world outside in the meanwhile. The whole atmosphere remains filled with the same old Nehruvian slogans, and the same old awe-struck reactions to them.

The Soviet Union, Pandit Nehru's promise of a paradise on earth, is now the haunting memory of a veritable hell in which millions of men, women, and children were terrorized, tortured and driven to death. The Great Socialist Experiment, Pandit Nehru's harbinger of the brightest era in human history, has turned out to be a calculated programme for mass pauperization in the service of a totalitarian state and an insatiable military machine. Lenin and Stalin, Pandit Nehru's heroes par excellence, stand exposed as monstrous criminals who organized mass murders, wide-spread witch-hunts, and cultural genocides.[4] The Communist Party of India, Pandit Nehru's favourite political platform, has been revealed by Soviet archives as a mercenary outfit hired and manipulated by whoever happened to be the master in Moscow. Secularism, Pandit Nehru's formula for national integration, has landed us with an Islamic revival which speaks the language of pre-Partition days, and threatens to tear apart the truncated India that has survived the Partition. Kashmir, Pandit Nehru's model of Secularism on the march, has exploded in our face, with almost every Kashmiri Muslim joining the *jihād* against Indian *kāfirs*, and almost every Kashmiri Hindu hounded out of his ancestral hearth and home. Similar explosions seem to be in store for West Bengal, Assam, and several States in the North-East where Muslim infiltration has already reached alarming proportions. The less said about Pandit

[4] Stanislav Govorukhin, director of the film *The Russia We have Lost*, cites a 1917 projection giving Russia a population of 323 million in 1950. He proceeds to say: "As it happened, a census was taken in 1950. It showed that Russia had a population of 178 million—where are those 150 million, where did all these people go?" (*The Sunday Statesman*, May 17, 1992). He agrees with Alexander Solzhenytsin in regarding Lenin and Stalin as great criminals. Sri Aurobindo had characterised Hitler as an instrument of the Devil. Someone asked him, "What about Stalin?" He replied, "Stalin is the Devil himself." And he was not joking.

Nehru's dearest dream for India — the Socialistic Pattern of Society —, the better. It has ended by ruining the country's economy and environment, and poisoning the nation's life with pervasive corruption.

Yet the political platforms, the media and the academia, in fact the whole establishment, continues to function as if none of these things has happened. The truth about the Soviet Union, Lenin, Stalin, and the Communist Party of India has been prevented from reaching even the intelligentsia, not to speak of the people at large.[5] It suffices for our Sham Lals, who had heaped no end of encomiums on the Soviet economy, to regret its mismanagement by the party and the bureaucracy; they have not a word to say about the human tragedy and the horrors that were enacted in the Soviet Union and its Satellites. Any worthwhile discussion of Islam, its Allah, its prophet, its scripture, its history, and its heroes continues to be a criminal offence. Islamic subversion in Kashmir is being explained away as alienation of its people brought about by India's high handedness, and Islamic terrorism is being blamed on Pakistan as a "party to the disputed territory" rather than as the vanguard of a renewed *jihād* sponsored by many Islamic countries. We hear a lot about state terror, fake encounters, and violation of human rights in Kashmir, but very little about the destruction of Hindu temples and the plight of Hindu refugees. The massive Muslim infiltration from Bangladesh is being credited to the "rumour mills of Hindu communalism" or, if admitted at all, to the "strength of India's economy". Scribes such as M.J. Akbar see in it a negation of the two-nation theory of the Muslim League. Socialism may have lost some of its self-confidence, but Secularism retains intact all its aggressive self-righteousness and continues to fire salvos which make most people run for cover. The one theme on which the whole establishment stands zeroed is the "menace of Hindu fundamentalism" which, we are told, "threatens the lives, properties and honour of an already harassed minority".

Had the Indian establishment purged itself of the poison that is Nehruism, this lapse of memory vis-a-vis the communist mafia would not have been possible. It would not have been possible for this mafia to continue its stranglehold on two strategic states, or

[5] *The Statesman* dated August 14, 1992 carried a story by Ishan Joshi — 'USSR is dead; long live the syllabus'. Courses offered at the Centre for Soviet (and East European) Studies in the Jawaharlal Nehru University continue to be the same even after the Soviet Union and its East European Satellites have ceased to exist.

retain its near monopoly on the media and the academia, or get grants and prizes for its fronts and fellow-travellers from the Government and private foundations, or strut around as *the* custodian of the nation's conscience and character. It is obvious that India's dominant intelligentsia which mans the establishment, refuses to learn from history. I wonder if this intelligentsia is out to prove the old adage that those who refuse to learn from history, will live to repeat it.

III

My readings and reflections since I studied and wrote on Pandit Nehru in 1961-62 have taken me much beyond his political biography. What has engaged my attention, more and more, is the phenomenon of a man hostile to everything Indian rising to the top in the Freedom Movement, and looking larger than life-size not only during the days of his dominance but also in the subsequent period. As I have stated earlier, Nehruism is nothing more than a mix of imperialist ideologies that have tormented this country for several centuries. Yet it has become a cult, and questioning its premises or propositions sounds as nothing short of blasphemy. The phenomenon cannot be explained in terms of Pandit Nehru's personal accomplishments, whatever they were, or in terms of the sacrifices supposed to have been made by his family. It needs a deeper probe.

After all, it has to be conceded that Pandit Nehru did not have to use brute force in order to beat down whatever opposition he faced from patriotic people, parties, and movements. His frowns combined with some pressure from his sycophants was all that he needed most of the time. It is anybody's guess whether he would have used force if he had been frustrated in implementing his policies and programmes. What we have to explain is the ease with which he succeeded. We have to answer a few question.

Why does Nehruism continue to flourish in spite of its manifest failure on every front? Does the flag of Nehruism continue to fly because the Nehruvian flock remains in power, or does the Nehruvian flock remain in power because Nehruism continues to represent the national consensus? Why has India's intellectual elite failed or refused to discuss Nehruism in some depth and detail, and evolve another ideology in keeping with the cultural, social, and political needs of an ancient people?

It is in an effort to find satisfactory answers to these questions that I have surveyed the propositions which Nehruism sponsors or supports in various spheres of national life — religion, culture, history, society, politics. I will present those propositions in the next volume. For now, I want to say only this much that none of these propositions squares with known facts or straight logic. All of them are fabrications of a mind which has lost its moorings in India's spiritual and cultural traditions, and her national history.

It is perfectly understandable that the Muslim and the Christian intelligentsia rallies round these propositions. For, these propositions work to the advantage of Islamic and Christian causes. What amazes, in fact intrigues me is that the Hindu intelligentsia by and large subscribes to them, or at least does not question them. For, they keep Hindu society and culture constantly on the defensive, and are bound to destroy whatever Hinduism has survived in the only Hindu homeland.

Of course, there are any number of Hindu scholars who take pride in Hindu history and heritage. There is no dearth of books on Hindu spiritual traditions, Hindu philosophies, Hindu sciences, Hindu architecture and sculpture, Hindu arts and crafts, Hindu social and political thought, Hindu history, Hindu heroes and heroines, and so on. But to the best of my knowledge, there is hardly any Hindu scholarship which processes propositions hostile to Hinduism from the Hindu point of view, directly or indirectly, and tries to show them up for what they really are. If one asks Hindu scholars to tackle these propositions, at least in the light of facts and logic, if not from the vantage point of Hindu spirituality one is either met with a stony silence, or dismissed as a "politician out to involve them in communal controversies and thus wreck their careers as scholars". It is not unoften that the same Hindu scholars advise people like the present author to say "something positive" and not to "waste your time on only the negative".

The result is that Hindu scholarship which deals with Hindu themes sympathetically and knowledgeably remains a private preserve most of the time. Once in a while this scholarship is praised in public ceremonies held primarily for the benefit of some politician in power. Occasionally, it is also honoured with awards and prizes. But, all the same, it fails to make an impact on public opinion, and is almost always eclipsed by the howls raised by Hindu-baiters. On the other hand, hacks who hawk half-truths or plain lies about Hindu history and heritage, win instant and widespread recognition and sell as know-alls.

I will give only one instance to illustrate my point. It was Mahatma Gandhi who coined and made current the proposition of *sarva-dharma-samabhāva* vis-a-vis Islam and Christianity, both of which he regarded as religions on par with his own Sanātana Dharma. The proposition has done immense mischief in as much it has given respectability to Islam and Christianity, which they had never enjoyed in the eyes of Hindu society before the Mahatma appeared on the scene. It has now become the stock-in-trade of Secularism in this country. Now, if you ask Hindu scholars to clear the confusion and state in unmistakable terms that, from the viewpoint of Sanātana Dharma and looking at their own doctrines and histories, Islam and Christianity are not religious at all, most Hindu scholars start looking the other way. Those few who agree with you privately, end by advising you not to bother about Islam and Christianity, but to concentrate on the greatness of Sanātana Dharma. If you tell them that Hindu saints and sages and scholars have been singing hymns of praise to *Sanātana Dharma* for ages and yet Islam and Christianity have retained all their aggressive self-righteousness, they terminate the discussion. They remain mortally afraid of mentioning Islam or Christianity except in what they regard as "positive" terms.

Coming back to the propositions sponsored or supported by Nehruism, one finds that most of them have been floated during and since his days, particularly in the field of history. There are, however, some propositions which are older than the birth of Nehruism. It has to be investigated as to when these propositions took shape, and who spread them among the Hindu intelligentsia. After all, Hindu intelligentsia was not born yesterday, that is, in the days of Pandit Nehru and his dynasty. This intelligentsia has a hoary history, much longer than we normally suspect. A history of the Hindu intelligentsia is the need of the hour. We can make a start with the shape in which we find it at present. I have tried to have a close look at the present-day Hindu intelligentsia, and like to present my comments on its character.

The present-day Hindu intelligentsia can be divided into two sections — the traditional and the modern. I find that there exists practically no contact between the two.

The traditional Hindu intelligentsia continues to deal with all sorts of Hindu themes. It produces studies which are sometimes written in Sanskrit but mostly in the latter's daughter languages. Some of these studies are outstanding for their sweep and depth and mastery over the subjects dealt with. The rest are of a sectarian character, keeping alive this or that spiritual tradition of Sanātana Dharma. On the whole, however, this scholarship covers a very wide range of subjects — religion, culture, society, history.

But this traditional scholarship flourishes in the backyards, and seldom receives recognition in the wide world. It also suffers from a serious drawback. It is almost incapable of understanding the modern world, or in dealing with forces which ideologies like Christianity, Islam, and Communism have unleashed. The other day, a friend presented to a traditional scholar an outline of the theology which prophetic creeds subscribe to in general. His response was one of surprise, having never come across such a thought-system in all his studies. His only comment was, "How can anyone think in this manner, or say all that?"

The modern section of the Hindu intelligentsia, on the other hand, is the dominant section at present. It consists almost exclusively of English-educated Hindus who consider themselves and are considered by the traditional intelligentsia as well, as constituting the elite in Hindu society. I find that apart from some scholars who keep contact with Hindu *śāstras* of old, most of this modern Hindu intelligentsia derives its knowledge of Hindu history and heritage from sources which, if not hostile, are at least alien. A large section of this intelligentsia can be characterised as follows:

1. It is not at all equipped with a framework of Hindu thought in terms of which it can process and evaluate the thought-systems competing with Hinduism, and thus assign the role of movements and personalities propped up by those thought-systems
2. It specialises in ignoring the unpleasant aspects of competing thought-systems, and selects from them or even invents for them some seemingly pleasant features so that it may live in a dream-world devoid of all dangers or unpleasant encounters.
3. Even if some members of this intelligentsia notice some unpleasant features of competing thought-systems, they keep the knowledge private and remain tongue-tied about them in public lest they invite accusations of being "communal" or "reactionary".
4. It is bothered only by the ugly behaviour patterns such street

riots and terrorism which people subscribing to competing thought-systems create, and never tries to examine the thought-systems from which the behaviour patterns spring.

5. If it develops critiques of competing thought-systems, it does so in terms of their own criteria and thus concedes their premises as well as most of their claims.
6. Quite often, it looks at Hindu history and heritage through categories provided by competing thought-systems, and ends by harbouring a deep-seated sense of inferiority vis-a-vis those thought-systems.
7. To a certain extent, it is also a cowardly lot which frowns upon those who disturb its complacence with unpleasant facts, and crawls or cringes before bullies whose crimes it ignores, or condones, or explains away.

I believe that it was this character of the dominant Hindu intelligentsia which enabled Pandit Nehru to prevail and impose his will on the Indian establishment. The fact that the Arya Samaj, the Ramakrishna Mission, and the Sangh *parivara* ended by bowing before him and toeing his line, has a story to tell. To me it appears that he succeeded because he represented, truly and in a large measure, the dominant Hindu intelligentsia of his day. And Nehruism continues to thrive because it reflects the ideological emaciation, and satisfies the psychological needs of the dominant Hindu intelligentsia at present. In fact, the relationship between the dominant Hindu intelligentsia on the one hand and Nehruism on the other turns out to be something like a symbiosis. The dominant Hindu intelligentsia has propped up Nehruism, and spread it farther afield. In turn, Nehruism has patronized the dominant Hindu intelligentsia, and helped it to proliferate further. The process is still on.

In this perspective, Pandit Nehru no more remains the progenitor of Nehruism, On the contrary, he becomes one of its more prominent products. In this perspective, it was not Communism which alienated Pandit Nehru from his ancestral society and culture. On the contrary, he plumped for Communism because he was already alienated from them. The dominant Hindu intelligentsia of his day did not have the capacity to bring him back to his moorings, or defy and dethrone him.

No, Pandit Nehru was by no means an accident, and Nehruism is not at all a fortuitous phenomenon. That is why I have renamed this reprint as *Genesis and Growth of Nehruism*, Volume I. In Volume II, I will trace the thoughts and actions of Pandit Nehru on many fronts, and try to relate the pattern to the history of Hindu intelligentsia.

The history of Hindu intelligentsia is a fascinating as well as a depressing subject.

Fascinating because, by and large, this is the only intelligentsia in the world today which has survived, howsoever battered and bruised, wave after wave of hostile assaults — the sweep of the sword of Islam, the force and fraud employed by Christian missions from many countries, the wiles of the White Man's Burden, and the blitzkrieg of the Big Lies let loose by the communist mafia. Many others have gone down, and disappeared from the scene under similar circumstances.

But depressing because this intelligentsia has also tried at times to retain or regain its self-confidence by borrowing ideological trappings from its sworn enemies, and often appeared in plumage which is not its own. Stalwarts of Hindu awakening in the nineteenth century — Swami Dayananda, Bankim Chandra Chatterjee, Swami Vivekananda, Sri Aurobindo — had sensed this self-alienation of the Hindu intelligentsia, and tried to re-orient it towards its own inimitable traditions. There was a good response to their call. But only for a short time. With the advent of Mahatma Gandhi it resumed its emaciated role once again.

IV

This reprint is by no means a retrieval of archival material. The series I wrote in 1961-62 in order to pin-point the ideology of Pandit Nehru is not yet out of date. On the contrary, it is still relevant because

1. Nehruism continues to inspire the dominant intelligentsia which controls our media and academia;
2. The communist categories of thought which form the core of Nehruism, are still vitiating our vision of India's spiritual traditions, India's cultural wealth, India's history, and India's indigenous society;
3. The current political parlance is still dominated by the swearology which the communists had coined in order to throw Indian nationalism on the defensive;
4. The communist mafia is still active in our midst, and fast moving towards forging a united front with Islamic imperialism;

5. An alternate system of thought as can make us see forces in the field for what they are, is not yet in sight.

In fact, the need for an alternate system of thought is not likely to be felt unless we see through and reject the communist categories of thought, consciously and all along the line. It is hoped that this reprint will help Hindu intelligentsia in that effort.

New Delhi
September 25, 1993

Sita Ram Goel

IN DEFENCE OF COMRADE KRISHNA MENON

(A Political Biography of Pandit Nehru)

SITA RAM GOEL

BHARATI SAHITYA SADAN
NEW DELHI

Publishers
Bharati Sahitya Sadan
30/90, Connaught Circus,
New Delhi – 110 001

December, 1963
Rupees Sixteen only

Printers
The Printsman
18A/11, Doriwalan,
Rohtak Road,
New Delhi – 110 005

Dedicated

to

NIKITA KHRUSHCHEV

who took us into confidence about Communism

BY THE SAME AUTHOR

World Conquest in Instalments (1952)
The China Debate: Whom Shall We Believe? (1953)
Mind-Murder in Maoland (1953)
China is Red with Peasants' Blood (1953)
Red Brother or Yellow Slave? (1953)
Communist Party of China: A Study in Treason (1953)
Conquest of China by Mao Tse-tung (1954)
Netaji and the CPI (1955)
CPI Conspire for Civil War (1955)

In Hindi
Patthar kĕ Devatā (translation of *The God that Failed)*
Kamyūnisṭ aur Kisān (translation of *Communism and Peasantry*)
Swādhīnatā kī Aur (translation of *I Chose Freedom*)
Unnīs-sau Chaurāsī (translation of *Nineteen Eighty-Four*)
Ekākī (novel)
Pathabhrashṭa (novel)
Saptashīla (novel)
Saṁskāra Saṁsada (novel)
Samyak Sambuddha (compiled from the Tripitaka)
Satyakāma Soctrates (translations from Plato)
Shaktiputra Shivāji (translation of *The Grand Rebel)*
Nala-Damayantī (compiled from the Mahabharata)
Pārasamaṇi (novel)
Praṇaya Aur Parigraha (novel)
Pashu kī Paramparā (novel)
Prāṇōṅ kā Pāsha (novel)
Pāṇḍavapriyā Pāñchālī (compiled from the Mahabharata)
Ritambharā (collection of poems)

FOREWORD BY PHILIP SPRATT

Why is there so much puzzlement about the politics of Jawaharlal Nehru? As Goel reminds us, and every newspaper reader can recall, he himself frequently says that he agrees in principle with the Communists. Why is he not taken at his word?

We do not take him at his word, because he says and does many other things, and so we do not realise how closely the relevant parts of his policy accord with this particular avowal. When I read the articles in this book, I was quite surprised. He is a very much more faithful Communist than I had realised.

But the principal reason why we do not fully accept his own statements that he is a Communist is that our image of the Communist is so different. We think of the Communist as a man with no interests ourside politics, a fanatic working furiously for the cause, an offensive, truculent person, or if he has to indulge in camouflage, a wily deceiver, and at all times a docile follower of the party line. That is not a false picture, but there are many whom it does not fit. Many Communists are also ambitious; many have a liking for the fleshpots; some have serious interests outside politics, though their theory assures them that there is nothing outside politics; no doubt there are some who do not accept the more abstract parts of the Communist theory, as there are certainly many who ignore it; and there are some, even within the party, who are not slavish followers of the party line.

Nehru is a Communist in this broader sense. He accepts increasing governmental power, socialisation and mechanisation, as both inevitable and desirable. He is strongly attached to the existing Communist governments, and when they clash with other governments he almost invariably supports them.He is in a sense aware of the dark side of Communism as it has existed up to now, but he neutralises this awareness by the Communist procedure of considering history in block-stages. The "bourgeois era" is thus made responsible for all the unpleasant things that have happened in the past few centuries, and the facts that some bourgeois systems have outgrown many of the old evils, and that it appears possible to achieve a bourgeois world system which would be much preferable to the Communist world system, are ignored. The Marxian scheme of block-stages does not contemplate such facts.

Here, it is true, Nehru may deviate somewhat from the orthodox Communist position. The bourgeois world system was sketched by Woodrow Wilson. It provides for substantially independent nations, running their internal affairs in their own way, under a very limited world authority, like the League or the U.N. The Communists insist on substantial uniformity, through a Communist Party monopoly of power, in the internal affairs of all nationas, and until the rise of "ploycentrism" they contemplated a highly centralised world government. Wisdom may be dawning on them now, but we do not yet know how far they will go.

In this controversy Nehru no doubt stands with the revisionists, but that is a matter of little immediate importance. On the questions that arise now, though he looks so different he is a Communist in practice. The figure in world politics who most resembles him is Castro. Castro got into power on false pretences. i.e. as a liberator, not as a Communist, but within a year or so he had liquidated his opponents and built up the Communists so far that he was able to drop the mask. Nehru got into power on the same false pretences, i.e. as a liberator, not as a Communist, and he has proceeded in the same direction, but far more cautiously. Castro succeed Batista; Nehru succeeded Gandhi on the one hand, and the legalistic British regime on the other. The two legacies between them have cramped his Communist style. Nehru has sometimes sighed for a cadre such as Mao Tse-tung built up during the Long March. With such a cadre he might not have lagged so far behind Castro. But such a cadre, while it might have enabled him to enforce Communism, would not have made it any more congenial to India. Communism is the policy of a small group of intellectuals, who are building a governing machine with a vested interest in Communism, but it remains wholly alien to this conservative, religious, individualistic, property-conscious, peasant-minded country. Just as in Russia and China, Communism can be forced upon India only by a usurper regime.

When I have argued in this way, people object that Nehru has made no attempt to impose the Communist policy in regard to religion, education, freedom of opinion, personal liberty, and so on. The Gandhian legacy has been too strong; if he had tried he would have been overthrown. But through a series of constitutional amendments, he has systematically cut down the right to property, which most theorists regard as a necessary bulwark, in the long run, of the other freedoms. As for civil, religious and intellectual liberty, the Communists always profess to respect them. They are fully provided for in the Soviet constitution. Stalin himself claimed to recognise the necessity for discussion and the clash of opinions. But in practice Communists concentrate all power in the hands of the government, leaving no countervailing force to balance it. Consequently, the libertarian provisions of their constitution cannot be enforced. They are totally ignored in practice, and it is more than anyone's life is worth to protest. Nehru's attitude in this matter is, therefore, in accordance with the abstract theory of Communism. What he would have done if he had enjoyed total power is anyone's guess.

An item of his policy which, I believe, testifies to Nehru's Marxist feeling, though it is no longer Communist orthodoxy, is his tolerance of corruption. Before the revolution the Bolsheviks obtained their funds by organising a prolonged campaign of dacoities, by seducing heiresses, and by taking big subsidies from the German Government. The last was kept quiet, though it has been proved recently from German Foreign Office documents, but the other two were well-known, and the party leaders had not objection: why bother about bourgeois financial prejudices? Nehru has the same bohemian attitude towards audit objections: they belong to the fussy bourgeois era of Gokhale and Gandhi.

Nehru's Communism is revealed in the extraordinary favour he shows to the Communist Party, as contrasted with his marked coolness towards the socialists who put democracy first, like the PSP. He allows the Russian Government, and apparently the Chinese too, to subsidise them. It has been admitted in Parliament that the Home Department knows about some of these foreign funds. No other ruler in the world tolerates this kind of thing. Why does Nehru?

His Communism has been clearly revealed in his foreign policy. He cannot go wholly over to the Communist bloc, but he will not take the protection of the free countries, so India remains defenceless. China's big attack came a year after Goel's articles, and fully bore out his warning. It even moved Nehru for the moment, but he quickly went back to the policy which made the attack possible.

His Communism is also shown in his economic policy. Its deficiencies in Russia and China have become generally known in recent years, but he still persists with it. He is not even disabused of collective farming, despite its spectacular failure everywhere. This over-centralised, one-sided, state-controlled economy is building up a great vested interest, political and bureaucratic and indeed capitalistic, which he doubtless relies upon to keep it going when he has stepped down.

Ten years ago the Congress Party was by no means socialistic. When the resolution on the socialistic pattern was passed at Avadi, an important Congressman compared it to the Emperor Akbar's Din Ilahi. Socialism, he said, is Nehru's personal fad, which will quickly be forgotten when he passes from the scene. It seemed a shrewd judgement at the time, but it overlooked the attraction of socialism for a ruling party of hungry careerists. The experience of socialism in the nine years since than has won many Congressmen over. But there are still many who oppose it, and its continuance in the future is not yet assured. That, I take it, is the real inwardness of the Kamaraj Plan. The purpose of the current goings-on is to arrange the succession to Nehru in such a way that the pro-communists retain control.

The dispute over this question is of the greatest importance for India's future. But the partisans on both sides are still afraid of speaking plainly, and many of the public are still unaware of what it is all about. Goel's book helps greatly in making clear what the groups in the Congress are fighting over. It is really whether India shall continue to be ruled by a Government of usurpers, who will go on pushing the country against its will towards Communism, or the Government shall follow a policy which genuinely commends itself to the majority of the public.

Bangalore
October 25, 1963

PHILIP SPRATT

FIRST PREFACE

The eighteen chapters of this book appeared originally as eighteen instalments of a series written by 'Ekaki' in the weekly *Organiser*, New Delhi, from June 5 to October 9, 1961. The nineteenth chapter, *Choosing Between USA And USSR*, was contributed by me to the Diwali 1962 issue of the *Organiser* which came out soon after the first wave of Chinese invasion on October 20, 1962. They have been reprinted with a few minor changes here and there.

While these articles were appearing in the *Organiser*, there was repeated demand from readers that the series should be brought out as a book as soon as it was complete and, if possible, translated into other Indian languages. A weekly magazine in Andhra, it was learnt later, was following the *Organiser* with a Telugu translation. In November 1962, Madaem Suzanne Labin, an international name in the campaign against Communism, offered to take up the series with publishers in France. It did not work out. Even now, full two years after the series was completed, frequent enquiries are received from friends asking when they can expect "that Krishna Menon Series" as a book.

It has not been possible to bring out this book before now due to a number of reasons. But this delay has in no way dated it. Subsequent events have only substantiated the central thesis presented in this series, namely that fellow-travelling Pandit Nehru and not Krishna Menon was the real author of those defence and foreign policies which led this country to a debacle in the face of communist China, and that if we wanted to change those policies and avoid greater debacles Pandit Nehru should be sacked. Krishna Menon has since been dismissed under the pressure of an outraged public opinion. But the policies for which he was held responsible are still there, leading the nation into a trap from which it will be a troublesome task to take her out. This series is, therefore, still relevant as a warning to the nation which is again becoming self-complacent and permitting Pandit Nehru to ride roughshod over voices of dissent, be they from within his own Congress Party or from other patriotic people.

I do not suffer from any illusion that this book will finally educated our people, particularly our intelligentsia, who have wilfully remained ignorant of the realities of present-day international politics. Nor do I harbour the hope that our politicians will be easily cured of those romantic notions about other nations which have persuaded them to practise blackmail in peace and servility in war. I am placing this book before our people, as I did so many others, simply because I want to be true to my own impulse for action in terms of my own lights. Rest is in the hands of Him who sends Saviours as well as Scourges according to His own inscrutable Law.

I am not unmindful of the tragedy which has forced me to take up my pen against one of the foremost names in India's fight for freedom. It is true that I have never been an admirer of Jawaharlal Nehru. It was as a teenager that I heard him shouting like an ordinary street bully and slapping a Congressman on the public stage simply because the mike had failed for a few minutes. I also saw him kicking and slapping our common people who had travelled long distances to have his *darshan* and touch his feet. I had sensed in him that snobbery which is so characteristic of our upstart "upper" classes and against which I have been in total revolt all my life. His admirers call him an aristocrat who has a right to be short-tempered and rude. For me, it is simply an absence of any culture, inherited or acquired.

Yet, Prime Minister Nehru is exactly as old as my own father. Normally, and in keeping with our Indian tradition, I should have been sitting at his feet and listening to words of wisdom dropping from his lips. It is a tragedy that it had to be otherwise. In a clash of larger loyalties, considerations of age and station have had to yield place to what I regard as weightier considerations. But lest people be led away by my polemics, let me confess that I have done what I have done with a very heavy heart. I still believe that Pandit Nehru can be as great an asset to India as he has been a liability, if he gives up his self-righteousness, admits his mistakes like Mahatma Gandhi whose company he kept for so many years, and stops haranguing others to march with the times while he himself remains a prisoner of outmoded categories of thought.

It was only as a result of first-hand political experience that I came to these conclussions about Prime Minister Nehru. They are the outcome of observation and contemplation of the political drama enacted in India after attainment of independence. Perhaps I would have never been able to see Pandit Nehru as a Soviet-addict, had I not been involved in a struggle against Communism which has been trying to engulf us all these years. I, therefore, think it proper to tell the story of that struggle which started in the second half of 1948 and which is far from finished as yet. Readers will thus be able to appreciate this series in its proper perspective. For, this series is only a sequel to a struggle waged in the past and, God willing, the forerunner of some more struggles in future.

II

The struggle started with a small pamphlet, *Let Us Fight The Communist Menace,* written and published by Ram Swarup[1] towards the end of 1948. It was an appeal to our political leadership to organise an "information service to supply objective data about communist Russia and the communist parties to the people" so that they may beware of the Soviet Trojan horse which was busy beguiling them towards a totalitarian tyranny unprecedented in human history. A publishing house, Prachi Prakashan, was floated in 1949 for the fulfilment of this objective. Its very first publication, *Russian Imperialism: How to Stop It* by Ram Swarup, was brought out in early 1950. It was blessed by Sri Aurobindo and recommended by Bertrand Russell, Arthur Koestler and Philip Spratt. Besides providing detailed data about the nature of Soviet society under Stalin, this book presented a thorough analysis of communist economic thinking which has been responsible for so much mischief and misery, and which has had such a strong hold over our thinking as a nation in recent years.

Sardar Patel was one of the recipients of a copy of *Russian Imperialism* which had been sent to all political leaders of note including Prime Minister Nehru. He responded speedily and very sympathetically. I still remember that morning in the summer of 1950 when an emissary of the Home Ministry at New Delhi came to my house in Calcutta with a message from the Home Minister. "The Home Minister wants me to convey ot you," he said, "that if the work started by you is not encouraged and assisted right now, it will have to be done by the Indian Army one day." That was very encouraging for our group. But, unfortunately for India, Sardar

---

[1] Not to be confused with Ram Swarup Sabharwal who has recently dropped his surname, who has added an "a" to his first name and made it "Rama", and who smiles meaningfully when asked if he is the same Ram Swarup who organised and led the biggest battle against Communism. Rama Swarup is now a representative of the Asian People's Anti-Communist League in India. [He was in front-page news in 1986 when he was taken into police custody for investigation as a spy in the service of foreigners.]

Patel did not live for long thereafter. The nation was fated, as it were, to see the day when its sons had to shed their blood in the snows of the Himalayas for no other reason than the folly of their Prime Minister, Jawaharlal Nehru. That story is too well known to need repetition here. But very few people know how seriously Sardar Patel had taken the Chinese occupation of Tibet, and what foresight was contained in the policies which he had formulated for the defence of our northern frontiers. Pandit Nehru was almost on the verge of leaving the Congress Party because he was finding it difficult to get reconciled to the Sardar's resolve to fight communist aggression, outside and inside, to the last ditch.

As soon as Sardar Patel was dead, Pandit Nehru reversed the stand we had taken over communist aggression in Korea. That was the forerunner of a similar reversal over Tibet. It was in this context that Ram Swarup wrote his article, *A Critique of India's Foreign Policy*, which was published in *Mother India*, a fornightly published by the Sri Aurobindo Circle at Bombay, on February 21, 1951. He floodit the false analysis on the basis of which our foreign policy was being formulated, and recommended a revision as follows:

"What is our foreign policy? It is difficult to be very exact about it but, summarised fairly, its premises are: that the world is divided between two power-blocs; that they are equally good and equally bad—more bad than good; that with very little to choose between the two, we do not choose at all but maintain an attitude of superiority and neutrality between them; that when we do have to choose we choose without alignment with any specific power-bloc and consider each happening and action on its individual merits or rather demerits.

"While we are essentially fighting for our own freedom and defence, this defence is closely bound up with the kind of world in which the continued defence of our freedom is automatically assured.

"The struggle that is being waged today is not primarly between the U.S.A. and the U.S.S.R., though they are parties to the struggle as we all are, whether we like it or not. It is a deeper struggle, a struggle between forces of freedom, democracy, equal co-opertion, economic advance through mutual aid and self-dependence on one hand and forces of darkness, slavery, fascism and progressive pauperization on the other. What we become tomorrow will depend on the outcome of this struggle, and the outcome of this struggle will depend on what we do and where we stand with regard to these basic issues today.

"We are faced with a situation in which we have been called upon to forget old quarrels in order to fight new dangers. It is suggested that the time has come when we must give up our peculiarly unrealistic and barren policy and base it on the recognition of the following solid facts:

1. that our freedom is at stake;
2. that this is a danger which we share with many free nations of the world;
3. that in the face of this global danger, a global strategy is needed;
4. that in order to make this global stragtegy effective, powerful and organic, it should be based on local strength and regional security.

"Not only do we stand for the defence of freedom and democracy in India and in the world, we also stand for redressing some old wrongs. We stand for the liberation of dependent countries, the economic advance of undeveloped areas, free communication between people of different countries. For achieving these posotive values, we should base our conduct in international affairs on the following:

1. Support to the cause of genuinely nationalist movements of old colonies.
2. Support to the nationalist struggle of the newly conquered countries in East Europe.
3. Refusal to accord recognition to governments which capture power by abolishing parliaments and maintain power by disallowing all opposition. In cases where we are forced to accord diplomatic recognition to such governments owing to world circumstances, we should never place them morally on par with governments based on free, unimpeded elections.
4. Peace in the world is impossible so long as the people of the free world cannot speak directly and freely to the people beyond the Iron Curtain, and vice versa. This is the most important single obstacle to peace.
5. Economic development of undeveloped countries must be related to the needs and resources of these areas. While we in

these areas can advance largely on the basis of our own efforts and sacrifices, we look to industrially developed nations to give such marginal catalytic help as is necessary. We on our part must educate our people to regard this step, if taken, as a friendly one which should be welcomed."

Meanwhile, a discussion had developed within our group that the danger of a world war to stop Communism was as grave as the danger of Communism itself. Ram Swarup summed up the conclusions of this discussion in another article, *Plea For A Fourth Force,* published in *The Statesman* of November 18, 1951. He wrote:

"To-day the free world is faced with a dilemma; the defence of freedom against a very total evil which is Communism, and a world war which this defence apparently involves and which would mean a probable destruction of the human race. Can we escape or transcend this dilemma? Can we both save freedom and avoid a third world war?

"The escape generally sought is either in minimising the evil nature of Communism, or in denying the horrible nature of the atomic third world war.

"There is no question of soft-pedalling either the one or the other. War threatens the existence of the race, while Communism threatens the spirit of man, negates and denies it completely. This point should be well understood. Communism is not an evil in the ordinary sense of the term like violating some social convention of monogamy or property. Its horror is deeper, more deadly than any physical pain. The whole spiritual evolution of man is at stake. Fashionable pacifism which is blind to this fact must be rejected.

"But can we combine anti-communism with anti-war and integrate both with the positive forces of love and justice? And can we combine all these sentiments into an effective programme of action? A programme of action which while uncompromising on principles is still plastic and patient enough to discuss and undertake gradual measures and make piecemeal efforts.

"We believe that such a synthesis is possible; and in the world situation to-day it is eminently desirable.

"The premises of what may be called the 'Fourth Force' is that Communism is an evil which must be resisted, that due to the total nature of present-day war, a war is the least effective method of resistance, that the best way of resistance is the intellectual and moral mobilization of the common people. This resistance involves the following:

1. A vastly expanded informational-interpretative programme. People should be told about the true conditions in Soviet Russia and her satellite countries;
2. A special programme for converting the communists and the fellow-travellers, particularly those who believe in Communism because of its original generous impulses. They should learn that Communism has failed and they should be invitied to start a reformist, revisionist movement from within;
3. Approaching communist leaders to encourage their giving up communist doctrines ex-cathedra, particularly those relating to tactics and strategy. So long as they believe in an amoral approach and primacy of ends over the means, they would always inspire fear and suspicion;
4. Calling upon the Soviet leaders to call off their local fifth-columns;
5. Calling upon the Soviet leaders to close down forced-labour camps, and introduce civil liberties and free elections in their country;
6. Calling upon the Soviet leaders to lift up the Iron Curtian. If there is no response, the free people should organise an international volunteer force ready to cross the Soviet borders;
7. Organising an agitational programme for a world Government among the peoples of the world. Non-governmental agencies may run their own candidates in local elections on the ticket of world Government. These agencies could also convene an experiemental world parliament, its members being elected directly by the people. During the time the idea of a world Government matures, we should be working for greater regional co-operation and larger political units. For example, let India, America and the British Commonwealth come into some kind of loose federal relationship;
8. Promoting progressive disarmament and international control of all dangerous weapons;
9. Promoting equality of productivity between individuals and nations by working for population control, free economic aid, and exchange of techniques."

A larger effort along these line was launched by our group in March 1952 from a new platform suggestively named Society for Defence of Freedom in Asia (SDFA). For, while the innate strength of the Western countries and the Atlantic Pact had stopped communist aggresesion and subversion in Europe and North America, the emergence of Red China had turned the whole of Asia into a battleground in which international Communism was making rapid advances. The Western Powers were bound to intervene in every country threatened by communist take-over, as they had already done in Korea, Indo-China and Malaya. No good could come to any independent Asian nation out of that intervention. In the case of Asian nations still under foreign rule, it meant a postponement of the day when they could attain independence. It was, therefore, in the interest of Asian nations themselves to remove the basic cause of that intervention, namely a powerful communist movement bent upon siezing power by violence and subterfuge and tilting the world balance of power further in favour of the Soviet bloc.

The SDFA was a national platform on which people from all our patriotic political parties and non-political movements cooperated in the service of a common cause. It published many books, pamphlets, handbills and posters, and, as a friend who did not approve of its effort put it, "placed anti-communism squarely on the map of political India". Although it did anti-communist work on several fronts, its main concerns were: (i) to start a peasant movement *against* Communism which has killed and enslaved vast peasant masses in Russia, China and East Europe, and *for* a prosperous countryside which programme was conspiciously missing from our Five Year Plans; and (ii) to awaken the nation against the communist danger developing all along our Himalayan frontiers in the wake of Red China's occupation of Tibet.

Ram Swarup had written his book, *Communism And Peasantry Implications of Collectivist Agriculture For Asia,* in 1950 to serve as the plank of a peasants' conference to be called for launching a peasant movement of our conception. But paucity of resources and other opportunities prevented us from going much farther than the publication of this "path breaking study" as the socialist leader and thinker, Ashoka Mehta, described it in 1954. The book received very good reviews.

As regards the security of our Himalayan frontiers, however, the SDFA was able to make considerable headway, thanks to the lead taken by Munshi Ahmed Deen and Professor Tilak Raj Chaddha of the Praja Socialist Party (PSP). A Tibet Committee was organised in August 1953 and a Tibet Day was observed in September that year when a demonstration and a meeting were organised in New Delhi.

In February 1954, the Tibet Committee called a Himalayan Borders Conference in New Delhi and it was resolved to hold such conferences in all parts of India till such time as our Government saw the danger and started doing something about it. Another Conference did materialise at Patiala later in the same year.

But the programme could not be carried further than that because Prime Minister Nehru sprang a surprise with his *Panchshila* surrender over Tibet in April 1954, and the *Hindi-Chini Bhai-Bhai* movement misled the whole country soon after. In an atmosphere seething with pro-Chinese communist propaganda done by goodwill missions going to and coming from Peking almost every week, it became increasingly difficult for us to convey our as yet weak voice to the Indian people at large. We would have continued the battle and waited for better times, but for the bitter hostility shown by Prime Minister Nehru personally. It was perhaps the most painful experience of our lives to see the Prime Minister of a democratic country openly patronising the Chinese lobby led by the Communist Party of India, and angrily denouncing tried and tested patriots of a long standing in India's freedom movement.

III

The communist press in India and abroad came out against the SDFA since its very inception. Both *Pravda* and *Izvestia* denounced it in their issues dated October 16, 1952.[2] On October, 26,1952 the communist weekly in India, *Cross Roads*, opened its famous campaign with a full front-page story which sprawled over the entire back-page as well. R.K. Karanjia could not lag behind in inventing and spreading the standard communist lies about a patriotic effort aimed at exposing the communist game. His yellow sheet, *Blitz*, set a new record in rascalism in a matter of few months. One of us had to spend some time in analysing Karanjia's "legitimate" sources of income through advertisements in the columns of *Blitz*. The results, published by D.F. Karaka's weekly *Current*, silenced this "vox populi" for the rest of the SDFA's tenure. He returned to the charge only after the SDFA was closed down in December 1955.

This communist hysteria gave us moral strength to wage the

[2] Both papers named Brij Mohan Toofan of the PSP and the present author as the "chief conspirators.

struggle with greater determination. We were really hitting the enemy where it hurt him most—the Soviet and the Chinese myths which were the only props of his false propaganda. Several years before Comrade Khrushchev and other Soviet leaders were free to agree with us publicly, we exploded the Soviet myth skyhigh and the explosion was heard throughout the length and breadth of India. The Russian and Chinese embassies started sending memoranda to our External Affairs Ministry protesting that their countries were being systematically "blackened" by the SDFA.

It took us some time to know the mind of Prime Minister Nehru about our anti-communist work. To start with, we were under the impression that like most of our busy politicians he had neglected his readings about the nature of Soviet society under Stalin. It did not occur to us that he was soon going to come out openly as an angry opponent of any effort to expose the Soviet myth. H.D. Malaviya, editor of the offical Congress fortnightly *AICC Economic Review,* had started heaping abuses on us under the pretext of reviewing some of our publications. But it was misunderstood by us to be the personal predelections of a known fellow-traveller rather than the expression of an avowed party policy approved by the Prime Minister. Prem Bhatia of *The Statesman,* another spokesman for Soviet Russia, Red China and Krishna Menon in those days, had also displayed malice towards our work in the columns of that important daily. But that, too, we did not immediately interpret as the authentic voice of official India.

Several events were, however, getting linked in a chain which unmistakably led to Prime Minister Nehru. I summarise them below:

1. We were using a slogan — *Communism has nothing to offer but chains* — on all our mail posted from our Calcutta office. The slogan had been duly applied for and approved by the General Post Office (GPO) when we bought a Franking Machine in June 1952. Early in 1953, *Cross Roads* published a photostat of this slogan on its front page, and a communist M.P. put a question in Parliament about its 'propriety' in view of India's friendship with Soviet Russia, Red China, and other communist countries. The very next day, an inspector from the GPO barged into our office and took away the plate bearing the slogan without assigning any reason whatsoever. Several days later a letter from the Post Master General, West Bengal, lied that "the use of the slogan has not been

authorised either in the Licence or otherwise".

2. In August 1953, the SDFA organised a Tibet Committee which announced a Tibet Day to be observed in September. As many as 12 M.Ps including Professor N.G. Ranga were associated with the Committee. The Prime Minister came out against the Committee the day after it was formed. He called upon Congressmen not to associate with the Committee in any way. He put pressure on Ranga to resign from the Committee. The use of the Constitution Hall on Curzon Road was refused for the meeting organised by the SDFA on Tibet Day. But since the SDFA could not be stopped from its own course of action, the Prime Minister used the floor of the Parliament to denounce the organisers of Tibet Day, and threatened them with Government action.

3. The Prime Minister had perhaps become wiser about the futility of these direct methods in a democratic country by the time the SDFA organised the first ever Himalayan Borders Conference in February 1954. So he resorted to indirect and insidious methods. The Himalayan Borders Conference was to be denied publicity in the Press under pressure from the Prime Minister's office. The event, however, happened to be so important that the Press could not ignore it. Now the Prime Minister was really desperate. So when a second Conference started taking shape in Patiala a few months later, he ordered Colonel Raghubir Singh, the then Chief Minister of PEPSU, who was closely associated with the Conference, to withdraw his support. The Colonel obeyed but not without confessing to the organisers that he was doing so under pressure from the Prime Minister.

4. In April 1954, Prachi Prakashan had rented a stall in the Government sponsored Industrial Exhibition at Eden Gardens, Calcutta, for selling its own and SDFA's publications which were always in good demand among our politically conscious intelligentsia. Such stalls had been rented by Prachi Prakashan in several Puja celebrations at Calcutta in 1952 and 1953. A stall at the Kalyani Congress session in January 1954 had shown record sales. Pandit Govind Ballabh Pant, the Chief Minister of Uttar Pradesh, and Shri Morarji Desai, the Chief Minister of Bombay, had visited the stall and recommended our publications to our people in comments they wrote on the visitors' book. The communist press in Calcutta had all along raised a hue and cry against these stalls but its harangues as well as threats had so far failed to force the sponsors of Pujas and

other exhibitions—private agencies—to deny us the normal facilities which the Communist Party of India itself had always enjoyed. But its outrary succeeded with the Government sponsored exhibition. A two-column attack on the stall was frontpaged in the Calcutta communist daily, *Swadhinata*, on May 10,1954. The paper particularly mentioned several books written by me on communist China. On May 11, an official of the Publicity Department, Government of West Bengal, asked our workers to close the stall. I myself had a talk with him in the evening that day. He offered to refund the entire rent we had paid for the duration of the exhibition but was absolutely firm that the stall should go. But as we refused to oblige him voluntarily, he issued an official order on May 20 for closing the stall immediately. We had no alternative except removing our books and furniture when we were told that they will be dumped on the street outside. The whole thing was very intriguing because the Government of West Bengal had so far been far from hostile to our work. Enquiries revealed that there was pressure from New Delhi where the communists had represented their case to the Prime Minister.

5. In February 1955, I received an invitation to attend the forthcoming Conference of the Asian People's Anti-Communist League in Formosa. I sent the entire correspondence — including a very warm letter written to me personally by President Chiang Kai-shek — to our External Affairs Ministry, saying that I would accept the invitation only under advice from them. Months passed and not a word came from New Delhi. Meanwhile, I had applied for a passport to the regional Bureau at Calcutta because I wanted to have the documennt in hand in case I was advised to go. Normally, a passport is issued by the regional passport Bureau to citizens residing in its jurisdiction. But when I approached the Bureau after more than two months to find out the status of my case, they told me confidentially that my case was receiving attention from the Prime Minister himself. I wrote an urgent letter to the Prime Minister on May 3 and followed it up with a telegram. My plane ticket for Formosa had already arrived. It was only on May 21 that I received a one-line memorandum from the Ministry of External Affairs stating that "Mr. Sita Ram Goel is hereby informed that passport facilities applied for cannot be granted". But hundreds of communists and fellow-travellers had been granted passports during this very period and very speedily, for joining delegations which were going out to various communist capitals almost every week.

IV

Having thus become aware of the Prime Minister's attitude towards our work, we enquired from friends in the Congress Party and the Government as to why he was so hostile. They told us that, the Prime Minister did not mind our anti-communist work as such but only disliked our "propaganda" against Soviet Russia and People's China which countries he was trying to befriend in pursuit of his foreign policy. They also assured us that so far as he was concerned, we could safely assail the Communist Party of India, but assailing the communist countries was a different matter because that embarrassed India's stand in international affairs.

We wanted these friends to find out a way in consultation with the Prime Minister by which we could fight the Communist Party of India without exploding the Soviet and the Chinese myths which were its only stock-in-trade. We did not insist on our democratic right to criticize India's foreign policy which we disliked. In fact, none of our publications had commented on India's foreign policy so far. But we received no guidance from our Congress friends, or the Prime Minister. Nor was the assurance that we could assail the Communist Party of India without arousing opposition from the Prime Minister, meant seriously. For, when we exposed communist infiltration in Kashmir, we were accused of doing propaganda for Pakistan! The fact that we had advocated full and final integration of Kashmir with India, was conveniently forgotten. Our response to vile attacks on us by fellow-travellers crowding the numerous communist fronts was interpreted as a "slader campaign" against "respectable citizens". It was as strange phenomenon indeed that all these "respectable citizens" happened to be famous fellow-travellers like Dr. V.K.R.V. Rao who in those days was advocating the Chinese path very aggressively, and shouting from the platform of the India-China Friendship Association that all those who criticised China were enemies of the country.

Another explanation of the Prime Minister's hostility was that the SDFA had become a platform for parties opposed to the Congress. But we could not help it. We had started with a wide support in the Congress as the letters on our files from leading Congressment could prove. These Congressment had to fall silent and avoid all association with us under pressure from the Prime Minister. We did not go in search of people from the opposition parties. We found anti-communist patriots wherever they existed and were prepared to participate in the movement. The fact that most of them belonged to the opposition parties was not a portent of any partisan spirit on our part but a sad reflection on the state of the Congress organisation. Moreover, the Prime Minister refused to see that some sections of the opposition parties were also opposed to our effort. We were far from representing the offical position of any opposition party. Nor did we have a complete political platform which could satisfy the opposition friends associated with us. In fact, some of these friends had accused us of being soft towards the Congress Party and the Government.

It was intolerance, pure and simple, towards any anti-communists effort which had persuaded the Prime Minister to become hostile towards our effort. His hostility went on mounting up as he saw our work having an impact on public opinion. Finally, Prem Bhatia was chosen to express the offical opinion in his weekly column, The Political Scene, in *The Statesman.* He wrote as follows on August 7, 1955:

"Over a period of some years now a group of indigenous MacCarthies have been operating in Inida, sometimes subtly, through rumour and scandal, but mostly by means of scurrilous writing. No means are repugnant to their conscience. 'Letters to the Editor' are manufactured by the dozen, other people's views distroted, misquoted and torn out of context and vile personal attacks launched in the crusading spirit of the farway idol whom they seek to emulate. My own information is that the Government of India has a dossier of the activities of such authors, journalists and writers of 'Letters to the Editor' and their connexions.

"Here is yellow journalism in one of its worst forms. Most of these 'journals' have small circulations, and whenever one of them makes a personal MacCarthy attack, the victim is obligingly supplied with a free copy of the publication with a neat printed slip on the cover inviting attention to page so-and-so. Essentially, the object of the attack is the Prime Minister's foreign policy, but placing discretion above valour, they direct their fury at correspondents whose professional decency may prevent them from engaging in an unclean controversy or who may be frightened into silence and discouraged from doing their job with honest objectivity.

"In the present stage of India's political development, the greatest amount of freedom of thought and expression is an essential requirement of our progress, but the main condition is an honesty of motives. Admittedly, political reporting has to be objective to win respect or influence public opinion, but objectivity does not necessarily mean either a crusade against one Power bloc or the other.

"In any case, Indian MacCarthies may soon find themselves left out in the cold as East-West tension decreases, much the same as the Communist Party of India will find itself out of step with the fountainhead of its inspiration if it does not quickly adjust itself to changed conditions. Meanwhile public opinion must beware of our Little MacCarthies and the Government take note of their *modus operandi*, which extends from personal blackmail to pontifical lectures on objective journalism."

It was an ultimatum from the Prime Minister whose unofficial spokesman Bhatia had become in those days. I wrote to Bhatia on August 22: "Anyone can easily descend to your level and call you a Russian agent, opportunist and all sorts of bad names in terms of that swearology to which the communists have given currency. But I do not believe in that technique and I do not use it. My only appeal to you is to practise a little charity and do a little self-examination before you feel so self-righteous and so cocksure. I am praying for your soul."

It was true that 'Letters to the Editor' written by our team were quite frequent and were published in many newspapers and periodicals of standing. That was our cheapest way of reaching large sections of our people. But we had no way of preventing the communist side from joining the debate in the same columns. Nor was the press reluctant to publish their side of the story. It was not our fault that the other side, although boasting all the time that it had many outstanding scholars in its ranks, did not try to rebut our facts and arguments. Compared to the far-flung communist phalanx, we were only a few. Their utter failure to refute the solid facts and straight logic presented us, could mean only one thing, namely that they had no case and had been selling plain lies for years. Prem Bhatia could have grasped the situation, had he used his own mind and some calm reflection. But time-servers have no minds of their own. They bark whenever and on whomsoever their masters bid them to do so. It is a great pity that people like Prem Bhatia continue to pass as "veteran journalists".[3]

Events in the political firmament of India were now moveing

[3] Para added in 1993.

very fast. Pandit Nehru's foreign policy had been approved by the whole country which had been swept off its feet by a flood of foreign dignitaries visiting New Delhi every now and then. Nobody seemed to notice that the Communist Party of India was in the vanguard of those who supported this foreign policy most vociferously. If the fact was pointed out by some doubting Thomases like ourselves in the SDFA, pat came the stock reply that the Communist Part had seen the error of its own ways and the wisdom of Pandit Nehru's policies. Some enthusiasts went even so far as to believe that Pandit Nehru's influence was fast spreading in the international communist movement and bringing about basic changes in communist theory and practice.

But we in the SDFA had closely followed those intra-party discussions of the communist movement in India which formed the background of communist support to "progressive" Congressmen led by Pandit Nehru as against "reactionary" Congressmen led by Morarji Desai, B.C. Roy, etc. The communists had absolutely no doubt that Pandit Nehru's foreign policy was serving their best interests and paving their way to power. In fact, this foreign policy was a communist plot planted in the heart of the Congress Party and the country through the agency of a fellow-travelling but popular Prime Minister.

It was in this atmosphere that I voiced the misgivings of our group in two articles published in the *Organiser,* one in August and the other in November, 1955. In the first article I traced *The Sources of Communist Power in India.* I summed up: "Our foreign policy, especially after the grant of American military aid to Pakistan, has become a powerful motive which simultaneously props up the Soviet myth and the American spectre. The Government of India now frowns upon efforts to explode the Soviet myth in the name of goodwill towards a 'friendly nation'. The outstanding newspapers in this country are increasinly employing communists and fellow-travellers in responsible positions to please the Prime Minister. Even a paper like *The Statesman* has been forced to accept an inveterate fellow-traveller like Prem Bhatia (who writes under various guises) as its reporter and columnist.[4] Quite a few editors and journalists have changed their tone, if not their opinion, to suit the

[4] I was mistaken about Prem Bhatia. It turned out that he was not a fellow-traveller but only a time-server. Fellow-travellers have some convictions. Time-servers have none; they serve the powers that be. (Footnote added in 1993.)

Prime Minister's taste. *In my opinion, the refusal of the opposition parties at this juncture to attack Nehru's foreign policy and the increasing influence of Communism in the country will prove ultimately the most disastrous event in the history of India.* Whether the refusal is an outcome of confusion, cowardice, or calculation is immaterial."

In the second article, *Nehru's Fatal Friendship,* I traced the history of countries like Spain, France, Czechoslvakia and China which had permitted their communist parties to grow strong under the pretext of friendship with the Soviet Union. There was a warning in the following words:

" 'I want with my vote to support Henderson in the same way as the rope supports a hanged man', wrote Lenin in what is considered to be his maturest work, namely *Left-wing Communism: An Infantile Disorder,* first published in June 1920. And this has been the guiding principle not only of the communist parties in their 'united front' tactics, but also of the Soviet state in its 'friendly' relations with other states.

"Ever since the signing of the U.S.-Pakistan Military Aid Agreement, our Government has, to all intents and purposes, abandoned its policy of neutrality and entered on a phase of enthusiastic friendship for the Soviet Union and its satellite, Red China. Whether there was a prediscposition for this change, and the U.S.-Pak Agreement provided merely a handy excuse, is a larger question which I do not want to discuss here. But this much is clear that our Government has recently started making earnest endeavours to popularise Soviet Russia and its satellites as a first step to inhibiting all efforts, howsoever small, at an objective estimate of these countries and their professed religion of Communism. Scores of offical delegations and missions have been recently swarming towards the Soviet Union and Red China, and one can discover a note of unity in their praise for the communist countries such as can only be masterminded by a deliberate propaganda effort. That effort is very much obvious in the news bulletins over the All India Radio and the documentaries released by the Ministry of Information for display in thousands of our cinema houses.

"Those who have made a close study of Communism, the Soviet Union, and the history of the international communist movement can see in this new policy nothing but disaster and ruination for independent, democratic India. I know that these people are scoffed at as 'Indian MacCarthies,' 'reactionaries obsessed with the spectre of social revolution', 'American Agents' and 'enemies of India'. I also remember that the very same scoffers has used the very same technique when they denounced people opposed to the Muslim League and its slogan of Pakistan as 'communalists', 'agents of British imperialism', 'disruptors of national unity', and so on. The Muslim League triumphed and Pakistan became a fact because the nation allowed the scoffers to triumph. It is an irony of history that the same people who created Pakistan are today leading the country into another disaster, this time in the name of opposition to Pakistan!"

But the warning went in vain. Politicians were drunk with power, social workers with the success of their own pet projects, and businessmen and industrialists with an unporecedented plunder in the name of fulfilling the "socialist plan". The public at large had been completely drugged by communist propaganda patronised by the Prine Minister. Slowly, the voices of warning also fell silent.

V

This, then, is the background against which this series was written. I had time between 1955 and 1960 to read the writings and speeches of Pandit Nehru which I had neglected earlier because he had never impressed me as a thinker of any consequence. It was in this way that I discovered for the first time the basic convictions of Jawaharlal Nehru, "the jewel of India". I could understand at last why Pandit Nehru had behaved the way he did. Normally, a fellow-traveller loses his appetite and sleep whenever the worth of his Soviet Fatherland is questioned. So the fellow-travelling Pandit Nehru was behaving according to his fundamental mental make-up, which is that of a self-righteous bully who surrounds himself with bourgeois luxury and flirts with Communism.

But all honour to the Prime Minister for showing the courage of his convictions. There have been only a few others who could combine their private convictions with public courage. If this country ever goes down, it will not be due to Prime Minister Nehru's fellow-travelling follies, but because of the cowardice of the other Indian leaders. I am sure that Pandit Nehru would not have dared go that far in pursuit of his policies had he been challanged by a healthy democracy inside the Congress Party and a free and frank debate in the country at large. In a way, all of us are as guilty, if not more, as Prime Minister Nehru. But the time for undoing that guilt is not yet past. We can still restore to this country and the Congress Party the freedom of debate and discussion over all those matters in which the Prime Minister chooses to be a contesting party. The communist conspiracy has never survived a democratic debate.

VI

I take this opportunity to ask my countrymen to recall the names of those patriots who came together in the SDFA and did their utmost to fight the floods let loose by Jawaharlal Nehru in collaboration with the Communist Party of India. My mind goes back to those days when Har Bhajan Singh, Brij Mohan Toofan, Bhajan Dasgupta, Jaswant Singh, Som Prakash Shaida, Samir Das, Jaigopal, Jagdish Mehta, Yudhisthir, Santosh Sahrai, Prem Pal Bhatia, Amlendu Dasgupta and Pran Sabharwal of the PSP; Naresh Ganguli, Dinkar Dange, Ajit Bhattacharya and Devi Singh Rana of the Jana Sangh; Binode Bihari Chakravarty and Gopal Mittal of the Congress Party; Vishwajit Datta of Bengal Volunteers; Gauri Shankar Mohta, C. Parameshwaran and J.G. Tiwari in their individual capacity as scholars; and many others from all parts of the country and belonging to all shades of patriotic opinion, came together and served a common cause.

I am also reminded of the goodwill which many outstanding leaders and men of note in our public life showed for the SDFA all along. It was very encouraging indeed to know that we had with us the blessings of Acharya Kripalani, Dr. Pattabhi Sitaramayya, Dr. Shyama Prasad Mukherjee, Jayaprkash Narayan and Ashoka Mehta. Dr. H.C. Mukherjee, Governor of West Bengal, and Mr. A.J. John, Chief Minister of Kerala, appreciated our work and gave us words of good cheer. Sajani Kant Das, editor of *Sonibarer Chitti* from Calcutta, was an unfailing friend to whom we could always go in moments of difficulty. Amal Home, Director of Publicity, Government of West Bengal at one time, was always sympathetic and helpful. Professor Balraj Madhok and Prabhakar Faizpurkar of the Jana Sangh stood by us squarely. The reviews of our publications which Philip Spratt frequently wrote in the weekly *Mysindia* from Bangalore assured us that we were keeping along the right path in tracking down the communist conspiracy of which only a few have had a better first-hand knowledge than he. And there were many others who were equally friendly but who may not like to be named now.

VII

In the end, I should like to express my heartfelt gratitude towards K.R. Malkani and L.K. Advani of the *Organiser* who gave 'Ekaki' freedom to say in their "fascist" paper what the "free press" in India was not prepared to publish. They might not have always agreed with what 'Ekaki' wrote on so many matters. But they are perhaps the only editors who are convinced about a person's right to say what he wants to say provided he can fortify his case with facts and figures. They took meticulous care to publish these articles as 'Ekaki' wrote them, and used their specialised skill to display them to the best effect.

19/11, Shaktinagar,
Delhi.
October 16, 1963

SITA RAM GOEL

ONE

IN SEARCH OF A CULPRIT

The communist and fellow-travelling press and platforms in this country are busy building up and defending India's Defence Minister, Mr. V.K. Krishna Menon, in the face of what the leftists describe as "an upsurge of rightist reaction". Krishna Menon himself struts about with an air of injured innocence, and frequently dons the mask of a much misunderstood martyr whose services to the nation have not been properly appreciated.

But the nation at large is not convinced. It is not only the politically conscious intelligentsia, concentrated in our patriotic parties, that suspects Krishna Menon as a sinister influence in our public life. Even the man in the street feels that there is something spurious about his masquerade as a servant of the nation. There is a widespread belief that he is the real author of that disaster which has recently overtaken India's *Panchashila* policy vis-a-vis communist China.[1]

A belief is abroad that if Krishna Menon is not immediately removed from his position of influence on the Government of India and the armed services, many more disasters of greater magnitude will follow in each other's trail.[2] And there has been a persistent demand in the popular press, by the partriotic parties of the opposition, and among an overwhelming majority of Congressmen that he should be sacked.

At the back of this continued clamour against Krishna Menon, there is a generally accepted assumption that, left to himself, Prime Minister Nehru is a clean and honest patriot who will do the right thing at the right time and in the right place. Krishna Menon has, therefore, become the central target of attack. All sorts of stories are current as to how he is trying to undermine the morale of the de-

---

[1] The reference here is to Red China's first public proclamation in January 1959 that she did not recognise the MacMahon Line and that Indian territories occupied by her in all sectors of the Himalayas were in fact Chinese territories. The Chinese started their aggression against India almost simulatneously with the signing of the *Panchashila* on April 29, 1954. But till the time they laid a legal claim to the large territories they had occupied, Prime Minister Nehru kept the facts of Chinese aggression a closely guarded secret. It was the Chinese claim which forced him to confess the truth before the Parliament in India.

[2] The belief has since been vindicated by what happened in the Himalayas during October-November 1962, only an year after the last of these articles appeared in the *Organiser* on October 9, 1961.

fence services, how he is leaking top secrets to the Russian and Chinese communists, and what decisive role he is playing in leaving our northern frontiers unguarded.

But no one has as yet bothered to contemplate the two important implications which follow from this generally accepted assumption about Pandit Nehru. The first implication is that he is a half-wit who readily and repeatedly surrenders his own judgement to the evil counsels of a scheming scoundrel. According to the second implication, although he knows what his Defence Minister is doing, he is too powerless to get rid of the man.

None of these implications squares with known facts. It is, therefore, legitimate to doubt the basic assumption that Pandit Nehru is not the guilty party. It is, therefore, wrong to reserve all our brickbats for Krishna Menon and all our bouquets for Pandit Nehru. If something is seriously wrong somewhere, Pandit Nehru and not Krishna Menon is the real author of it. *If we are in search of a culprit, we should get at Pandit Nehru and not at Krishna Menon.*

For, even the worst critic of Pandit Nehru cannot call him a half-wit. He has proved himself to be easily the most astute politician among a legion of leaders left to this country during thirty long years of Mahatma Gandhi's stewardship. He has tamed, or beaten, or driven into wilderness not only the so-called "mature and hard-headed men" of the Congress Right but also the "fire-eating rabble-rousers" of the Congress Left. He has reduced the mighty Congress Party to his private harem in a matter of less than ten years. The other top Congress leaders may still continue to intrigue against each other for the Grand Moghul's favours, but all of them put together are too weak and demoralised to challenge his authority.

Nor is Pandit Nehru, by any stretch of imagination, a powerless man vis-a-vis Krishna Menon. It is only his personal favour that has catapulted Krishna Menon into such and important position in so short a time. Krishna Menon was nobody in the national struggle for freedom, and as such has never wielded any entrenched influence or personal following in the Congress Party. Nor is he distinguished for any extraordinary talent such as can hold its own in the political or administrative set-up of the country after independence. Left to himself, he would have been a garrulous non-entity with whom no one would have willingly shared a table in the coffee house. Even today, after all these years of power and publicity, he can be dropped at will by Pandit Nehru without so much as arousing even a stray dog to bark in protest. If anything, the whole country will heave a sigh of relief and rejoice over the event.[3]

The simple and stark truth is that Pandit Nehru is wilfully sticking to Krishna Menon in the face of an overwhelming national demand for latter's immediate dismissal. Not only that. Pandit Nehru has been going out of his way to defend his Defence Minister, in season and out of season, inside and outside the Parliament.

What is the explanation? Why has Pandit Nehru shown such extraordinary fondness for Krishna Menon? Why did he ignore the advice of such devoted friends as the late Rafi Ahmed Kidwai and Maulana Azad against what they regarded as the evil influence of Krishna Menon? Why did he estrange his relations with his devoted sister and life-long follower, Vijayalakshmi Pandit, on account of Krishna Menon? Why did he come down on his beloved daughter simply because Krishna Menon disapproved of her stand against the communist Government in Kerala? These are some of the questions that must be answered.

Some people take resort to depth psychology whenever they are faced with such questions. They say that Pandit Nehru is a man of honour who believes in standing by an old friend against the insinuations of the latter's political rivals and personal enemies. But his life-story as a whole leaves no doubt that he has never bothered about such "sentimental nonsense" as a sense of honour. He has made friends and deserted them in their hour of need with the casualness of a hardened street harlot.

Some others say that Pandit Nehru is under a debt of gratitude for the various jobs of publicity which Krishna Menon did for him at a time when he was not so important in terms of international stature. But, again, Pandit Nehru's life-story reveals that whatever other virtues the man may possess, at least gratitude has never been his strong point. He has often kicked the ladder that lifted him up and bitten the hand that fed him.

The history of various missionary movements as well as the known examples of great personal friendships go to prove that the strongest bond between human beings is forged by a meeting of minds, by common convictions, by sharing together of a common ideology. Normal human bonds are likely to disintegrate when subjected to controversy. But the bonds created by common con-

---

[3] This conclusion has been confirmed by the nationwide rejoicing that followed Krishna Menon's dismissal from the Union Cabinet on November 20, 1962.

victions grow stronger with every additional strain.

We should, therefore, seek an explanation of Nehru-Menon comradeship at the level of convictions. That is the one point where we are most likely to strike at the truth. We should make a serious attempt at digging out the basic beliefs of Pandit Nehru from under a mass of verbiage that has been his stock-in-trade whenever he is acting on the public stage. If the two persons are found to be holding certain common convictions, the problem of Nehru-Menon relationship stands solved in a simple and straightforward manner. But if there is a divergence between the two at that level, the Nehru-Menon relationship must remain a mystery for all time to come.

Now, what does Krishna Menon stand for? The task of pinpointing him is somewhat difficult because the man has so far abstained from writing a book that sets out his beliefs in an unmistakable manner. He has also refused to give a straight answer when asked if he is a communist. He has always shouted a counter-question: Are you a fascist? But those who have known him during his long sojourn in London have absolutely no doubt that the man is a convinced communist. The Labour Government in Britain was considerably perturbed when it became known to it that Pandit Nehru was adamant on appointing Krishna Menon as India's High Commissioner in London.

Mr. Philip Spratt who came to India in 1926 as a top Comintern Agent, who was the first architect of the Communist Party of India, who was tried as the chief accused in the Meerut Conspiracy Case, and who later on turned against Communism, says: "For nearly twenty of his years in London, he was known as a close supporter of the communists. People change their minds, but Mr. Menon's recent speeches do not suggest that he has changed his. *I should guess that he is one of that considerable band of people in important positions in the free world who, though not technically party members, are in fact disciplined communists.* Even if this is disputed, it will be agreed that there is something anomalous in a convinced partisan of the aggressor masquerading as a neutral mediator, and contriving so regularly to serve the aggressor's purposes. I hope people will not think I am suffering from a conspiracy mania; after all, Communism is a conspiracy."[4]

[4] Philip Spratt, *Blowing Up India: Reminiscences of a Comintern Agent,* Prachi Prakashan, Calcutta, 1955, p. 111. Italics added.

The public image of Krishna Menon in India also squares with Mr. Spratt's estimate of him. He has always received unmitigated support from the Communist Party of India. The group that cherishes him inside the Congress Party is the so-called Ginger Group which consists of communists and crypto-communists. The papers with which he is associated in India, namely R.K. Karanjia's *Blitz* and the newly brought out weekly *Link*, are without a doubt mouthpieces of Communism.[5] We can, therefore, take it as a settled fact that the man is a communist. That is what the common man in India, his admirer as well as his opponent, believes about him.

At this stage, a clarification about the definition of a communist may be helpful. Ever since the days of Senator MacCarthy, most people feel a distrust towards those who spot a communist without a party card. According to a widely accepted but essentially American definition, a communist is he who either publicly displays his party membership or whom the secret police can locate in the party apparatus by means of a standard system of check-up. No one else should be labelled a communist, particularly if he or she is not an ill-fed, ill-clad, illiterate, oppressed, and exploited poor person. Persons in power in a non-communist country are not supposed to be communists.

The Soviet Union, however, happens to have a different definition. According to this definition, the party members and the men of the apparatus are, of course, communists. But there are many others, more numerous than the party members and apparatus men, who believe in Communism and who regard the Soviet Union as an ideal country where all the miracles have already happened. For the Soviet Union, all these people are communists, to be cherished, encouraged, assisted, and anointed as "progressive people struggling for a better world". The Soviet scriptures pose only one question before every person: Are you *for* or *against* the Soviet Union?

Those who have doubts on this score may read one little pamphlet, *Patriotism and Internationalism*, by the Russian writer S. Titasenko, available for one anna from any communist bookstall. It says: "Love of country, native land, we call patriotism. But not every one speaks of the concept of patriotism in the same way. In

[5] Now we can enlarge the list by adding papers like *Patriot*, *Mainstream*, and *Century* which have appeared after the Chinese invasion and Krishna Menon's dismissal.

our times only the Communist and Workers' Parties, adhering to the platform of Marxism-Leninism, cherish and give expression to patriotic ideas. A patriot is one who exposes the aggressive plans of the Anglo-American imperialists and their accomplices. Proletarian internationalism not only does not deny patriotism but, on the contrary, is indissolubly connected with it. An internationalist is one who always and under all circumstances subordinates the national interests to the interests of the struggle for victory of the working class over the bourgeoisie. Internationalism places above everything else the interests of international proletarian solidarity. *The Communist and Workers' Parties regard the fostering of love for the USSR—the fatherland of the working people—as one of their cardinal tasks. Devotion to the Soviet Union, the true place of socialism, a determined struggle against any anti-Soviet machinations by the enemies of the working class is the touchstone, the criterion of true proletarian internationalism."*

Or read the pamphlet, *Are You For or Against the Soviet Union,* by Otto Kuusinen. He says: "The Soviet State not only differs radically from all previous states. It represents the materialisation of a great historic aim which the finest progressive minds of mankind had cherished for centuries. Politically conscious workers in all countries are aware that the Soviet State is the first Socialist State in the world, the vanguard of the progressive forces of humanity. That is why their deep devotion to the cause of Socialism and Communism is inseparable from an equally profound devotion to the Soviet Union. *The need for solidarity with the Soviet Union is not a debatable question. For the situation all over the world is such that without solidarity with the Soviet Union there can be no loyalty to Socialism."*

It need not be pointed out that, in standard Soviet parlance, the terms "internationalist" and "socialist", like the terms "people", "proletariat", and "progressive", mean the same as the term "communist". So those who stand for the Soviet Union are communists for all practical purposes. Whether one carries a party card or not is a matter of minor detail.

We accept the Soviet definition of a communist as the only authentic definition. After all, it is Soviet Union which defines as to who shall be a "friend of the people" and who shall be denounced as a "lackey of imperialism". The American definition misses the mark and leads to mischief because it ignores what one carries in one's head and gloats only on whatever outer trappings one may have. We think that it is one's system of *belief* and *thought* and not one's situation in life that ultimately determines what one shall do, and towards which end one shall use one's position and opportunity.

Krishna Menon is undoubtedly a communist according to the Soviet definition. He has all along been serving the Soviet cause — as an editor of the Penguin Series, as a left-winger in the British Labour Party, as India's High Commissioner in England, as India's leading spokesman in the UNO, and as India's Defence Minister. But what about his boss, Jawaharlal Nehru?

Here we are, fortunately, on a very much easier ground. Panditt Nehru has done a lot of writing and speaking and although a complete record is not available for purposes of this review, whatever we have before us establishes beyond a shadow of doubt that the man is a communist in terms of the Soviet definition. He has been and remains an admirer not only of the Soviet socio-political and economic system but also of the Marxist-Leninist-Stalinist ideology on which, according to communist theoreticians, the Soviet system is based. The lines that follow will mostly be devoted to sifting his ideology all through his nearly thirty-five years in the public life of India and the world.

Two

A PILGRIM TO THE SOVIET PARADISE

The first job is to find out how Pandit Nehru has looked at the Soviet Union and the creed of Communism all through these years. For purposes of this investigation we have chosen five basic books written by him, namely *Soviet Russia* (1929), *Glimpses of World History* (1934), *An Autobiography* (1936), *Unity of India* (1941), and *Discovery of India* (1946). All these books, except the first and the fourth, have been reprinted many times and still constitute the basic reading for anyone who wants to understand Pandit Nehru. We shall take these books one by one.

The book *Soviet Russia: Some Random Sketches And Impressions* was compiled from a series of articles that Pandit Nehru wrote in various Indian newspapers after his return from a visit to Moscow in November 1927.[1] A reprint of this book was brought out in 1949 and is even now recommended as well as readily made available by communist bookshops. I have myself seen translations of this book in several Indian languages brought out by communist publishing houses as late as 1954. So far as I know, Pandit Nehru has never withdrawn, or disclaimed, or dated this book. We can, therefore, conclude that he still regards as valid the views he expressed in it.

He had spent altogether three or four days in Soviet Russia and that too in Moscow. But in his book he expresses very definite opinions about every important aspect of what he eulogises as "the Soviet Experiment". No one who is familiar with the torrent of books written by communists and fellow-travellers after brief visits to this or that communist country, can fail to see that while writing this book Pandit Nehru had depended entirely upon official Soviet handouts that were heaped upon him while he was in Moscow. He added to this official version the version of various "progressive" writers from outside the Soviet Union.

The book opens with a chapter "Fascination of Russia". Russia, he says, is "a country which has many points of contact with ours and which has launched one of the mightiest experiments in history. All the world is watching her, some with fear and hatred, and

---

[1] Jawaharlal Nehru, *Soviet Russia: Some Random Sketches and Impressions*, reprinted by Chetana, Bombay, 1949, p.1.

others with passionate hope and longing to follow in her path." Then identifying himself with the second group, he theorises: "Much depends on the prejudices and preconceived notions which he brings to his task. But whichever view may be right, no one can deny the fascination of this strange Eurasian country of the hammer and sickle, where workers and peasants sit on the thrones of the mighty and upset the best-laid schemes of mice and men."[2]

Again: "For us in India the fascination is even greater, and even our self-interest compels us to understand the vast forces which have upset the old order of things and brought a new world into existence, where values have changed utterly and old standards have given place to new. We are a conservative people, not everfond of change, always trying to forget our present misery and degradation in vague fancies of our glorious past and immortal civilisation. But the past is dead and gone and our immortal civilisation does not help us greatly in solving the problems of today."[3]

And again: "Russia thus interests us because it may help us to find some solution for the great problems which face the world today. It interests us specially because conditions there have not been, and are not even now, very dissimilar to conditions in India. Both are vast agricultural countries with only the beginnings of industrialisation, and both have to face poverty and illiteracy. If Russia finds a satisfactory solution for these, our work in India is made easier."[4]

Then he bursts out against non-communist news agencies which, in his opinion, are preventing India from knowing the truth about the Soviet Union. He says: "It is right therefore that India should be eager to learn more about Russia. So far her information has been largely derived from subsidised news agencies inimical to Russia, and the most fantastic stories about her have been circulated."[5] Comrade Khrushchev, however, informed us in 1956 that it was not these news agencies but communist propagandists like Pandit Nehru who had been telling the most fantastic stories about Stalin's Soviet Russia.

Before entering the Soviet Union, Pandit Nehru had to pass through Poland which had committed the "crime" of being anti-

[2] Ibid., p.2
[3] Ibid.
[4] Ibid., p. 3.
[5] Ibid., pp. 3–4.

communist because she had been invaded by the Red Army in 1920 and had freed herself only after a grim struggle. He writes: "We went from Berlin and crossed the whole of Poland. It was an uneventful and dreary journey. Poland looked a desolate and dismal country. Except for Warsaw, the stations were small wayside buildings with very few houses in the neighbour-hood. It may be, however, that the cheerless aspect of the country was due to the season; it was the beginning of winter. But even winter could not have made much difference to an industrial country and from what we could see from the train there were few evidences of industrialism."[6]

Soviet Russia too had hardly any industries worth the name at that time. But that did not diminish his enthusiasm. He himself tells us the reason: "We had already taken our dinner but the station staff produced large quantities of food and, after the Indian fashion, would have no refusal. We had to comply with their wishes....Our berths had been reserved by our hosts and we had a very comfortable journey. There is only one class in Russia but they have some special sleeping cars and we had been provided with these. We travelled the whole night and the greater part of the next day, arriving at Moscow the next afternoon. All the stations *en route* were decorated with flags and pictures in honour of the anniversary. The men and women and children we saw at the stations were well-clad and most of them had great coats reaching to their ankles and big Russian boots up to the knees."[7] In exchange for this wining, dining and welcome, he could very well forgive Soviet Russia for not having any industries.

But he arrived late. The big *tamasha* in the Red Square of Moscow was already over. So he weeps: "Our first feeling was of great regret that we had not come a day or two earlier. The real anniversary celebration had taken place the day before and we had missed it.... Effigies there were of Chamberlain and Briand and Baldwin, some of them very clever. One of these showed Chamberlain wedged in a sickle with the hammer falling on his head.... Such were the accounts that we heard, and the more we heard them the more we regretted having missed this magnificent spectacle."[8]

---

[6] Ibid., pp. 6–7.
[7] Ibid., pp. 7–8.
[8] Ibid., pp. 9–10.

From all accounts the poverty in Russia at that time was appalling. But he has always been able to find a justification for every shortcoming in the Soviet Union. He rationalises: "Generally the goods displayed in the shops were simple and modest and had no pretensions to fashion or smartness. There were none of the dainties of the Rue de Rivoli or of Bond Street. People in the streets and indeed everywhere were clad regardless of fashion, many without collars or ties. Many of them of course could not afford to buy any thing expensive. But apart from the question of expense it was considered a bourgeois failing to waste time and money on clothes."[9] It did not occur to him that even if the people in Moscow had become prepared to "waste time and money" on clothes, there were no clothes which they could buy. If he had tried to sell his old garments in Moscow at that time, he could have easily obtained a fabulous price. Many others did, and the Muscovites not only paid but were also extremely thankful. The Bolsheviks had completely disrupted Russia's economy and there was an all-round shortage of consumer goods.

He visited Lenin's mummy in Moscow. This new *avatara* of Chingiz Khan, who was responsible for seven million deaths in Russia, bewitched him completely. He writes: "He lies asleep as it were and it is difficult to believe that he is dead. In life they say he was not beautiful to look at. He had too much of common clay in him and about him was the 'smell of the Russian soil'. But in death there is a strange beauty and his brow is peaceful and unclouded. On his lips there hovers a smile and there is a suggestion of pugnacity, of work done and success achieved. He has a uniform on and one of his hands is lightly clenched. Even in death he is the dictator. In India, he would certainly have been canonised, but saints are not held in repute in Soviet circles, and the people of Russia have done him the higher honour of loving him as one of themselves."[10] Knowing nothing about India at that time, or ever since for that matter, he alone could believe that the Indian people would have hailed as a saint a mass-murderer like Lenin.

Not only that. Thinking of Lenin and his deeds, he becomes bitter about his own Congress Party in India. He complains: "It is

---

[9] Ibid., pp. 14–15.

[10] Ibid., pp. 40–41. Incidentally, Lenin, like most of our communists in India, came from the lanndlord class, and never worked in a field or factory. No one else has ever accused him of having the "smell of the Russian soil". (Footnote added in 1993.)

difficult for most of us to think of our ideals and our theories in terms of reality. We have talked and written of Swaraj for years, but when Swaraj comes it will probably take us by surprise. We have passed the independence resolution at the Congress, and yet how many of us realise its full implications? How many belie it by their words and actions? For them it is something to be considered as a distant goal, not as a thing of today or tomorrow. They talk of Swaraj and independence in their councils but their minds are full of reservations and their acts are feeble and halting."[11] He was looking around in India for a similar spectacle as had drowned Russia in rivers of innocent blood during 1917-21.

This self-appointed leader of the peasantry in U.P. was angry with the Russian peasants because, at that time, they were resisting the Bolshevik bandits from depriving them of their land and whatever meagre amounts of grain they had managed to save and hide. Repeating the most mendacious communist lies against "counter-revolutionary *Kulaks*", he writes: "The city proletariats of Leningrad and Moscow were the spear-heads of the revolution and the peasantry was for some time poorly represented in the soviets. Immediate advantage, however, was taken by the peasantry of the Soviet decree to nationalise land, and even without the intervention of the central authority they ejected the landlords and divided the land amongst themselves. Having done so the more prosperous of them were content and had no desire for further change or more revolution. Many of them knew little about communism and cared less, and gradually they developed hostility to the Soviet power which did not view with favour the hoarding of corn and the profiteering in which the richer peasantry was indulging."[12]

It was, however, the criminal law and prison administration of Soviet Russia which simply bewitched him. He enthuses: "Nothing is perhaps more confusing to the student of Russia than the conflicting reports that come of the treatment of prisoners and of the criminal law. We are told of the Red Terror and ghastly and horrible details are provided for our consumption; we are also told that the Russian prison is an ideal residence where anyone can live in comfort and ease and with a minimum of restraint. *Our own visit to the chief prison in Moscow created a most favourable impression*

[11] Ibid., p. 47. Belittling others was always this small man's cheap way of becoming big in his own eyes. (Comment added in 1993.)
[12] Ibid., pp. 57–58.

on our minds."[13]

Again: "As we were very much pressed for time we were unable to see as much of the jail as we wanted to. We had an impression that we had been shown the brighter side of jail life. Nonetheless, two facts stood out. One was that we had actually seen desirable and radical improvements over the old system prevailing even now in most countries and the second and even more important fact was the mentality of the prison officials, and presumably the higher officials of the government also, in regard to jails. Actual conditions may or may not be good but the general principles laid down for jails are certainly far in advance of anything we had known elsewhere in practice. Anyone with a knowledge of prisons in India and of the barbarous way in which handcuffs, fetters and other punishments are used will appreciate the difference. The governor of the prison in Moscow who took us round was all the time laying stress on the human side of jail life, and how it was their endeavour to keep this in the front and not to make the prisoner feel in any way dehumanised or outcasted. I wish we in India would remember this wholesome principle and practise it in our daily lives even outside jail.... *It can be said without a shadow of doubt that to be in a Russian prison is far more preferable than to be a worker in an Indian factory, whose lot is 10 to 11 hours work a day and then to live in a crowded and dark and airless tenement, hardly fit for an animal.* The mere fact that there are some prisons like the ones we saw is in itself something for the Soviet Government to be proud of."[14]

One wishes that the British Government of India had adopted the Soviet system of criminal law and prison administration, at least so far as Pandit Nehru was concerned. In that event, he would not have had the opportunity to write the voluminous amounts of abominable nonsense he did in later years while serving short sentences in the cool comfort of Dehra Dun District Jail. No one has yet heard of a book written by a prisoner in a Soviet jail. Even most of the prisoners have never been heard of once they went behind the bars in the Soviet Union. In any case, we have first hand accounts of conditions in Soviet jails from the few who were for-

---

[13] Ibid., p. 63. Italics added. "Red Terror" was not a term invented by anti-communists. It was Trotsky who used this term in order to glorify his slaughter of sailors in St. Petersburg. (Footnote added in 1993.)

[14] Ibid., pp. 74–76. Italics added.

tunate enough to come out.. They tell a different and dismal story.

He is not sure that his own account of the Soviet Union is sufficiently convincing. He knows that the truth about the Bolshevik butchers has leaked out into the wide world. So he recommends to his readers larger doses of the dope which has paralysed his own mind. He writes: "I remember attending a banquet given by the scientists and professors in Moscow. There were people from many countries present and speeches in a variety of languages were made. I remember specially a speech given by a young student who had come from far off Uruguay in South America....He spoke in the beautiful sonorous periods of the Spanish language and he told us that he was going back to his distant country with the red star of Soviet Russia engraved in his heart and carrying the message of social freedom to his young comrades in Uruguay. Such was the reaction of Soviet Russia on his young and generous heart. And yet there are many who tell us that Russia is a land of anarchy and misery and the Bolsheviks are assassins and murderers who have cast themselves outside the pale of human society."[15]

He wants his readers not to bother about communist theory while contemplating communist creations in Soviet Russia. According to him: "But to understand the great drama of the Russian Revolution and the inner forces that shaped and brought the great change about, a study of cold theory is of little use. The October Revolution was undoubtedly one of the great events of world history, the greatest since the first French Revolution, and its story is more absorbing, from the human and the dramatic point of view, than any tale or phantasy."[16] A critique of Soviet Russia in terms of what Marx or even Lenin had promised after the proletarian revolution is likely to be too disturbing. So he says: to hell with the theory of Communism! But, later on, when he is faced with the ugliness of Soviet Russia in too overwhelming a manner, he will ask his readers to forget the reality on the ground, and contemplate the promise which communist theory holds for mankind!

He recommends that his readers should read *Ten days That Shook The World* which the American communist, John Reed, had written in 1920 and which was, incidentally, for some time an officially prescribed text-book for children in Soviet schools. Reviewing this propaganda book, he says: "And as one reads, with horror

---

[15] Ibid., p. 33.
[16] Ibid., p. 36.

and pain at times, the wonder grows that such a miracle could have happened and succeeded. And above all there is admiration for the group of men who did not flinch at the mightiest of obstacles, and, in the midst of war and rebellion, with a cruel death and disaster continually facing them, set down to evolve a socialist order out of the chaos that surrounded them. They had time even on the fourth day of the revolution, with firing going on in the streets, to establish the eight hour day for the workers and formulate their policy for a system of popular education. Within a week they had tackled the problem of minorities, which like the poor is always with us in India."[17]

Prof. Anton Karlgren's book, *Boshevist Russia*, is, in his opinion, "patently anti-Bolshevik propaganda"[18]. But he recommended a book which he himself has not read! "A recent book," he writes, "well recommended but which I have not read, is Maurice Dobb's *Russian Economic Development Since the Revolution* (Routledge). Dobb is an eminent economist with considerable sympathy for the basic ideas of the revolution, but withal critical and scientific."[19] He forgets to tell his readers that Maurice Dobb is a communist.

Or, better still people could read *Soviet Russia Today*. "It is frankly a report of the friends of Russia, but is nonetheless valuable and full of information. It is signed by 92 representatives of workers' organisations in England and Scotland and no such document however partisan it may be can be lightly treated. It is only not very critical and is full of enthusiasm for what they saw...That Russia should produce such a reaction on representative hard-headed workers is itself a significant fact. It gives us a glimpse of how the Russian Revolution is creeping into the hearts of workers in different countries and Moscow is becoming the Mecca of the proletariat. Soviet Russia by translating their dreams into reality has given them a new hope and a new courage."[20] He does not know or tell us that these "hard-headed workers" were picked up and quite often paid by the world-wide communist network for saying precisely the things they said.

Thus whatever the facts, his conclusions are the same. He is out of sell Soviet Russia to his own countrymen.

---

[17] Ibid., pp. 37-38.
[18] Ibid., p. 50.
[19] Ibid., p. 51.
[20] Ibid., pp. 51–52.

Three

HISTORIAN WITH COMMUNIST GLASSES

Pandit Nehru's second book, *Glimpses of World History,* was first published in India in 1934 and later on in England in 1939. The second edition which was "revised and, to a considerable extent, rewritten", carried a foreword from Krishna Menon who was mainly responsible for getting it published in England. Krishna Menon says: *"Glimpses of World History* is no mere narrative of events, valuable as the work is in this respect, but also a reflection of the author's personality."[1]

When Pandit Nehru rose to unrivalled power and position in India his toadies recommended this book as a reliable reference work for advanced students of history in our universities. As this book has been reprinted many times, translated into several languages of India, and poisoned successive generations of Indian intelligentsia, the ideas it lays down about Communism and Soviet Russia are of particular interest and deserve to be presented in some detail.

In this book, he dismisses non-Marxist schools of Socialism in a single chapter while he devotes two chapters to Marx and Marxism. He is infatuated with the "arresting personality" of Karl Marx, notwithstanding the fact that most of Marx's contemporaries found him intolerant, cantankerous, and abusive. Marx's labyrinthine work, *Das Capital* (which, we are absolutely sure, he has never read), is for him "a purely scientific work" in which "he dealt with the development of history and economics dispassionately and scientifically, avoiding all vagueness and idealism".[2]

In his opinion, "Marx did not preach class conflict. He showed that in fact it existed, and had always existed in some form or other. His object in writing *Capital* was 'to lay bare the economic law of motion of modern society', and thus uncovering these fierce conflicts between different classes in society. These conflicts are not always obvious as class struggles, because the dominant class al-

[1] Jawaharlal Nehru, *Glimpses of World History,* Lindsay Drummond, London, 1949, p. vi. On p.2 of this book he congratulates his daughter, Indira, in the following words: "The year you were born in — 1917 — was one of the memorable years of history.... In the very month you were born, Lenin started the great Revolution which has changed the face of Russia and Siberia." (Footnote added in 1993.)

[2] Ibid., p. 539.

ways tries to hide its own class character. But when the existing order is threatened, then it throws away all pretence and its real character appears, and there is open warfare between the classes. Forms of democracy and ordinary laws and procedures all disappear when this happens. Instead of these class struggles being due to misunderstanding or the villainy of agitators, as some people say, they are inherent in society, and they actually increase with better understanding of the conflict of interests."[3]

He is very critical of the leaders of the Second International as against those of the Third International or the Communist International (Comintern). He says: "This International had many people in its ranks who later took high office in their countries. Some used the labour movement for their own advancement and then deserted it. They became prime ministers and presidents and the like; they had succeeded in life; but the millions who had helped them on and had faith in them were deserted and left where they were. These leaders, even those who swore by the name of Marx or were fiery syndicalists, went into parliament or became well-paid trade-union chiefs, and it became more and more difficult for them to risk their comfortable positions in rash undertakings. So they quietened down, and even when the masses of the workers, forced by desperation, became revolutionary and demanded action, they tried to keep them down. Social democrats of Germany became (after the War) president and chancellor of the Republic; in France Briand, fiery syndicalist preaching the General Strike, became prime minister eleven times and crushed a strike of his old comrades; in England, Ramsay MacDonald became prime minister, and deserted his own Labour Party which had made him, so also in Sweden, Denmark, Belgium, Austria. Western Europe today is full of dictators and people in authority who were socialist in their earlier days. But as they aged, they mellowed down and forgot their old-time colleagues. Mussolini, the Duce of Italy, is an old socialist; so also is Pilsudski, the Dictator of Poland."[4]

It did not occur to him that the leaders of the Third International had also become presidents and prime ministers and had come to occupy "high office". The communist leaders, of course, did not *desert* the working class. They *destroyed* the working class movement itself by a mass murder of its vanguard and by depriving

[3] Ibid., p. 547.
[4] Ibid., pp. 541–42.

it of the right to form trade unions and go on strike against oppression and exploitation. Compared to the communist dictatorships, the dictatorship of Mussolini and Pilsudski sounded like liberal democracy. But for Pandit Nehru a dictator meant a patriot who destroyed the communist Trojan horse in order to save his country from Soviet imperialism.

Next, he comes to the Soviet Union. And this is what he writes about Stalin's Russia of the thirties: "Russia today is a Soviet country, and its government is run by representatives of the workers and peasants. *In some ways it it the most advanced country in the world.* Whatever actual conditions may be, the whole structure of government and society is based on the principle of social equality".[5] How did this Russia happen to come into existence? Not as a result of a *coup d'etat* staged by a traitorous gang of assassins equipped with plentiful German gold. For Pandit Nehru, what happened in Russia in the November of 1917 was a "unique revolution" which he wishes to see spread over many more countries. He says: "Apart from its effect on the war, the Revolution was in itself a tremendous event, unique in world history. Although it was the first revolution of its kind, it may not long remain the only one of its type, for it has become a challenge to other countries and an example for many revolutionaries all over the world."[6] Again: "The March Revolution had been a spontaneous unorganized one, the November one had been carefully planned out. *For the first time in history the representatives of the poorest classes, and especially of the industrial workers, were at the head of a country.*"[7]

His opinion about Lenin, the author of a premeditated civil war and slaughter on an unprecedented scale, is equally enthusiastic. "There was," he says, "no doubt or vagueness in Lenin's mind. His were the penetrating eyes which detected the moods of the masses; the clear head which could apply and adapt well-thought-out principles to changing situations; the inflexible will which held on to the course he had mapped out, regardless of immediate consequences."[8] Again: "It is not many years since he died, and already Lenin has become a mighty tradition, not only in his native Russia, but in the world at large. As time passes he grows greater; he has

[5] Ibid., p. 597. Italics added.
[6] Ibid., p. 638.
[7] Ibid., p. 649. Italics added.
[8] Ibid., p. 643.

become one of the chosen company of the world's immortals. Petrograd has become Leningrad, and almost every house in Russia has a Lenin corner or a Lenin picture. But he lives, not in monuments or pictures, but in the mighty work he did, and in the hearts of hundreds of millions of workers today who find inspiration in his example and the hope of a better day."[9]

Coming to the post-war period, he writes: "What are the outstanding events, then, of these past fourteen years? First in importance, I think, and most striking of all, has been the rise and consolidation of the Soviet Union, the U.S.S.R. or the Union of Socialist and Soviet Republics, as it is called. I have told you already something of the enormous difficulties which Soviet Russia had to face in its fight for existence. That it won in spite of them is one of the wonders of this century. The Soviet system spread all over the Asiatic parts of the former Tsarist Empire, in Siberia right up to the Pacific and in Central Asia to within hail of the Indian frontier. Separate Soviet republics were formed, but they federated together into one Union, and this is now the U.S.S.R. This Union covers an enormous area in Europe and Asia, which is about one-sixth of the total land area of the world. The area is very big, but bigness by itself does not mean much, and Russia, and much more so Siberia and Central Asia, were very backward. The second wonder that the Soviets performed was to transform great parts of this area out of all recognition by prodigious schemes of planning. *There is no instance in recorded history of such rapid advance of a people. Even the most backward areas in Central Asia have gone ahead with a rush which we in India might well envy.*"[10]

He accepts the Leninist doctrine of an irreconcilable conflict between "capitalism" and "socialism". He writes: "But the conflict has not ended and the fight between the two rival forces—capitalism and socialism—goes on. There can be no permanent compromise between the two although there have been, and there may be in the future, temporary arrangements and treaties between the two. Russia and communism stand at one pole, and the great capitalist countries of Western Europe and America stand at the other. Between the two, the liberals, the moderates, and the centre parties are disappearing everywhere."[11]

[9] Ibid., p. 660.
[10] Ibid., pp. 685–86. Italics added.
[11] Ibid., p. 787.

Talking about the rise of dictatorships in Europe, he says: "*I have not included the Soviet Union in the above list of dictatorships, because the dictatorship there, although as ruthless as any other, is of a different type.* It is not the dictatorship of an individual or a small group, but of a well-organised political party basing itself especially on the workers. They call it the 'dictatorship of the proletariat'."[12]

Justifying this judgement, he quotes the communist theory in the following words: "I have referred to democracy as 'formal' in the preceding paragraph. The communists say that it was not real democracy: it was only a democratic shell to hide the fact that one class ruled over the others. According to them democracy covered the dictatorship of the capitalist class. It was plutocracy, government by the wealthy. The much-paraded vote given to the masses gave them only the choice of saying once, in four or five years, whether a certain person, X, might rule over them and exploit them or another person, Y, should do so. In either event the masses were to be exploited by the ruling class. Real democracy can only come when this class rule and exploitation end and only one class exists. To bring about this socialist State, however, a period of the dictatorship of the proletariat is necessary so as to keep down all capitalist and bourgeois elements in the population and prevent them from intriguing against the workers' State. *In Russia this dictatorship is exercised by the Soviets in which all the workers and peasants and other 'active' elements are represented. Thus it becomes a dictatorship of the 90 per cent over the remaining 10 or 5 per cent.* That is the theory. In practice the Communist Party controls the Soviets and the ruling clique of communists controls the party. And the dictatorship is as strict, so far as censorship and freedom of thought or action are concerned, as any other. *But as it is based on goodwill of the workers it must carry the workers with it. And, finally, there is no exploitation of the workers or any other class for the benefit of another.* There is no exploiting class left. If there is any exploitation, it is done by the State for the benefit of all."[13]

The Soviet Union was, in his eyes, the model of a peaceful nation. He says: "Soviet policy with other nations was one of peace at almost any cost, for they wanted time to recuperate, and the great task of building up a huge country on socialistic lines ab-

[12] Ibid., p. 822. Italics added.
[13] Ibid., p. 824. Italics added.

sorbed their attention. There seemed to be no near prospect of social revolution in other countries, and so the idea of a 'world revolution' faded out for the time being. With Eastern countries Russia developed a policy of friendship and co-operation, although they were governed under the capitalist system."[14]

The Soviet Union had produced a "miracle" by solving her problem of minorities. He writes:

"This Soviet solution of the minorities problem has interest for us, as we have to face a difficult minority problem ourselves. The Soviets' difficulties appear to have been far greater than ours, for they had 182 different nationalities to deal with. Their solution of the problem has been very successful. They went to the extreme length of recognizing each separate nationality and encouraging it to carry on its work and education in its own language. This was not merely to please the separatist tendencies of different minorities, but because it was felt that real education and cultural progress could take effect for the masses only if the native tongues were used. And the results achieved already have been remarkable.

"In spite of this tendency to introduce lack of uniformity in the Union, the different parts are coming far nearer to each other than they ever did under the centralized government of the Tsars. The reason is that they have common ideals and they are all working together in a common enterprise. *Each Union Republic has in theory the right to separate from the Union whenever it wants to, but there is little chance of its doing so, because of the great advantages of federation of socialist republics in the face of the hostility of the capitalist world...*

"These Central Asian republics have a special interest for us because of our age-old contact with Middle Asia. They are even more fascinating because of the remarkable progress they have made during the past few years. Under the Tsars they were very backward and superstitious countries with hardly any education and their women mostly behind the veil. *Today they are ahead of India in many respects.*"[15]

But his greatest admiration is reserved for the First Five Year Plan in implementing which Stalin murdered millions of peasants and workers. He writes at length: "This Five Year Plan had been drawn up after the most careful thought and investigation. The

[14] Ibid., pp. 847-48.
[15] Ibid., pp. 850–51. Italics added.

whole country had been surveyed by scientists and engineers, and numerous experts had discussed the problem of fitting in one part of the programme into another. For, the real difficulty came in this fitting in... But Russia had one great advantage over the capitalist countries. Under capitalism all these activities are left to individual initiative and chance, and owing to competition there is waste of effort. There is no co-ordination between different producers or different sets of workers, except the chance co-ordination which arises in the buyers and sellers coming to the same market... The Soviet Government had the advantage of controlling all the different industries and activities in the whole Union, and so it could draw up and try to work a single co-ordinated plan in which every activity found its proper place. There would be no waste in this, except such waste as might come from errors of calculation or working, and even such errors could be rectified far sooner with a unified control than otherwise."[16]

The wanton and wholly unnecessary starvation forced on the people of the Soviet Union was, for him, only an evidence of "a spirit of sacrifice". In his own words:

"For Russia, therefore, this building of heavy industries at a tremendous pace meant a very great sacrifice. All this construction, all this machinery that came from outside, had to be paid for, and paid for in gold and cash. How was this to be done? The people of the Soviet Union tightened their belts and starved and deprived themselves of even necessary articles so that payment could be made abroad. They sent their food-stuffs abroad, and with the price obtained for them paid for the machinery. They sent everything they could find a market for: wheat, rye, barley, corn, vegetables, fruits, eggs, butter, meat, fowls, honey, fish, caviare, sugar, oils, confectionery, etc. Sending these food articles outside meant that they themselves did without them. The Russian people had no butter, or very little of it, because it went abroad to pay for machinery. And so with many other goods...

"Nations have, in the past, concentrated all their efforts on the accomplishment of one great task, but this has been so in times of war only. During the World War, Germany and England and France lived for one purpose only — to win the war. To that purpose everything else was subordinated. *Soviet Russia, for the first time in*

[16] Ibid., pp. 853–54.

history, concentrated the whole strength of the nation in a peaceful effort to build, and not to destroy, to raise a backward country industrially and within a framework of socialism."[17]

But the credit for these "achievements" should, in his opinion, go to Stalin and Stalin alone. In his own words: "But the privation, especially of the upper and middle-class peasantry, was very great, and often it seemed that the whole ambitious scheme would collapse, and perhaps carry the Soviet Government with it. It required immense courage to hold on. Many prominent Bolsheviks thought that the strain and suffering caused by the agricultural programme were too great and there should be a relaxation. But not so Stalin. Grimly and silently he held on. He was no talker, he hardly spoke in public. *He seemed to be the iron image of an inevitable fate going ahead to the predestined goal.* And something of his courage and determination spread among the members of the Communist Party and other workers in Russia."[18]

And Stalin's victims were only "capitalist elements and saboteurs". According to Pandit Nehru, "But, as I have told you, this Five Year Plan brought much suffering, and difficulties and dislocation. And people paid a terrible price willingly and accepted the sacrifices and sufferings for a few years in the hope of a better time afterwards; some paid the price unwillingly and only because of the compulsion of the Soviet Government. Among those who suffered most were the *kulaks* or richer peasants. With their great wealth and special influence, they did not fit into the new scheme of things. *They were capitalistic elements which prevented the collective farms from developing on socialist lines.* Often they opposed this collectivization, sometimes they entered the collectives to weaken them from inside or to make undue personal profit out of them. The Soviet Government came down heavily on them. The Government was also very hard on many middle-class people whom it suspected of espionage and sabotage on behalf of its enemies. Because of this, large numbers of engineers were punished and sent to gaol."[19]

Now we know the truth about Stalin's collectivization and forced industrialisation. We know that the people who resisted this totalitarian tyranny were not capitalists or *kulaks* but millions of

[17] Ibid., p. 855. Italics added.
[18] Ibid., pp. 855–56. Italics added.
[19] Ibid., p. 857.

ordinary workers and peasants who were given a bad name by Stalin so that they could be liquidated. But Pandit Nehru's brain had been washed by communist propaganda so systematically and so completely that he became a willing victim of this semantic fraud and wanted to share his own imbecility with his countrymen at large. And he did succeed to a significiant extent with the active assistance of the communist propaganda machine which was fast multiplying inside India of the thirties.[20]

[20] Pandit Nehru has seen the history of many countries including India through the same communist glasses. He drops those glasses only when he comes to the rise of Islam and its imperialism. (Footnote added in 1993.)

Four

AN INDEFATIGABLE SOVIET ENTHUSIAST

We have seen in the foregoing chapter that Pandit Nehru held up the "Soviet experiment" up to 1934 as being of special interest to India because in his opinion "conditions in this country [India] are very much the same as in Russia before the Revolution". What were the similarities? First of all, Russia before the Revolution was a backward country as India was in 1934. Secondly, Russia before the Revolution had a huge language and minorities problem, the same as we had in India in 1934. Russia had solved both these problems. India might, he argued, very well learn a lesson from her.

Now, it is very doubtful if Soviet Russia had solved any of these two problems which obsessed Pandit Nehru in India in the year 1934. First of all, as regards economic development, the standard of living of the broad masses in Soviet Russia is even today, in the year 1961, somewhat lower than that which obtained there in 1913 so far as consumer goods are concerned. It was almost at starvation level in 1934. All official Soviet statistics admit this glaring truth. The Soviet apologists argue that the Soviet Government had to concentrate overwhelmingly on heavy industry in order to speedily build up an invulnerable defence system against what they describe as "the capitalist encirclement". How "invulnerable" this defence system was became known to the whole world when it collapsed against the very first onslaught of Hitler's armies. And the "defensive" purpose it served was revealed when, after the defeat of Hitler, the Red Army moved into many East European countries and installed one puppet regime after another.

Secondly, as regards the solution of language and minorities problem inside the Soviet Union, the way the various linguistic and cultural groups have been steam-rollered into a pre-determined communist pattern by means of overwhelming force and ceaseless terror, may very well appeal to certain people, but it can hardly be called a solution. Today, no nationality in the Soviet Union retains its age-old script. Every age-old language has been heavily Russianised through a slanted system of centralised education. The right to religious worship has been retained in theory but abolished in practice. And even the homelands of these national minorities have been, over the years, heavily colonised by an increasing number of

Russian settlers. Moreover, all these areas have been ruthlessly exploited in terms of manpower and raw-materials etc. so that today they are no better than colonial dependencies of an imperial metropolis which is Russia proper. That sort of solution is possible anywhere in the world and at any time. The fact that the democratic conscience of many countries rules out that sort of solution is a fact in their favour and not a fact against their capacity, as people like Pandit Nehru presuppose.

But let us suppose that Soviet Russia has solved her economic and minorities problems. Does that mean anything to India? For anyone who is aware of the deep dissimilarities between the two countries, the Soviet experiment should be of no significance to India. India is several times smaller in size than the so-called Soviet Union, but has twice that much population. How can a capital-intensive development such as has been tried in the Soviet Union achieve anything in India except mass unemployment and widespread misery such as is already obvious as a result of the Second Five Year Plan which was largely based on the Soviet model? The frightful folly involved in recommending the Soviet model to India should be crystal clear to anyone except such juveniles as Jawaharlal Nehru.

Nor has India ever had a minorities or language problem like that which Soviet Russia inherited from the Czarist days. The large number of smaller nationalities inside the Soviet Union, with the possible exception of Ukrain and Byelorussia, had nothing in common with Russia proper or with each other in terms of language, and were more or less self-contained in respect of religion, culture, and society. Most of them were specific nations conquered by the Czarist armies. The Bolsheviks promised them self-determination and the right to secede from Russia, and thus obtained their help in overthrowing the Czarist regime. But as soon as the Bolsheviks were in power their claims for self-determination were denounced as "bourgeois consciousness instigated by imperialism", their elites were systematically destroyed, and their revolts drowned in rivers of blood.

The so-called minorities inside India have never been separate nations in any sense of the term. India might have been divided into so many separate states several times in her long history. But every linguistic and cultural group inside India has always claimed a common ancestry since times immemorial. All of them have always been parts and parcels of one single nation which is characterised by a genius for unity in diversity. Even our Muslims and Christians who have been responsible for creating communal discord have nothing to distinguish them in terms of language and a large part of their culture. It is only their religion which stands apart from the religion of the vast majority of India. But a religion like Hinduism is quite capable of curing these creeds of their common vice of intolerance, and accomodating them in its vast mansion of catholic spirituality. What is needed is a revival of the religious spirit and the true traditions of India's past. It is only because India's leadership during the last 40 or 50 years has been in the hands of self-alienated people like Pandit Nehru that this solution has not been tried and a monstrosity like Pakistan has come into existence. But that is another story. That does not prove that India has any minorities or language problem like that of Soviet Russia.

The only explanation for Pandit Nehru's nonsensical admiration of Soviet Russia is that his mind was rendered imbecile because he refused to read anything which was not straight-forward communist propaganda. Had he cared even to glance at an array of highly objective and analystic studies of the Soviet Union such as had appeared in the West and were available in India several years before he compiled his *Glimpses* by copiously copying from communist handouts, he would not have remained such a juvenile regarding the Soviet Union as he is even today, in the middle of 1961. But, perhaps, Pandit Nehru who had been denied fairy tales in his childhood because Motilalji wanted him to be educated on the most modern pattern from the West, was in search of a fairyland. Communist propaganda informed him that such a fairyland existed in Soviet Russia. And he closed his eyes and went into a trance from which he has never descended, notwithstanding his sycophants' recurring reassurance that he has been "maturing of late". To the majority of his intelligent countrymen, his "mature mind" is revealed in his writings about Soviet Russia, particularly in the *Glimpses of World History* which he has not had the decency to disclaim even after reading Khrushchev's verdict on Stalin's Russia about which he has been most enthusiastic. We give a few more samples.

The Five Year Plan, according to Pandit Nehru, brought many good results with it. One such good result was the growth of population which phenomenon he loathes so much in his own country.

Says he: "The tremendous growth of the Soviet Union was in itself a remarkable sign of prosperity. It was not due, as in America, to immigration from outside. It showed that in spite of the privations and hardships of the people there was, as a general rule, no actual starvation. A severe system of rationing managed to supply the absolutely necessary articles of food to the population. *Competent observers tell us that this rapid growth of population is largely due to a feeling of economic security among the people.* Children are no longer a burden to the family, as the State is prepared to look after them, to feed them and educate them. Another reason is the growth of sanitation and medical facilities, which have resulted in reducing the infant mortality rate from 27 to 12 percent. In Moscow the general mortality rate in 1913 was over twenty-three per thousand; in 1931 it was under thirteen per thousand."[1]

Population experts the world over are unanimous that there is some universally observable correlation between increasing poverty and rapidly expanding population. We are observing this phenomenon in India before our own eyes. But for Pandit Nehru, all laws of Nature had changed in Soviet Russia simply because she had a communist regime.

Another good result, according to him, was spiritual solace: "Work remains, and must remain, though in the future it is likely to be pleasanter and lighter than in the trying early years of planning. Indeed, the maxim of the Soviet Union is: 'He that will not work, neither shall he eat.' But the Bolsheviks have added a new motive for work: the motive to work for social betterment. In the past, idealists and stray individuals have been moved to activity by this incentive, but there is no previous instance of society as a whole accepting and reacting to this motive. The very basis of capitalism was competition and individual profit, always at the expense of others. This profit motive is giving place to the social motive in the Soviet Union and, as an American writer says, workers in Russia are learning that, 'from the acceptance of mutual dependence comes independence from want or fear'. This elimination of the terrible fear of poverty and insecurity, which bears down upon the masses everywhere, is a great achievement. *It is said that this relief has almost put an end to mental diseases in the Soviet Union.*"[2]

---

[1] Ibid., p. 859. Italics added. Now we know, that the population in Stalin's Russia had declined steeply. (Footnote added in 1993.)

[2] Ibid., p. 861. Italics added.

At this point, even he felt that he had waxed too eloquent about Soviet achievements. He wrote: "I feel tempted to tell you about the progress in education and science and culture generally in the USSR, but I must restrain myself."[3] His enthusiasm, however, refused to accept any restraints. And he went on: "I shall tell you just a few odd facts which might interest you. *The educational system in Russia is supposed by many competent judges to be the best and most up-to-date in existence.* Illiteracy has almost been ended, and the most surprising advances have been made in backward areas like Uzbekistan and Turkmenistan in Central Asia."[4] The Soviet system of brain-washing and regimentation was never noticed by him.

The Soviet children could not have possibly missed this paradise. Pandit Nehru wrote: "The old palaces of the Tsars and the nobility have now become musems and rest-houses and sanatoria for the people... I suppose the old palaces now serve the purpose of children and young people. Children and the young are the favoured persons in Soviet land today, and they get the best of everything, even though others might suffer lack. It is for them that the present generation labours, for it is they who will inherit the socialised and scientific State, if that finally comes into existence in their time."[5] He never heard of those more than a million orphaned children who wandered all over Soviet Russia after Stalin's forced collectivization had either killed off their parents or sent them to forced labour camps. Quite a large number of these children were later on physically destroyed by Stalin's orders because they were "spreading disease". Nor did he ever learn about those "child heroes" who were acclaimed in the Soviet press and by the Soviet Government because they betrayed their parents to the Soviet secret police.

So, all in all, "The Soviet Union is an exciting land with all these changes taking place from day to day and hour to hour. But no part of it is so exciting and fascinating as the desert steppes of Siberia and the old-world valleys of Central Asia, both cut off for generations from the drift of human change and advance, and now bounding ahead at a tremendous pace."[6] He said all this without

---

[3] Ibid.
[4] Ibid. Italics added.
[5] Ibid., p. 862.
[6] Ibid.

ever visiting these areas, though it is a safe bet that such a visit would have hardly helped him to descend from his trance. He would not have noticed the slave labour camps with which Siberia stood dotted, or he would have found some high-sounding explanation for them also, as he did for so many other Soviet crimes.

Finally, he returned to the eternal communist chorus of the "peaceful" intentions of his ideal land. Soviet Russia had been fomenting treason and trouble in every country of the world with the help of her communist fifth-columns. But he could not see it. He said: "Soviet Russia has been behaving internationally very much as a satisfied Power, avoiding all trouble, and trying to keep peace at all costs. This is the opposite of a revolutionary policy which would aim at fomenting revolution in other countries. It is a national policy of building up socialism in a single country and avoiding all complications outside. Necessarily, this results in compromises with imperialist and capitalist Powers. But the essential socialist basis of Soviet economy continues, and the success of this is itself the most powerful argument in favour of socialism."[7]

But on his own saying the Soviet Union did not have to bother itself about the outside world. The capitalist system, according to him, was involved in a crisis from which it could never salvage itself. He wrote: "The conflict between capitalism and democracy is inherent and continuous; it is often hidden by misleading propaganda and by the outward forms of democracy, such as parliaments, and the sops that the owning classes throw to the other classes to keep them more or less contented. A time comes when there are no more sops left to be thrown, and then the conflict between the two groups comes to a head, for now the struggle is for the real thing, economic power in the State. When that stage comes, all the supporters of capitalism, who had so far played with different parties, band themselves together to face the danger to their vested interests. Liberals and such-like groups disappear, and the forms of democracy are put aside. *This stage has now arrived in Europe and America, and fascism, which is dominant in some form or other in most countries, represents that stage.* Labour is everywhere on the defensive, not strong enough to face this new and powerful consolidation of the forces of capitalism. And yet, strangely enough, the capitalist system itself totters and cannot ad-

[7] Ibid., pp. 864-65.

just itself to the new world. It seems certain that even if it succeeds in surviving, it will be but another stage in the long conflict. For modern industry and modern life itself, under any form of capitalism, are battlefields where armies are continually clashing against each other."[8] He could not foresee this very "fascism" in Europe and America coming to Stalin's rescue when Stalin and his Soviet experiment were almost destroyed by the Nazi hordes.

He was under the spell of communist theories about the "capitalist" world, and went on: "The Soviet Union in Europe and Asia stands today a continuing challenge to the tottering capitalism of the western world. While trade depression and slump and unemployment and repeated crises paralyse capitalism, and the old order gasps for breath, the Soviet Union is a land full of hope and energy and enthusiam, feverishly building away and establishing the socialist order. And this abounding youth and life, and the success the Soviet Union has already achieved, are impressing and attracting thinking people all over the world."[9] Naturally, he imagined that he and his type represented "thinking people all over the world". But what he represented at that time or, for that matter, even today is a band of self-alienated Soviet-addicts whom materialistic education from the West is multiplying fast in every corner of the globe.

He added a Postscript to this book on November 14, 1938. It carried his comments on many countries of the world. Coming to the Soviet Union, he admitted: "The First Five Year Plan met with general success though it failed in particulars, especially in regard to the quality of the goods produced. There were untrained mechanics, and transport also largely failed. The concentration on heavy industry led to shortage of goods for consumption and to a lowering of standards."[10]

But the very next moment he burst out with hope: "But this plan laid the foundations of future progress by rapidly industrialising Russia and collectivizing her agriculture. The Second Five Year Plan (1933-37) changed the emphasis from heavy to light industry, and aimed at getting rid of the deficiencies of the first plan and at producing consumer's goods. *Great progress was made and the standards of life went up, and are continually going up. Culturally*

[8] Ibid., p. 935. Italics added.
[9] Ibid., pp. 939-40.
[10] Ibid., pp. 965-66.

and educationally, and in many other ways, the advance all over the Soviet Union has been remarkable. Anxious to continue this advance and to consolidate its socialist economy, Russia consistently followed a peace policy in international affairs. In the League of Nations it stood for substantial disarmament, collective security, and corporate action against aggression. It tried to accommodate itself to the capitalist Great Powers and, in consequence, Communist Parties sought to build up 'popular fronts' or 'joint fronts' with other progressive parties."[11]

He himself sounded a jarring note. He wrote: "In spite of this general progress and development, the Soviet Union passed throught a severe internal crisis during this period. I have already told you of the conflict between Stalin and Trotsky. *Various people, dissatisfied with the existing regime, gradually drew together and it is said that some of them even conspired with the fascist Powers.* Even Yagoda, the chief of the Soviet Intelligence (the G.P.U.), is stated to have been associated with these people. In December 1934, Kirov, a leading member of the Soviet Government, was murdered. The Government took stern action against its opponents, and from 1937 there were a series of trials which provoked great controversy all over the world, as many famous and prominent individuals were involved in them. Among those tried and sentenced were those who were called Trotskyites, and rightist leaders (Rykov, Tomsky, Bukharin), and some high army officers, the chief of whom was Marshal Tuchachevsky."[12]

Had he been really objective he would have suspended his judgement on these trials. But objectivity vis-a-vis the Soviet Union has never been possible for him. He theorised: "It is difficult for me to express a definite opinion about these trials or the events that led up to them, as the facts are complicated and not clear. But it is undoubted that the trials disturbed large numbers of people, including many friends of Russia, and added to the prejudice against the Soviet Union. *Close observers are of opinion that there was a big conspiracy against the Stalinist regime and that the trials were bonafide.* It also seems to be established that there was no mass support behind the conspiracy, and that the reaction of the people was definitely against the opponents of Stalin. Nevertheless, the extent of the repression, which may have hit many innocent persons

---

[11] Ibid., Italics added.
[12] Ibid., Italics added.

also, was a sign of ill-health, and injured the Soviet's position internationally."[13]

Now we know and on no less an authority than that of Comrade Khrushchev that these trials in the Soviet Union were monstrous frame-ups staged by Stalin to establish his totalitarian dictatorship. Even at that time, Pandit Nehru had only to read a small pamphlet by Trotsky, *I Stake My Life,* to realise that every case so carefully built up by Stalin had been conclusively proved to be a framework of filthy lies. But he had no time for "traitors" like Trotsky. For him, Stalin was the "driver of the locomotive of history", as Soviet propaganda at that time presented that fiend. And even today these shameful passages appear in every reprint of his book. Anyone else would have at least added a foot-note. But Pandit Nehru is Pandit Nehru. He cannot admit that he ever made a mistake.

---

[13] Ibid., Italics added.

FIVE

AN INCURABLE SOVIET-ADDICT

If we contemplate the several varieties of Soviet-addicts, we can classify them into three clear-cut categories.

In the first place, we have those dupes who believe that all the dreams which mankind has ever dreamt have become physical reality inside the Soviet Union. These people can talk and write endlessly about the miracles that have materialised in Soviet society. But no one can ever involve them into a discussion based on known facts. Faced with facts, they either denounce you in the choicest terms of communist swearology or simply turn away their faces and get back into their trance.

We find lots of such people in every communist party and quite a few in the communist fronts. There is no way of curing such people except unloading them physically inside the Soviet borders where the Soviet Secret Police and the Slave Labour Administration is quite capable of bringing them back to sanity. In a democratic society, such Soviet-addicts cannot be dealt with without outraging the conscience of our liberals and leftists.

The second type of Soviet-addict hardly ever talks of the Soviet Union. His mind is always preoccupied with the "plenty of evil" prevailing in "your so-called democracies". You point out a single drawback in the Soviet system and this fellow starts reading out an endless inventory of drawbacks in the "so-called democracies". If you point out that two evils can never explain away or abolish one another and that the Soviet Union does not become white simply because the rest of the world is (or has been painted) black, he sees no merit in this logic. In fact, this fellow lives in a dark night and sees darkness everywhere. It is only when you praise the Soviet Union that his face brightens up.

We find quite a few such Soviet-addicts in the ranks of the card-carrying communists. Their strength, however, is concentrated generally in the communist fronts. The only effective way of dealing with such people is to subject them to at least some of the evils they imagine as existent in non-communist countries. For, most of these people come from classes which have really never known hardship but which, due to some sickness in their mental make-up, become enemies of the system which provides them protection and privilege. But, again, a democratic society cannot deal with this type of sickness without raising a hue and cry amongst our liberals and leftists.

The third type of Soviet-addict is somewhat more sophisticated. He is prepared to listen to most of the criticism levelled against the Soviet Union by a capable critic. He is also prepared to admit that quite a large part of that criticism is valid so far as facts are concerned. But he insists that one should look at the Soviet Union somewhat "more objectively" and in a "larger historical perspective". Is it not true, he starts by saying, that the Soviet Union is carrying on an experiment which is unique in human history and which, if successful, will lead the whole of humanity out of "capitalist slavery" and into "socialist freedom"? Is it not true, he proceeds, that the Soviet Union is surrounded by a hostile capitalist world which stops the flow of foreign capital into the Soviet Union, which smuggles into the Soviet Union all sorts of saboteurs, which has been always preoccupied with preparations for a new war against the Soviet Union, etc? And if the Soviet Union, he explains, has been forced into committing some mistakes either due to the vastness of its vision, or due to its "imperialist encirclement", one should not view the Soviet Union in a hurried and hostile manner. One should, he concludes, try to understand the vision which inspires the Soviet Union, and take into account the overwhelming odds against which the Soviet Union has been struggling ever since its birth.

Such apologists of the Soviet Union have more or less completely swamped the universities of the Western world, particularly those of the Anglo-Saxon countries. Today, nobody can be counted a scholar in any field unless he is prepared to "study the Soviet system, objectively and sympathetically". Harold Laski of the British Labour Party spent a life-time apologising for and explaining away the crimes of the Soviet Union in terms of this or that "compulsion of events" or "historical necessity". And Laski has been copied wholesale and on a large scale in almost all our strongholds of scholarship. These "scholars" are very hard to crack because their gaze "is fixed on the distant goal", while their opponents "cannot see beyond their own nose". These "scholars" refuse to deal with "dirty facts". Their proper province is "the sweep of the human vision and human history". And the only way to deal with these "philosphers" is to apply the whip on their bare backs. Only a touch of cold physical reality can bring them down from their sojourn in the stratosphere and make them feel in their flesh that the mass murder of millions of innocent human beings should never be philosophised out of existence. But, alas! we are no longer living in medieval times. Alas! we have become too modern to deal methodically with these monsters masquerading as sociologists, economists, and historians. You cannot mention the whip to a modern democrat without being branded as a fascist.

Now, most non-communist countries of the world have their own fair share of these various kinds of Soviet-addicts. But, fortunately, these sick people exist singly and separately in most of the places. India alone has the privilege of having all the three categories of Soviet-addicts rolled into a single personality — that of its Prime Minister and unrivalled leader, Pandit Jawaharlal Nehru. We have seen how he can get into a trance about the "Soviet experiment". We shall now see him trying the other tricks. That takes us to his autobiography which he started writing in 1934 and which was first published in England in early 1936. It was immediately became a bestseller and ran into many reprints. Till 1955, the edition from which we shall quote, it had been reprinted as many as twenty times. In the Preface written by Pandit Nehru himself in January 1936, he says: "My intention was to trace, as far as I could, my own mental development and not write a survey of recent Indian history."

Coming to the one philosophy of life which finally gripped him, he writes: "My thoughts travelled more to other countries, and I watched and studied, as far as I could in gaol, the world situation in the grip of the great depression. I read as many books as I could find on the subject, and the more I read the more fascinated I grew. India with her problems and struggles became just a part of this mighty world drama, of the great struggle of political and economic forces that was going on everywhere, nationally and internationally. In that struggle my own sympathies went increasingly towards the communist side."[1]

But unfortunately for his trance, some ugly facts about the Soviet Union were too obvious and they forced themselves on his attention. He at once turned his face towards the capitalist world and wept: "I had long been drawn to socialism and communism,

[1] Jawaharlal Nehru, *An Autobiography*, The Bodley Head, London, 1955, p. 361.

and Russia had appealed to me. Much in Soviet Russia I dislike — the ruthless suppression of all contrary opinion, the wholesale regimentation, the unnecessary violence (as I thought) in carrying out various policies. *But there was no lack of violence and suppression in the capitalist world, and I realised more and more how the very basis and foundation of our acquisitive society and property was violence.* Without violence it could not continue for many days. A measure of political liberty meant little indeed when the fear of starvation was always compelling the vast majority of people everywhere to submit to the will of the few, to the greater glory and advantage of the latter."[2]

There has been a widespread belief that Pandit Nehru, the successor of Mahatma Gandhi, does not approve of violence and that while he likes communist goals, he disapproves of communist methods, particularly communist violence. But we have his own confession in this context. He himself says: *"Violence was common in both places, but the violence of the capitalist order seemed inherent in it; whilst the violence of Russia, bad though it was, aimed at a new order based on peace and cooperation and real freedom for the masses.* With all her blunders, Soviet Russia had triumphed over enormous difficulties and taken great strides towards this new order. While the rest of the world was in the grip of the depression and going backward in some ways, in the Soviet country a great new world was being built up before our eyes. Russia, following the great Lenin, looked into the future and thought only of what was to be, while other countries lay numbed under the dead hand of the past and spent their energy in preserving the useless relics of a bygone age. In particular, I was impressed by the reports of the great progress made by the backward regions of Central Asia under the Soviet regime. In the balance, therefore, I was all in favour of Russia, and the presence and example of the Soviets was a bright and heartening phenomenon in a dark and dismal world."[3]

In an earlier article we have seen how he wanted his readers not to bother about communist theory but to contemplate only communist creations. Now he did a right-about-turn and asked his readers to concentrate on communist theory alone. He wrote: "But Soviet Russia's success or failure, vastly important as it was as a practical experiment in establishing a communist state, did not af-

---

[2] Ibid., Italics added.
[3] Ibid., pp. 361–62. Italics added.

fect the soundness of the theory of communism. *The Bolsheviks may blunder or even fail because of national or international reasons and yet the communist theory may be correct.* On the basis of that very theory it was absurd to copy blindly what had taken place in Russia, for its application depended on the particular conditions prevailing in the country in question and the stage of its historical development. Besides, India, or any other country, could profit by the triumphs as well as the inevitable mistakes of the Bolsheviks. Perhaps the Bolsheviks had tried to go too fast because, surrounded as they were by a world of enemies, they feared external aggression. A slower tempo might avoid much of the misery caused in the rural areas. But then the question arose if really radical results could be obtained by slowing down the rate of change. Reformism was an impossible solution of any vital problem at a critical moment when the basic structure had to be changed, and however slow the progress might be later on, the initial step must be a complete break with the existing order, which had fulfilled its purpose and was now only a drag on future progress."[4]

And contemplating the communist theory himself, he again went back into his trance. He warmed up:

"Russia apart, the theory and philosophy of Marxism lightened up many a dark corner of my mind. History came to have a new meaning for me. The Marxist interpretation threw a flood of light on it, and it became an unfolding drama with some order and purpose, howsoever unconscious, behind it. In spite of the appalling waste and misery of the past and the present, the future was bright with hope, though many dangers intervened. It was the essential freedom from dogma and the scientific outlook of Marxism that appealed to me. It was true that there was plenty of dogma in official communism in Russia and elsewhere, and frequently heresy hunts were organised. That seemed to be deplorable, though it was not difficult to understand in view of the tremendous changes taking place rapidly in the Soviet countries when effective opposition might have resulted in catastrophic failure.

"The great world crisis and slump seemed to justify the Marxist analysis. While all other systems and theories were groping about in the dark, Marxism alone explained it more or less satisfactorily and offered a real solution."[5]

---

[4] Ibid., p. 362. Italics added.
[5] Ibid., pp. 362–63.

Next, he fitted India's struggle for independence into the Marxist frame of history. According to him, "As this conviction grew upon me, I was filled with a new excitement and my depression at the non-success of civil disobedience grew much less. Was not the world marching rapidly towards the desired consummation? There were grave dangers of wars and catastrophes, but at any rate we were moving. There was no stagnation. *Our national struggle became a stage in the longer journey, and it was as well that repression and suffering were tempering our people for future struggles and forcing them to consider the new ideas that were stirring the world.* We would be the stronger and the more disciplined and hardened by the elimination of the weaker elements. Time was in our favour."[6]

At long last he had a "philosophy" of life. And this "philosophy" enabled him to see a "fascist danger" in India as soon as he was released from jail in September 1935. Taking his aim at Subhash Chandra Bose who was, in later years, to break the morale of the British Indian army and install this nincompoop on the throne of independent India, he wrote: "There are already clearly marked fascist tendencies in India's young men and women, especially in Bengal, but to some extent in every province, and the Congress is beginning to reflect them. Because of fascism's close connection with extreme forms of violence, the elders of the Congress, wedded as they are to non-violence, have a natural horror of it. But the so-called philosophical background of fascism — the Corporate State with private property preserved and vested interests curbed but not done away with — will probably appeal to them."[7] Fortunately for him, "the elders of the Congress" did not understand his language and, therefore, failed to cure him out of his self-righteousness.

Making his own choice of communism quite clear, he now bewailed his "bourgeois background" which prevented him from becoming a better communist. He said: "*As between fascism and communism my sympathies are entirely with communism.* As these pages will show, I am very far from being a communist. My roots are still perhaps partly in the nineteenth century, and I have been too much influenced by the humanist liberal tradition to get out of it completely. This bourgeois background follows me about

[6] Ibid., p. 363. Italics added.
[7] Ibid., p. 590.

and is naturally a source of irritation to many communists. I dislike dogmatism, and the treatment of Karl Marx's writings or any other book as revealed scripture which cannot be challenged, and the regimentation and heresy hunts which seem to be a feature of modern communism. I dislike also much that has happened in Russia, and especially the excessive use of violence in normal times. *But still I incline more and more towards a communist philosophy.*"[8]

The communists themselves were saying repeatedly that Marx had failed to see the future course of history quite clearly because, in his life-time, capitalism had not become "monopoly capitalism" or "a world imperialist system". The prophet par excellence of this "imperialist era", according to official communist dogma, was Comrade Lenin. Yet Pandit Nehru went on waxing eloquent on the beauties of Marxism as a scientific system which could lay bare many secrets. In his own words, "Marx may be wrong in some of his statements, or his theory of value; this I am not competent to judge. But he seems to me to have possessed quite an extraordinary degree of insight into social phenomena, and this insight was apparently due to the scientific method he adopted. This method, applied to past history as well as current events, helps us in understanding them far more than any other method of apporach, and it is because of this that the most revealing and keen analysis of the changes that are taking place in the world today come from Marxist writers. It is easy to point out that Marx ignored or underrated certain subsequent tendencies, like the rise of a revolutionary element in the middle class, which is so notable today. But the whole value of Marxism seems to me to lie in its absence of dogmatism, in its stress on a certain outlook and mode of approach, and in its attitude to action. That outlook helps us in understanding the social phenomena of our own times, and points out the way of action and escape."[9]

But he was perhaps too conscious of recent history to miss the point that Marx had been proved wrong on every single count as far as the course of contemporary history was concerned. So, he took refuge in Lenin who had tried to force history into the Marxist mould, as soon as it was seen that history on its own did not pay much attention to the mumblings of Marx. He wrote: "Even that

[8] Ibid., p. 591. Italics added.
[9] Ibid., pp. 591–92.

method of action was no fixed and unchangeable road, but had to be suited to circumstances. That, at any rate, was Lenin's view, and he justified it brilliantly by fitting his action to changing circumstances. He tells us that, 'To attempt to answer yes or no to the question of the definite means of struggle without examining in detail the concrete situation of a given moment at a given stage of its development, means to depart altogether from the Marxian ground.' And again he said: 'Nothing is final; we must always learn from circumstances.' "[10]

He could now place the communist mafia as an entity apart and above the ordinary run of "bourgeois" politicians. He philosophised: "Because of this wide and comprehensive outlook, the real understanding communist develops to some extent an organic sense of social life. *Politics for him cease to be a mere record of opportunism or a groping in the dark. The ideals and objectives he works for give a meaning to the struggle and to the sacrifices he willingly faces.* He feels that he is part of a grand army marching forward to realise human fate and destiny, and he has the sense of 'marching step by step with history'. Probably most communists are far from feeling all this. Perhaps only Lenin had this organic sense of life in its fullness which made his action so effective. But to a small extent every communist, who has understood the philosophy of his movement, has it."[11] It need not be said that he included himself in this "grand army".

And finally he hugged the "proletarian politicians" to his own "bourgeois" bosom in the following words: "It is difficult to be patient with many communists; they have developed a peculiar method of irritating others. But they are a sorely tried people and, outside the Soviet Union, they have to contend against enormous difficulties. *I have always admitted their great courage and capacity for sacrifice. They suffer greatly, as unhappily untold millions suffer in various ways, but not blindly before a malign and all-powerful fate. They suffer as human beings, and there is a tragic nobility about such suffering.*"[12]

This fraternisation with the communists has ever since been a permanent feature of Pandit Nehru's politics, national and international. He has never failed to *understand* the communists even

[10] Ibid., p. 592.
[11] Ibid. Italics added.
[12] Ibid. Italics added.

when they have indulged in large-scale murder, arson, loot, and rape, even when they have openly preached and practised high treason against his own country. And he also believes that howso-ever badly the communists may behave towards others, he himself can always bring them round by means of his superior understand-ing. He is like that eighth wife of a Chinese landlord who, when told that her husband had strangled his seven earlier wives, smiled and said, "Oh, they didn't understand the old dear!"

Six

AN APOLOGIST FOR SOVIET SINS

An ordinary apologist for Soviet sins always points out the "progressive character of Soviet foreign policy" whenever he is faced with an overwhelming evidence of Soviet crimes in the domestic sphere. And he generally turns towards "Soviet achievements at home" whenever he finds that a defence of Soviet foreign policy at some point is a somewhat more difficult job. But Pandit Nehru is no ordinary apologist. He does take the first turn and tries to draw people's attention towards Soviet foreign policy whenever the ugliness of the domestic Soviet scene becomes too obvious even to his indoctrinated "insight". But whenever it comes to defending the defects in Soviet foreign policy, he comes out as quite an extraordinary apologist. In fact, Soviet foreign policy has been his one permanent fixation all through these nearly thirty-five years during which he has worshipped at the altar of Communism. This will become more than amply evident when we take up his foreign policy in the later part of this series. Just now we are analysing his various books for finding out his basic beliefs.

His fourth book, *The Unity of India*, is a collection of articles and speeches from 1935 to 1940 in the context of various national and international issues. Its compilation and publication in London in early 1941 was also arranged by Krishna Menon who says in the Foreword: "Jawaharlal Nehru entrusted to me the task of making the necessary selection of his writings and putting them together for the publishers. I had no opportunity of consulting him about the form of this book, nor has he seen any of its proofs...To Jawaharlal Nehru I am deeply grateful for his generous confidence."[1]

In the same Foreword, Krishna Menon gives a warning to those people who had started holding that recent happenings inside the Soviet Union as well as the doings of the Soviet Union abroad had cured Pandit Nehru of his old addiction. As we shall see later on, there was also at this time an acute difference of opinion inside the Congress High Command regarding the so-called "radicalisation" of Congress policy under pressure from Pandit Nehru and his leftist

[1] Jawaharlal Nehru, *The Unity of India*, Lindsay Drummond, London, 1948, p. 5.

followers, for all of whom Mahatma Gandhi harboured a more than blind fondness. Says Krishna Menon: "It should help those who are prone to think that Jawaharlal Nehru can be cajoled or coerced or that the movement of Indian awakening can be diverted from its basic purposes to discover their tragic error. Such a discovery would be the beginning of an understanding of renascent India."[2] What he meant by the terms "awakening" and "renascent India" should be clear to everybody. He was pointing out that by the year 1941 the Soviet Trojan horse inside India had travelled too far to beat a retreat simply because some "reactionaries" objected to its transgressions. And the "basic purposes" he had in mind meant a steady colonisation of the Indian National Congress by the Communist Party of India so that in due course this country could be converted into a Soviet satellite.

This book was published by the same firm which had earlier brought out Pandit Nehru's *Glimpses of World History*. A second impression was printed in 1941 and a third one in 1948, by which time world events had clearly shown the intrinsic character of the Soviet Union as a totalitarian tyranny and an imperialist monster for which human history held no example. But that did not deter Pandit Nehru from going on parading the Soviet Union as a paradise at home and a force for peace abroad.

This book is very important in so far as it is a close paraphrase of Georgi Dimitroff's *United Front* published by this General Secretary of the Communist International at the end of 1937. Dimitroff's exercise depicted "development of the political line of the Communist International" after August 1935 when the Comintern did a volte-face against its earlier pro-fascist performances and propounded, in its Seventh World Congress, the policy of "anti-fascist people's united front". We shall have occasion to review Pandit Nehru's advocacy of a "united front" in India. In the present context we are reproducing only his record as an apologist for Soviet sins.

On March 5, 1938 he had given an Address to the National Academy of Sciences at their Annual Meeting held in Allahabad. He could not miss this opportunity for doing a bit of clean communist propaganda. He said: "We have seen how a consciously held objective, backed by coordinated effort, can change a backward country into an advanced industrial State with an ever rising standard of living. *Some such method we shall have to pursue if we are*

[2] Ibid.

to make rapid progress."[3] He was to redeem this promise when he rose to supreme power and launched his Five Year Plans after the Soviet style. Of course, we have witnessed inside India during 1956-61 the "ever-rising standard of living" and the record of "rapid progress". The Soviet Union up to 1938 had put up a better performance because she had managed to kill millions of peasants, and workers and to discover "plots and counterplots" of unprecedented magnitudes.

During February-March 1939, Pandit Nehru had published a long article — *A Survey of Congress Politics, 1936-39.* Coming to his survey of the international scene, he wrote: "I had been considerably upset by the course of events in the Soviet Union, the trials and the repeated purges of vast numbers of Communists. *I think the trials were generally bonafide and there had been a definite conspiracy against the regime and widespread attempts at sabotage.* Nevertheless, I could not reconcile myself to what was happening there, and it indicated to me ill-health in the body politic, which necessitated an ever-continuing use of violence and suppression. Still the progress made in Russian economy, the advancing standards of the people, the great advance in cultural matters and many other things continued to impress me. I was eager to visit the Soviet Union, but unfortunately my daughter's illness prevented me from going there."[4]

No one should imagine that he wanted to visit the Soviet Union in order to discuss his doubts. For, doubts he had none. He himself said so in the next paragraph of the article: *"Whatever doubts I had about internal happenings in Russia, I was quite clear in my mind about her foreign policy.* This had been consistently one of peace and, unlike England and France, of fulfilling international obligations and supporting the cause of democracy abroad. The Soviet Union stood as the one real effective bulwark against Fascism in Europe and Asia. Without the Soviet Union what could be the state of Europe today? Fascist reaction would triumph everywhere and democracy and freedom would become dreams of a past age."[5]

But unfortunately for him, the Soviet Union, "the sole defender of democracy" and "the one real effective bulwark against Fascism", signed a non-aggression pact with Nazi Germany and threw

[3] Ibid., pp. 181-82. Italics added.
[4] Ibid., p. 116. Italics added.
[5] Ibid., Italics added.

Europe into the throes of the Second World War. By the normal laws of human psychology, he should have felt ashamed of himself and admitted his mistake publicly like his master, Mahatma Gandhi. But, as we have already pointed out, he is no ordinary Soviet-addict. His psychology, therefore, has also been extraordinary. He had up his sleeve an apology for the Soviet Union, and he produced it as early as September 21, 1939 when he wrote: "Soviet Russia is at present a mystifying factor in the world situation. It is obvious that whatever Russia does will have important and far-reaching results. But as we do not know what she is going to do, we have to leave her out of our present calculations. *The Russo-German Pact came as a shock and surprise to many. There was nothing surprising in it except the manner of doing it and the moment chosen for it.* At any other time it would have naturally fitted in with Soviet foreign policy. But there can be little doubt that at that particular moment it brought dismay to many friends of Russia. There seemed to be too much over-reaching, cynicism and opportunism about it. That criticism applied to Hitler also, who overnight had dropped his fierce anti-Communism and apparently made friends with the Soviet. A cynic said that Russia had joined the Anti-Comintern Pact; another that Hitler was turning Communist as well as a patron of the Jews. All this seems to us fantastic nonsense, for there can be, and there is going to be, no real alliance between Hitler and Stalin. But both are willing enough to play at the game of power politics. Russia has suffered enough at the hands of England to resent it bitterly."[6] So, Russia had committed no crime; she was simply repaying England in the latter's own coin!

But the rape of poor Poland by the "socialist and anti-imperialist" Soviet Union was somewhat more difficult to defend. The admirers of the Soviet Union had constantly pointed out that she did not covet foreign territory. They had, of course, forgotten that the Soviet Red Army had tried to occupy Poland as early as 1920 and only the weakness of the Red Army had prevented it from playing its essentially imperialist role. And Soviet propaganda had turned this necessity into a virtue. Now all of a sudden the Red Army had marched into Poland which had not offended the Soviet Union in any way except refusing to ally with the Soviet Union which was Poland's sovereign right. Moreover, Poland had seen the fate of

[6] Ibid, pp. 308-09. Italics added.

Czechoslovakia which was allied with the Soviet Union, and which the latter had done nothing to save from Hitler. It was no fault of Poland that she saw no protection in a Polish-Soviet Alliance. She had instead depended on the protection promised by England and France which nations at least showed a sense of honour by declaring war against Nazi Germany.

Pandit Nehru was, of course, shocked. But like every inveterate Soviet-addict, he was quite capable of absorbing this shock also. He guessed and philosophised as follows: "The Soviet's march into Eastern Poland was another shock. But it is yet difficult to say whether this was to counter the German army or to weaken the Poles or merely to take advantage of a particular situation from the nationalist point of view. From the meagre information that we possess it seems, however, that Russia's advance into Poland has certainly come in the way of German designs. *It has prevented German occupation of Eastern Poland and cried a halt to the German army. More important still is the occupation of the entire Polish-Rumanian frontier by the Soviet army. This has made it certain that Germany cannot take possession of the Rumanian oil-fields which she coveted, and probably that she cannot draw upon the vast wheat supplies of Rumania.* The Balkans are saved from German aggression, and Turkey breathes with relief. All this may mean little today, but in the future, as the war progresses, it will have a vital significance. It may be thus that Soviet Russia has rendered a great service to the cause of the Western Allies, and Bernard Shaw's dictum that Stalin has made a cat's-paw of Hitler has some truth in it."[7] He had nothing to say when, after the fall of France, the German armies occupied Rumania and the Balkans, and Soviet Russia kept on looking the other way.

Everyone except Pandit Nehru and his communist comrades could see that the Nazi-Soviet Pact alone had given a free hand to Hitler for his triumphant march into Western Europe and the Balkans. The Pact had also strengthened Hitler's resources so that he could turn back and devour the Soviet Union. The nemesis came very soon. And it is recorded history how the poor and down-trodden people of Russia rose against Nazi hordes in defence of their Fatherland after the Red Army had collapsed all along the front, and after Stalin, who was responsible for inviting the German armies, ran away from Moscow like a rat.

[7] Ibid., pp. 309-10. Italics added.

Again, everyone knew in 1948 how Stalin had conspired with Hitler for a division of Europe and Asia between Germany and Russia. The records of the Ribbentrop-Molotov talks had been published by that time. They did not betray any socialist or democratic intentions on the part of the Soviet Union. If anything, they showed that Soviet Russia was as ruthless in pursuit of her imperialist designs as Hitler's Nazi Germany. Her record in Eastern Europe and China during 1945-47 had further confirmed that Soviet Russia intended to streamline her system of imperialism. But for Pandit Nehru all these facts did not mean a fig. He quietly permitted his minion to bring out another reprint of his "philosophisations" in the middle of 1948. He had become the Prime Minister of an independent India by that time due to the good graces of a British Government. And Krishna Menon was by now a responsible representative of the Indian Republic in his capacity as India's High Commissioner in England.

We do not know if there have been any more reprints of this book in India or abroad. Pandit Nehru has been a bestseller for years now. We should not be surprised if this book runs into more reprints without a comma being erased or a footnote being added, as if it were not a piece of puerile journalism but a sacrosanct scripture. Even in 1948, it was obvious that old copies of this book should have been hidden away from the public. But that sort of discretion demands a sense of shame. And Pandit Nehru has prospered without that sense over the past forty or more years.

The fifth book by Pandit Nehru, *The Discovery of India,* was published in early 1946. In this book, after taking his autobiographical thread upto 1936, he suddenly switches over to India's past history and culture till he reaches the point at which he had left. Then he resumes his commentary on events in India and abroad and comes up to the year 1942. This book, too, has seen many reprints and is supposed to bring into high relief Pandit Nehru as, "the statesman-philosopher".

In the very first chapter he wrote: "A study of Marx and Lenin produced a powerful effect on my mind and helped me to see history and current affairs in a new light. The long chain of history and of social development appeared to have some meaning, some sequence and the future lost some of its obscurity. The practical achievements of the Soviet Union were also tremendously impressive. Often I disliked or did not understand some development there and it seemed to me to be too closely concerned with the opportunism of the moment or the power politics of the day. But despite all these developments and possible distortions of the original passion for human betterment, *I had no doubt that the Soviet Revolution had advanced human society by a great leap and had lit a bright flame which could not be smothered, and that it had laid the foundation for the 'new civilisation' towards which the world would advance.* I am too much of an individualist and believer in personal freedom to like overmuch regimentation. Yet it seemed to me obvious that in a complex social structure individual freedom had to be limited, and perhaps the only way to real personal freedom was through some such limitation in the social sphere. The lesser liberties may often need limitation in the interest of the larger freedom."[8]

And again, when he returned to modern India: "We realized in our hearts that we could not do much till conditions were radically changed—hence our overwhelming desire for independence—and yet the passion for progress filled us and the wish to emulate other countries which had gone so far ahead in many ways. We thought of the United States of America and even of some eastern countries which were forging ahead. But most of all we had the example of the Soviet Union which in two brief decades, full of war and civil strife and in the face of what appeared to be insurmountable difficulties, had made tremendous progress. Some were attracted to communism, others were not, but all were fascinated by the advance of the Soviet Union in education and culture and medical care and physical fitness and in the solution of the problem of nationalities—by the amazing and prodigious effort to create a new world out of the dregs of the old."[9]

Thus we see that Pandit Nehru was quite a Soviet-addict up to the eve of his becoming the first Prime Minister of independent India in August 1947. Since then he has not written any major book from which we may find out his basic beliefs, but his speeches on foreign policy and other subjects leave little doubt that, by and large, his fascination for the Soviet Union has remained undiminished.

[8] Jawaharlal Nehru, *Discovery of India*, Signet Press, Calcutta, December 1947, pp. 12-13. Italics added.

[9] Ibid., p. 311.

SEVEN

A PERSISTENT PRO-SOVIET SPEAKER

Pandit Nehru's admirers are prepared to admit that he was influenced by communist thought to quite an extent before he became the first Prime Minister of independent India in August 1947. But they maintain (of course, in a purely *a priori* fashion) that since that event his sense of responsibility as leader of a major democracy has considerably diluted his devotion to purely theoretical questions, and developed in him a sense of proportion regarding the Soviet Union.

These people tell us that Pandit Nehru's unceasing tirades against the various Western alliances have been inspired not by his addiction to the Soviet Union but by his strong anti-imperialist inclinations coupled with his faith in non-violence. They add that he has been considerably annoyed with the West due to the latter's pro-Pakistan stand on the Kashmir question. He, they say, had come to put considerable trust in Western good faith after the British withdrawal from India. But the West has, over the past few years, frittered away that fund of goodwill by committing one folly after another. If, therefore, he has spoken against the West it must be due to his bitterness against the West rather than to any pro-Soviet proclivities on his part.

The Western nations, particularly the U.S.A., have gradually come to accept this explanation of what they describe as Pandit Nehru's neutralism. They are, therefore, vying with each other to "heal the wounds" which they think they have unwittingly inflicted on Pandit Nehru's "sensitive mind". And in that process Pandit Nehru's India has become the "bastion of democracy" in Asia and he himself the only firm guiding star for the destiny of what they describe as the underdeveloped nations. More recently, his "dynamic neutrality" is gaining prestige in the West as a model for all newly independent nations in Asia and Africa.

Independent India would have very much liked her Prime Minister to be inspired neither by the West nor by the East. India may be a newly independent country, but she is no new nation. In fact, in terms of her culture and civilisation, she is the only nation on earth which has still maintained an unbroken continuity with her ancient traditions. Those traditions have their own solutions to offer for most of the ills from which the world has been suffering ever since Christianity, Islam, and the materialist civilization of the modern West managed to unhinge nation after nation from their deeper moorings.

But that, perhaps, is too idealistic an aspiration. India does cherish her ancient traditions but is no longer alive to them. She may, therefore, not be able immediately to bring those traditions to bear on current controversies. But she can at least strive to preserve her independent identity and "judge each issue on its own merits", as Pandit Nehru is so fond of saying so often. To that end, it is necessary that India should understand the true nature of Communism as a streamlined system of neo-imperialism, and show some appreciation for the struggles of those nations which have to fight the communist menace for their very self-preservation. That is the minimum we should expect from an independent India.

But under Pandit Nehru's leadership, India has shown neither a will for self-preservation against the increasing communist threat to her own integrity, nor a minimum of sympathy for those who have had to stand up against Communism. And that is no accident. It is not due to any lack of information about the communist menace that India has kept her eyes shut towards it. Nor is it due to any lack of moral sense in the nation as a whole. If an explanation is to be found for this phenomenon of an independent India siding with the communist camp, we have to look into the mind of that man who has been the sole architect of India's policies since Sardar Patel died in December 1950. Let us see how that man's mind has functioned vis-a-vis the Soviet Union and Communism after he became our Prime Minister.

If we could present all of his speeches and statements after he assumed office, we would have more than adequate evidence to prove conclusively that he has continued to be a Soviet-addict all through these post-independence years. But that is a big job. We have before us only his selected speeches from 1946 to 1957 compiled and published by the Government of India in three volumes. To these volumes, then, we must turn.

Pandit Nehru announced his Interim Government on September 7, 1946. His statement on this occasion contained greetings to both the U.S.A. and the Soviet Union. He said: "We send our greetings to the people of the United States of America to whom destiny has given a major role in international affairs. We trust that this tremendous responsibility will be utilized for the furtherance of peace and human freedom everywhere. To that other great nation of the modern world, the Soviet Union, which also carries a vast responsibility for shaping world events, we send greetings. *They are our neighbours in Asia and inevitably we shall have to undertake many common tasks and have much to do with each other.*"[1]

Thus the U.S.A. was a country whom "destiny" had chosen to play a "major role", while the Soviet Union was willingly shouldering "a vast responsibility". Further, Pandit Nehru had doubts in his mind whether the U.S.A. would use her power and opportunity for the good of mankind. He had no such misgivings about the Soviet Union. But, above all, while the U.S.A. was a far-away nation, which had no common tasks to undertake with us, the Soviet Union was a "neighbour in Asia" and India had "much to do with her". The slant was quite meaningful for all those who had the intelligence to pick it up.

A few months later, on December 13, he moved the Objectives Resolution in the Constituent Assembly which was meeting in order to frame independent India's constitution. Talking of American, French, and Russian revolutions, he employed the same slant. He said: "I think also of the various constituent assemblies that have gone before and of what took place at the making of the great American nation when the fathers of that nation met and fashioned a Constitution which has stood the test of so many years, more than a century and a half, and of the great nation which has resulted, which has been built up on the basis of that Constitution. My mind goes back to that mighty revolution which took place also over 150 years ago and the Constituent Assembly that met in that gracious and lovely city of Paris which has fought so many battles for freedom... Then my mind goes back to a more recent revolution which gave rise to a new type of State, the revolution that took place in Russia and out of which has arisen the Union of Soviet Socialist Republics, another mighty country which is playing a tremendous part in the world, not only a mighty country, but for us in India, a neighbouring country."[2]

So, the Soviet Union was still "a new type of State" and "a neighbouring country". Any average student of politics knows that

[1] *Jawaharlal Nehru's Speeches, 1946-49*, The Publications Division, Government of India, New Delhi, Second Edition, November 1958, p. 3. Italics added.

[2] Ibid., pp. 9–10.

neighbourliness of States leads to mutual hostility more often than to mutual trust. If neighbourliness were a test, there were so many other countries which were nearer to India at that time. In a few more months Pakistan was to be India's neighbour on both sides of her borders. It has never occurred to Pandit Nehru to emphasize the neighbourliness of Pakistan. And for obvious reasons. Geographical nearness is never meaningful unless it is accompanied by ideological nearness. What he was referring to in his speech was the ideological nearness of the Soviet Union.

Next year, on March 5, 1947, he gave an inaugural address to the Asian Relations Conference at New Delhi. Delegates from the Soviet Union had been admitted to that Conference on his plea that Russia was an Asian country as well and not a European Power which had colonised and subjugated vast areas of the Asian continent. Welcoming the various delegations, he said: "We welcome you, delegates and representatives from China, that great country to which Asia owes so much and from which so much is expected; from Egypt and the Arab countries of Western Asia, inheritors of a proud culture which spread far and wide and influenced India greatly; from Iran whose contacts with India go back to the dawn of history; from Indonesia and Indo-China whose history is intertwined with India's culture, and where recently the battle of freedom has continued, a reminder to us that freedom must be won and cannot come as a gift; from Turkey that has been rejuvenated by the genius of a great leader; from Korea and Mongolia, Siam, Malaya and the Philippines; *from the Soviet Republics of Asia which have advanced so rapidly in our generation and which have so many lessons to teach us*."[3]

Thus, while every other country had only past achievements to its credit, the Soviet Union alone had "so many lessons to teach us". The significant slant was once more very obvious to the intelligent ear.

Very soon India became independent as a result of Britain's voluntary and peaceful withdrawal. Pandit Nehru's sister, Vijayalakshmi Pandit, was appointed India's Ambassador in Moscow. But by that time the Kremlin had become intensely hostile to India. India had given no offence to the Soviet Union, except that the Indian National Congress rather than the Communist Party of India

[3] Ibid., p. 300. Italics added.

had come to power. One had to read the weekly *New Times,* a journal published from Moscow, to realise the depth of Kremlin's displeasure with Indian leaders. The Congress was being accused of selling India to "Anglo-American imperialism" in order to forestall a "people's revolution". In a few months, the Communist Party of India was to launch its famous 1948 insurrection on direct orders from Moscow. Naturally, Moscow could not be expected to be courteous to India's Ambassador.

Like her brother, Mrs. Vijayalakshmi Pandit had so far hobnobbed with various communist fronts in India. Even so, she was given a very cold reception in Moscow. She was not able to meet Stalin despite her repeated requests. And by the time she came back from her post in her brother's Fatherland, she was completely cured of her communist inclinations. She resented the fact that Moscow was refusing to accept India as an independent country. Moscow made its hostility patent even in petty matters. One such matter was the supply of furniture to the new Indian Embassy. She had to buy all the furniture she needed from Stockholm, and incur heavy expenditure on that account. Pandit Nehru was aware of the inside story.

But when some members in India's Assembly raised a question as to why the Indian Ambassador in Moscow had to spend so much for importing furniture from abroad, he did not tell the truth. Instead, he apologised for the Soviet Union. He rebuked the House for failing to understand Soviet Russia. He said: "A great deal of criticism has been made about our Ambassador in Moscow getting furniture from Stockholm. Well, how a house has to be furnished in Moscow, of course, Hon. Members do not realize. It just is not possible to furnish it easily in Moscow. You get an empty house. We thought of sending things from India, but it was almost a physical impossibility unless you spent vast sums on aeroplanes to carry chairs and tables from here. Of course, it could have been furnished alternatively with Russian furniture. *The Russian people, and all credit to them for this, ever since the war, are so intent on doing what they consider to be the fundamental things that they refuse to waste their time on the accessories of life.* They have to rebuild their country after the most horrible suffering and damage suffered in the war and they are concentrating on major undertakings. They go about in patched-up clothes and worn-out shoes. It does not matter, but they are building dams, reservoirs and factories and the rest which they consider more important. So it is not easy to get any of these small accessories of life for the moment. The only things you can get in Russia are antique pieces of Czarist days which are frightfully expensive. The result is that our Embassy in Moscow had to go to Stockholm for its chairs and tables, and as these were urgently required — office equipment, etc. — our Ambassador had to go there."[4]

It would have been difficult for anyone except an incurable Soviet-addict to believe that the Soviet Government could not supply ordinary furniture for a small embassy such as we had initially established in Moscow. There is ample evidence that other embassies in Moscow were buying a lot of furniture at that very time. Even if furniture was not readily available from stock a dictatorial government like that of the Soviet Union could have got it fabricated overnight, had it so wished. There are many instances of the Soviet Government performing such "miracles" at short notice.

The simple truth was that Moscow at that time was not favourably inclined to having an embassy from a country which in its estimation was no more than a "semi-colony of Wall Street imperialism". Moscow knew that Pandit Nehru had all along been its own minion. But Moscow also knew that Pandit Nehru was powerless so long as Sardar Patel wielded the Congress Party machine and exercised his "reactionary" influence against the "progressive people". And Moscow was angry with Pandit Nehru for his failure to put up a fight against Sardar Patel by making a common cause with the Communist Party of India. So Moscow behaved as it did. But all these studied insults heaped on his country and on his own sister presented no occasion to Pandit Nehru for having second thoughts about the Soviet Union. He only felt called upon to invent yet another apology for Moscow. In fact, he went further and praised Soviet Russia's preoccupation with "fundamental things" after the fashion of a straight-forward sycophant. Moscow's manners towards a newly independent country were not at all "fundamental" in his scheme of things.

As regards the Russian people, they had gone about in "patched-up clothes and worn-out shoes" ever since the Bolsheviks seized power in Russia. They had no say in the matter and they could not come in the way of the Kremlin selling furniture to the Indian Embassy. On the other hand, the communist bosses in

[4] Ibid., p. 211. Italics added.

Soviet Russia were, even during those days of post-war shortages, living in great comfort and enjoying all the amenities of civilised life. Things of luxury were being produced for them in plenty. If the bosses had wanted to sell furniture to the Indian Embassy, they had only to issue an order and all that was needed could have been manufactured in a day.

Then came the communist insurrection inside India and an avalanche of malicious Soviet propaganda against the Congress Party, its leaders, and its Government. Pandit Nehru was now portrayed as a "co-partner in Sardar Patel's crimes". Next year, that is in 1949, China went communist. Mao Tse-tung at once sent a message to B.T. Ranadive, General Secretary of the CPI, that India, too, was going to be "liberated before long". A few months later, Peking was describing Pandit Nehru as a "running dog of American imperialism". It was, therefore, natural that opinion inside the Congress Party became pretty hostile against Communism and the communist countries. Sardar Patel was still alive. So Pandit Nehru had to stop singing his hymns in praise of the Soviet Union. But he also refused to utter a word against Communism or the communist "paradise".

Had he been in possession of normal mental faculties, here was an opportunity for him to see the truth about the Soviet Union. He had admired that country for more than 20 years. He had refused to protest publicly even when, in his private opinion, the Soviet Union had acted in a way which he did not consider right. Yet, without any provocation whatsoever from him, the Soviet press had launched a malicious campaign against him personally, and the Kremlin had directed its hired hounds to overthrow his Government — a Government for which he had fought and suffered for many years.

It is the tragedy of Soviet-addicts that they can seldom overcome their infatuation. They always have an explanation for Soviet misdeeds. Now the explanation for which Pandit Nehru plumped was that the Soviet Union had been committed to a wrong line by an obstinate and die-hard faction in the Kremlin, and that Stalin was personally opposed to it. So he had only to wait and watch.

His next opportunity came in 1952. Sardar Patel was dead, and the Congress Party was fast heading towards becoming his pocket organisation. Meanwhile, the fiasco of the new communist line in Korea had moved the world communist camp towards wooing the newly independent nations in Asia. Early in 1952, it was more than clear that the Party line in India was changing towards "parliamentarianism". He immediately broke his silence and resumed his rhetoric in the service of the Soviet Union.

India had her first Parliament in session now. More than two dozen communist M.Ps were occupying the Opposition benches in New Delhi. They were bitterly critical of Government policies. Addressing these traitors on May 22, 1952, Pandit Nehru said on the floor of the Parliament: "I am sure that the honourable Members of the Opposition remember that Lenin is believed to have described Communism as soviets plus electricity. I am anxious to impress on the House that whatever has been done in India in these five years cannot be dismissed as insignificant. *Foreigners, even those from the great lands of Russia and China, have often been surprised at the measure of our achievements*. Not that they necessarily agreed with our policy. Unfortunately their access to news about India is limited and those who do supply them with information about this country are full of their own ideas and only too readily condemn everything we have done."[5] It sounds strange that the Soviet Government should, at that time, be misinformed about India. India had become a fully democratic country in which information was readily available to anyone who cared for it. And Moscow was now maintaining an Embassy in New Delhi and Consulates in several other cities. Unlike Russia, India was maintaining no Iron Curtain.

Slightly later, but during the same speech, he proclaimed: "I can say with some confidence that there is hardly any other country in the world, *perhaps including Russia also,* which can claim to have laid the foundations of scientific progress as we have in so short a period of time. It is true that Russia is far more advanced than we are but I am referring to the initial stages of development."[6] So the model to be admired and seek comparison with was still the Soviet Union. The sins of the Soviet Union towards the new Republic of India were explained away as due to lack of proper information. Only he could believe that Moscow was guided by the misinformation provided by its hirelings in India! The plain truth was that these hirelings were prepared to see the white as black and vice versa at Moscow's bidding.

[5] *Jawaharlal Nehru's Speeches, 1949–53,* The Publications Division, Government of India, New Delhi, Second Impression, June 1957, p. 34. Italics added.

[6] Ibid., p. 35. Italics added.

EIGHT

A DEVOTED DISCIPLE OF STALIN

The question may be asked that if Pandit Nehru was not very important in the Congress organisation so long as Mahatma Gandhi and Sardar Patel were alive, how did he come to dominate the organisation within a very short time after Sardar's death, and to swing the country fast towards his Soviet Fatherland. An answer to this question needs an analysis of the character of our nationalism during our struggle with British imperialism.

The negative content of our nationalism in those days was one for all — the British must go and Indians should rule India. But when it came to postulating the positive content of our nationalism, the nationalist ranks had split apart into two opposite camps. And the two camps had struggled for supremacy ever since the Indian National Congress started becoming a radical organisation at the turn of the nineteenth century.

To one camp of nationalism belonged the various kinds of worshippers of the West. For them, India's geography alone was of some significance because that geography placed some limits on India's progress towards becoming a carbon copy of this or that country in the West. For the rest, India was a clean slate on which this or that ideological language could be transcribed at will. India's hoary history, India's ancient traditions, India's characteristic culture, India's philosophy and religion, had no meaning for them except in so far as they could be interpreted to fit neatly into some western model. These worshippers of the West called themselves liberals and constitutionalists so long as the British system of parliamentary democracy dominated the ideological climate in the Western world.

But as soon as the Bolsheviks seized power in Russia, the leading sections of Western intelligentsia were swept into the stream of a new ideology — that of Communism. The ground for this ideological shift had been prepared by half-a-century of socialist propaganda, particularly in the universities of the West. Those intellectuals who could not stomach Bolshevik barbarism became socialists of one brand or the other. But, none the less, the socialists were like the protestant sects surrounding a monolithic Catholic Church. They had their points of difference with communist doctrine and communist ritual, but, by and large, they always rallied round Communism whenever it was under attack from any opposite ideology.

This ideological revolution in the West had a powerful impact on the worshippers of the West in India. They increasingly tended to become communists and recommended what they thought was a revolutionary programme for the regeneration of India. Pandit Nehru has been the leader of this camp ever since he was pushed forward by Mahatma Gandhi to become the President of the Indian National Congress in 1929. There are many sects and sub-sects within this camp — the liberals, the radicals, the socialists and the communists — and their mutual quarrels are quite often very bitter indeed. But whenever they are faced with the opposite camp of Indian nationalism, they try to close their ranks and present a united front of "all progressive forces".

The opposite camp of Indian nationalism was in revolt not only against Western imperialism but also against Western civilization. For these nationalists, India could regenerate herself and rise again only if she succeeded in recapturing her ancient spirit, and revitalising her age-old traditions and institutions. And to start with, this camp had very powerful spokesmen and leaders, so much so that at the Surat Congress in 1907 it succeeded in capturing the Congress organisation and driving the Westernisers into wilderness. But the victory was short-lived. By the time of the Bolshek Revolution, the leaders of this camp were either in retirement, or mauled. The path seemed to be clear for the Westernisers to stage a comeback.

The Westernisers could not capture the Congress organization immediately. The hold of Mahatma Gandhi on the Congress and the common masses was too deep to permit that development. And the Mahatma was instinctively suspicious of whatever came from the West. Nevertheless, in the ideological struggle that followed, the Westernisers were in a clearly advantageous position. The moralisings of the Mahatma were no match for a monolithic system of thought with which the Westernisers were now armed. Increasing amounts of material support from Soviet Russia made a decisive difference.

Moreover, the Congress organisation under Mahatma Gandhi gradually passed into the hands of politicians who had, by and large, no clear-cut ideological moorings, and who pursued power to the utter neglect of any battle for the minds of men. Thus, in due course, we had the anomaly of powerful politicians who were unpopular and powerless politicians who were popular. The Western education imparted in our universities was fast multiplying an intelligentsia which supported the camp of the Westernisers. In due course, the opposite camp was left with no intelligentsia to support its case. In fact, that camp seemed to have no case at all. Mounting communist propaganda made that camp look like a crowd of mindless people serving "reactionary" causes.

That was not the truth. The camp of the Congress Right as they came to be described in latter-day political parlance had, on the whole, a larger number of clean and honest patriots in its ranks. The camp of the Congress Left was, by and large, composed of communist traitors and woolly headed socialists who were perpetually split between their loyalty to India and their addiction to the Soviet Union. But the case of the Congress Right went by default. It had no philosophy of its own and no intellectual equipment to present or defend its case. On the other hand, the Soviet apparatus in India was busy providing all the philosophy and propaganda that was needed by the Congress Left for addressing itself to the intelligentsia.

This contradiction between power and popularity continued till Sardar Patel died in December 1950. So long as he was alive, he kept the Congress Left at bay. But as soon as he was gone, the Congress Right was left with no leader who could rally its ranks. Pandit Nehru saw his opportunity and, using his popularity as a powerful handle, he forced the Congress Right to surrender the Congress organisation to him. And by the year 1954 when the Avadi Congress passed its resolution in support of the "socialistic pattern of society", the Congress Right had already ceased to exist except in communist and socialist propaganda. The old leaders of the Congress Right ended by becoming Pandit Nehru's clever courtiers, which they have remained ever since and which they continue to be today.

Thus the contradiction between power and popularity was at last resolved with the victory of a Westerniser inside the Congress Party. Pandit Nehru had been popular ever since he started leaning towards the communist camp. Now he rose to unrivalled power as well inside the Congress organisation. Now he could go ahead with his hymns to the Soviet Union without fear of any serious resistance from any quarters. And very soon he attained his old poetic heights in praise of the Soviet Union once more.

On June 7, 1952, he addressed the Scheduled Tribes and Scheduled Areas Conference in New Delhi. Coming to the language problem, he said: "It is absolutely clear to me that the Government must encourage the tribal languages. It is not enough simply to allow them to prevail. They must be given all possible support and conditions in which they can flourish must be safeguarded. We must go out of our way to achieve this. *In the Soviet Republic we have the example of a country that has adopted such a policy with success.* Lenin and other leaders in his time were exceedingly wise in this respect. Regardless of their ultimate objective, they wanted to win the goodwill of the people and they won it largely by their policy of encouraging their languages, by going out of their way to help hundreds of dialects, by preparing dictionaries and vocabularies and sometimes even by evolving new scripts where there were none. They wanted their people to feel that they were free to live their own lives and they succeeded in producing that impression."[1]

He had never bothered to have a second look at the Soviet prison-house of nationalities. He was still repeating the slogans he had learnt during his first visit of Moscow in November 1927. If he had cared to study the latest data from the Soviet Union he would have known how all non-Russian languages had been heavily Russianised till they had come to retain only their outer shells.

A month later, on July 7, 1952, he gave a repeat performance in the Parliament. Replying to the point raised by the fellow-travelling M.P., Dr. Meghnad Saha, he said: "Professor Saha referred to the separate republics in the Soviet Union in support of the theory of linguistic provinces in India. The two are not really comparable, because India is much more of a unity than the Soviet Union. *The Soviet Union is no longer a single empire but the union of a number of entirely different countries.* They have formed a political unit and are happy about it. That is very good. They proceeded on the basis of independent republics federating together. Now, India cannot function on that basis."[2]

He was right about India being different. But he did not refer to, or refute, the communist proposition, entertained by the likes of Dr. Saha, that India too was a bundle of nationalities. And only a

[1] Ibid., p. 46. Italics added.
[2] Ibid., p. 61–62. Italics added.

Soviet-addict could believe, as late as July 1952, that the Soviet Slave Empire was a "federation of independent republics". The autocratic manner in which Stalin had created and abolished Soviet republics had failed to leave any impression on his mind.

On November 1, 1952, he addressed the Harijan Convention at Wardha. Speaking about the dignity of labour, he cited the Soviet precedent in the following words: "After the revolution of 1917, the Russians had to work tremendously hard before they could reach their present position. They had their Five Year Plans and laboured with diligence and patience for them. *The people gladly endured hardship and suffering so that the foundations of their Republic may be true and strong*. The Russian Revolution took place 35 years ago and it is only now that the people are beginning to gather the fruits of their labours. For the first decade, they had to work hard and suffer even more than they did under the old regime, but they had courage and confidence."[3]

Only a Soviet-addict could believe, at the end of 1952, that the forced labour extracted by Stalin from whole masses of a terrorised people was a symbol of sacrifice and willingly accepted hard work. For others, the story of Soviet slave-labour camps was too well documented to leave them in any doubt about the "dignity of labour" in Soviet Russia.

But the clearest evidence that he was still an unrepentant Soviet-addict came on March 6, 1953. Stalin, the blood-thirsty dictator of Soviet Russia for twenty-five years, had died (or been murdered) the previous day. The Russian people and even the Russian communists heaved a sigh of relief at the passing away of this fiend, as we were to know in 1956 when Khrushchev made his famous speech about Stalin. But the communists and fellow-travellers outside the Soviet Union felt orphaned. And in that list of orphans, Pandit Nehru stood almost at the top.

Using the floor of a democratic parliament for paying tribute to the most terrible tyrant in human history, he said on March 6, 1953: "When we think of Marshal Stalin all kinds of thoughts come to our minds, *at least to my mind* and the panorama of history for the last 35 years passes before our eyes. *All of us here are children of his age*... We have grown up not only participating in our struggles in this country but participating in other ways with the mighty

---

[3] Ibid., p. 63. Italics added.

struggles that have taken place in this world, and been affected by them. And so looking back at these 35 years or so, many figures stand out, but perhaps no single figure has moulded and affected and influenced the history of these years more than Marshal Stalin... He proved himself great in peace and in war... He was, I believe, technically not the head of the Soviet State — but Marshal Stalin was something much more than the head of a State... *I believe that his influence was exercised generally in favour of peace. When war came, he proved himself a very great warrior, but from all information that we have had, his influence has been in favour of peace.*"[4]

Nothing could be more shameful and sad than this praise of Stalin by the Prime Minister of a democratic country in which the large majority of people still professed a faith in *Sanatana Dharma*. For Pandit Nehru personally, it was doubly shameful. For, Stalin was the only world leader who had kept mum when Mahatma Gandhi was murdered in 1948. The incident revealed that his real Master all these years had been Marshal Stalin and not Mahatma Gandhi as many people had believed and continue to believe even today.

It was a foregone conclusion that once a Soviet-addict like Pandit Nehru rose to supreme power in India, the Communist Party of India would have full opportunity for spreading its poison and expanding its apparatus. All through 1952 and 1953, a spate of cultural delegations passing between India and this or that communist country. The communist fronts became frantically active. Communist literature from Soviet Russia and Red China started pouring into India in an increasing torrent. Very soon, the atmosphere was surcharged with communist slogans. And an American explanation was abroad that Pandit Nehru was striking at the very roots of the Communist Party of India by "taking the wind out of its sails", that is, by shouting communist slogans more loudly and adopting communist policies more enthusiastically than even the communists themselves.

It was a measure of the atmosphere at that time that when Pandit Nehru's old and trusted friend, Shaikh Abdullah, had to be dismissed and jailed, he was dismissed and jailed not as a traitor to India, which he was, but as an American agent, that is, as a traitor

[4] Quoted by C. Parameshwaran, *Nehru's Foreign Policy X-Rayed*, New Delhi, 1954, pp. 82-83. Italics added.

to the communist camp. That was a lie of course, and Shaikh Abdullah's opponents have still to provide proof that this spoilt child of Pandit Nehru's perverted Secularism was conspiring with anyone except his own unlimited ambition. But this lie passed unchallenged because the atmosphere had become full of much bigger lies.

There were certain other developments which we shall take up when we come to Pandit Nehru's foreign policy. As a result of all these developments, the stage was set by the middle of 1954 for Chou En-lai to make a dramatic dash from Geneva to New Delhi and sign the famous *Panchashila*. Towards the end of the year Pandit Nehru paid a return visit to Red China. He had now found a new communist Fatherland in Mao's New China in addition to his old Fatherland in Stalin's Soviet Russia.

So far he had been harping that conditions in India were very much similar to conditions in Soviet Russia. Now he started sounding a different note. The conditions in India were no more similar to conditions in Soviet Russia, but compared very favourably with conditions in communist China. Speaking at a press conference on November 13, 1954, he said: "The nature of problems is similar between India and China. *They are not so similar between India and Russia*. The Soviet Union is a vast territory but very thinly inhabited, compared to India. We have the problem of vast numbers of human beings but limited land. The Soviet Union has plenty of land. See the consequences of this, apart from communism. If they in Russia want to deal with their land problem, it is very easy, because the population is small and land plentiful. With us human beings are too many, and land is little. That is a basic difference. Take our Gangetic Valley, which is heavily populated. The problem of our introducing, let us say, tractor cultivation in a heavily populated area is completely different from the problem of introducing tractor cultivation in a sparsely populated area, which the Soviet Union is. One has to approach the problem by taking into consideration various factors, quite apart from theories. That is why I say that the problems of India and China in regard to land development, industries, and even in regard to floods, are rather similar."[5]

It is a truism that problems are not universal and objective, that

[5] *Jawaharlal Nehru's Speeches, 1953-57*, The Publications Division, Government of India, New Delhi, Second Impression, 1958, p. 277. Italics added.

is, they do not exist irrespective of the ideological manner in which we look at them. The Chinese were now presenting their problems in a communist perspective that had been imposed on them by a Soviet-built political apparatus. The problems presented by India could not be similar unless India was also starting to look at them through communist glasses. So when Pandit Nehru invited his countrymen to put their problems on par with problems of China, he was simultaneously suggesting a communist solution. And the communist professors led by Prasant Mahalonobis and aided by Soviet experts were, in fact, hammering out a communist plan inside the Planning Commission in those very days.

Next year, Pandit Nehru visited the Soviet Union as a state guest. He described the visit as a "pilgrimage", the second on his part. He had been pining to be in the Soviet Union since a very long time. But circumstance after circumstance had conspired to prevent him from this fulfilment. Now he had his *darshan*. He received a hero's reception. That was his due after all the services he had rendered to the Soviet cause inside India and on the international stage. And he paid rich tributes to his dreamland. Speaking in Moscow on June 22, 1955, he admired the Soviet Union in the following words: "I have been deeply impressed by the great achievements of the Soviet Union. I have seen the transformation of this vast land through the industry of its people and the great urge that drives them forward to better their own condition. I have admired the music, dancing and superb ballets that I have seen. I have been impressed most of all by the great care taken by the State and by the people of children and the younger generation of this great country."[6]

A few months later, Bulganin and Khrushchev were in India. he gave them a reception which these people had never known in the whole of their lives. One has to look at his photographs on this occasion and compare them with his photographs on other occasions in order to find out how hilarious he was feeling all along. Something of that hilarity flowed out into his speeches. Speaking at a banquet given in Rashtrapati Bhavan on November 22, 1955, he addressed Bulganin and Khrushchev in the following words: *"This is not a mere formal matter of welcome. Events have demonstrated that there is a deeper friendship and understanding between the*

---

[6] Ibid., p. 305.

people of our two great countries which are more significant than the formality of welcome. That understanding and friendship has progressively grown, even though the paths we have pursued in our respective countries have varied. But in spite of this difference of approach in dealing with our problems, which was inevitable in the circumstances which conditioned our countries and our peoples, there has been no element of conflict between us and there has been an approach to each other in many important fields of human activity. I am happy that this is so, and I hope it will be so in the future. We are neighbour countries and it is right that there should be a feeling of neighbourliness and friendship between us for the mutual advantage of both our countries and our peoples. I believe also that this friendship is good for the larger causes of the world, and more particularly for the most vital cause of all, the peace of the world."[7]

One wonders what friendship could be possible between a country like India which had no ambitions outside her natural borders, and a country like Soviet Russia which had been conspiring to add India to her empire ever since 1920 and which was maintaining a hired fifth-column inside India. Bulganin and Khrushchev must have felt fulfilled as they watched this performance on the part of their most prominent dupe in India..

On January 7, 1956, he again cited communist China and Soviet Russia as models for India in the following words:

"It is agreed by all—and that indeed is our firm policy—that we should go towards a socialist structure of society. We want that not because of some emotional feeling but for very practical considerations. We cannot meet the social problem of the day except in that direction. I hope everybody realizes that to achieve socialism or indeed to achieve any kind of a really high standard in this country is a long-term process. It is not good to delude the public that we can achieve it quickly. Even in China Chairman Mao repeatedly talks of achieving socialism in twenty years in spite of all the authoritarian powers that they have had and the tremendous capacity of the Chinese people for work.

"We talk of Russia, but we forget that it is 38 years since they have been at it, apart from communism and other considerations. I asked the Soviet leaders who were here, when they thought they

---

[7] Ibid., p. 309. Italics added.

would achieve their objective of a communist society and they said that it would take fifteen or twenty years more—whatever their idea of a communist society is. *Perhaps it means abundance for everybody.*"[8]

But Khrushchev dropped a bomb on believers like Pandit Nehru. He revealed the misdeeds of Stalin before the 20th Congress of the Soviet Communist Party. This must have been a moment of supreme mental crisis for Pandit Nehru. He had worshipped and worked for Stalin for thirty years. But he was no ordinary devotee. He gritted his teeth and quietly absorbed the shock. Stalin might have been a monster, but there could be no doubt that the Soviet society which Stalin had created was a very great piece of work! Speaking before the Lok Sabha on March 20, 1956, he welcomed the "new trends" in Soviet Russia in the following words: "I should like to take this opportunity of drawing the attention of the House to a very important event in recent weeks. I refer to the Twentieth Congress of the Communist Party of the Soviet Union which met recently in Moscow. There can be no doubt that this Congress has adopted a new line and a new policy. This new line, both in political thinking and in practical policy, appears to be based upon a more realistic appreciation of the present world situation and represents a significant process of adaptation and adjustment. According to our principles we do not interfere in the internal affairs of other countries, just as we do not welcome any interference of others in our country. But any important development in any country which appears to be a step towards the creation of conditions favourable to the pursuit of a policy of peaceful co-existence is important for us as well as others. It is for this reason that we feel that the decisions of the Twentieth Congress of the Soviet Union are likely to have far-reaching effects. I hope that this development will lead to a further relaxation of tension in the world."[9] Not a single word about the sins of Stalin!

So far he had been praising the Soviet Union because Stalin was there. Now he was praising it on the plea that Stalin was no more there! He conceded, although indirectly, that the old critics of Stalin's Russia whom he had attacked and ridiculed as reactionaries for more than thirty years, were right. But in the next breath, he took a right-about-turn and came back to his old position of admi-

---

[8] Ibid., p. 76. Italics added.
[9] Ibid., p. 318. Italics added.

ration for the Soviet Union. He barked back at the critics that now that Stalin had been denounced they should have no cause for complaint. All his Marxism could not help him to see that a whole epoch of human history could not be blamed upon an individual. Stalin was as much a creature as a creator of Communism. And Soviet Russia was still swearing by that ideology.

Thus he had passed the supreme test laid down by the Soviet bosses: Are you for or against the Soviet Union? The dethronement of Stalin was a disillusionment for many men and women of weaker mettle. He was not one of them. He had qualified for that class of Soviet-addicts who will always stand by the Soviet Union till either the Soviet Union breaks down under the weight of its own crimes or they themselves suffer a fall due to their frightful follies.[10]

---

[10] Alas! Pandit Nehru suffered a fall and passed away before the Soviet Union broke down. One wonders what he would have said in 1991, had he lived to see the collapse of Communism. I am sure he would have joined the club of morons who maintain that the failure of Soviet practice does not invalidate communist theory. (Footnote added in 1993).

NINE

A FELLOW-TRAVELLER OF SOVIET FOREIGN POLICY-1

The Gita has laid down a profound principle in the following words: "The person is characterised by his credo. Whatever is a person's credo, that he is."

And a person's credo can be identified not so much in the words he speaks or writes as in the actions that flow freely out of him. The speaker or the writer who fails to act in terms of the faith he propounds in his speeches and writings is no more than a sophist who may be successful with some people or for some time but who is sure to be found out sooner or later. The tragedy of a sophist is that his own words fail to sink into the inner recesses of his being and inspire his actions in life.

Most of us ordinary human beings are sophists to a certain extent. We speak and write many words which we never mean. But some of our own words do find a way within, and we act in terms of the credo contained in those words. So if our professions are compared with our practices, a residue can always be discovered where the two correspond with one another. If the rest of our professions are peeled off, the core of our personality stands revealed.

Now, if we were to identify Shri Jawaharlal Nehru's person in terms of the professions put forward in his books and speeches, we must, like his American admirers, come to the conclusion that he is without a doubt a very complex person. For, in his written and spoken words, he has not been an unadulterated admirer of the Soviet Union and the creed of Communism. In fact, he as a writer and speaker seems to be an admirer of many things which completely contradict the communist credo.

He has composed some essays on the beauties of Buddhism as he understands it. Whenever he has turned his face to the "materialistic" West, he has talked fondly of India's "ancient heritage" and "moral-spiritual values". As and when there has been tension on the international stage, he has dramatised himself as a devoted disciple of Mahatma Gandhi. He has also spoken and written a lot about the profundities of parliamentary democracy. On an occasion, particularly in moments of frustration in his whole-time pursuit of power, he has contemplated the cosmos and mumbled about the mysteriousness of it all.

But he has never been so complex in his actions. In fact, he in action has been more straight and simple than most of us moderns are. There has never been a trace of tortuousness in his actions, which have always travelled along a single track. He might have often failed to have his own way because this nation has yet to fully affirm his own cherished faith. But he has never failed to charter the nation's course in very clear-cut terms.

Had he been a Soviet-addict only in his writings and speeches, he would have presented no serious problem. We have had so many socialists who in their speeches or writings have been, till recently, like blue-blooded communists in their admiration for the Soviet Union. But whenever the interests of the Soviet Union have clashed with the interests of their own nation, our socialists have acted like true nationalists. Whenever the Soviet Union has outraged their sense of human values, our socialists have denounced the Soviet Union.

But Pandit Nehru has never been like our socialists whom he has often pooh-poohed as a "debating club". He has always tried to translate his admiration for the Soviet Union into clear and concrete action. That is the point, and the only point, where his professions have corresponded with his practice. The whole history of his career in national and international politics is characterised by this close correspondence. We shall review that history in the following articles.

Pandit Nehru had entered the Comintern network for the first time in 1924-25 when he was clandestinely contacted by Eileen Roy, the first wife of M.N. Roy, who had set up in Paris the *Comite Pro-Hindou* in collaboration with the famous French communist, Henri Barbusse. This organisation was a communist front financed by the Comintern for planting the communist conspiracy in India. He left for Europe in March 1925, ostensibly for the medical treatment of his wife but really in order to establish a liaison with the world communist movement. He himself admits: "Further treatment in Switzerland was recommended for my wife. *I welcomed the idea for I wanted an excuse to go out of India myself.* My mind was befogged, and no clear path was visible; and I thought that, perhaps, if I was far from India I could see things in a better perspective and lighten up the dark corners of my mind."[1]

[1] *An Autobiography*, p. 147. Italics added.

Those were the days when the socialist parties affiliated to the Comintern were being Bolshevised in keeping with the decisions of the 5th Congress of the Comintern held in June 1924. Soviet Russia's attempt to turn these socialist parties into mere mouthpieces of Soviet foreign policy had split the socialist movement. The Social Democrats in most European countries were getting separated from the communist cliques, and the Second International was getting revived as a challenge to the Third or the Communist International. So the Comintern was moving towards denouncing all Social Democrats as Social Fascists who were, in its own terminology, "imperialism's second line of defence".

The Comintern called a Congress of Oppressed Nationalities in February 1927 to crystallise its new line in the colonies of the various Western Powers. The Congress met in Brussels and Pandit Nehru attended it on behalf of the Indian National Congress. He writes: "Towards the end of 1926 I happened to be in Berlin, and I learnt there of a forthcoming Congress of Oppressed Nationalities, which was to be held at Brussels. The idea appealed to me, and I wrote home, suggesting that the Indian National Congress might take official part in the Brussels Congress. My suggestion was approved; and I was appointed the Indian Congress representative for this purpose."[2]

And he swallowed the Comintern line against the Social Democrats — hook, line and sinker. He himself confesses: "The Brussels Congress, as well as the subsequent Committee meetings of the League, which were held in various places from time to time, helped me to understand some of the problems of colonial and dependent countries. They gave me also an insight into the inner conflicts of the Western Labour world. I knew something about them already; I had read about them, but there was no reality behind my knowledge, as there had been no personal contacts. I had some such contacts now, and sometimes had to face problems which reflected these inner conflicts. *As between the Labour worlds of the Second International and the Third International, my sympathies were with the latter.* The whole record of the Second International from the War onwards filled me with distaste, and we in India had had sufficient personal experience of the methods of one of its strongest supports—the British Labour Party. *So I turned in-*

[2] Ibid., p. 161.

evitably with goodwill towards Communism, for whatever its faults, it was at least not hypocritical and not imperialistic. It was not a doctrinal adherence, as I did not know much about the fine points of Communism, my acquaintance being limited at the time to its broad features. These attracted me as also the tremendous changes taking place in Russia."[3]

This unflinching faith in the Comintern qualified him for an important position in the League against Imperialism, the permanent organisation created by the Congress of Oppressed Nationalities. He was elected to the Executive Committee of the League and attended several of its meetings while he was staying in Europe. He had also qualified as a worthy visitor to the Soviet Union, where he was taken in November 1927.

He returned to India in December 1927 to attend the Madras session of the Indian National Congress which was being held that month. Now he was a man with a firm faith. He says: "I was returning from Europe in good physical and mental condition. *I felt I had a clear perception of world affairs, more grip on the present day world, ever changing as it was.* I had read largely, not only on current affairs and politics, but on many other subjects that interested me, cultural and scientific. I found the vast political, economic, and cultural changes going on in Europe and America a fascinating study. *Soviet Russia, despite certain unpleasant aspects, attracted me greatly, and seemed to hold forth a message of hope to the world.*"[4]

The first job he did for the Comintern on his return to India was to draft a number of resolutions in keeping with the Comintern line and present them to the Madras Congress. All of them were passed. He records: "I presented a bunch of resolutions to the Working Committee—resolutions on Independence, War Danger, association with the League against Imperialism, etc.—and nearly all of these were accepted and made into official Working Committee resolutions."[5]

By now the Comintern had finalised its thesis on the "capitalistic encirclement of the Soviet Union" according to which the lead-

[3] Ibid., p. 163. Italics added.

[4] Ibid., p. 166. Italics added. It was not long before he started attacking his colleagues in the Congress as reactionaries and the rest. He was even reported to have said that the Mahatma had gone senile. The exchange of letters between him and the Mahatma provides an interesting episode — how he aggressed, how he took fright, and how he retreated fast. (Footnote added in 1993.)

[5] Ibid., p. 167.

ing Western Powers, particularly Britain and France, were getting ready for waging an "imperialist war" against the Soviet Union. That thesis was to be proclaimed by the VI Congress of the Comintern held in 1928. Meanwhile, the Comintern network everywhere had been instructed to raise a hue and cry against the "impending imperialist war". According to the "information" brought to India by Pandit Nehru, the British Government was getting ready to invade the Soviet Union from the North-West Frontier Province of India and the Persian Gulf.

He incorporated this "information" and its implications for India in the War Danger resolution which he presented to the Madras meeting. The resolution read:

"This Congress has noted with grave concern the extraordinary and extensive war preparations which the British Government is carrying on in India and in the eastern seas, specially in the North-West Frontier of India. These preparations for war are not only calculated to strengthen the hold of British Imperialism on India in order to strangle all attempts at freedom, but must result in hastening a disastrous war in which an attempt will be made to make India again a tool in the hands of foreign imperialists.

"The Congress declares that the people of India have no quarrel with their neighbours and desire to live at peace with them, and asserts their right to determine whether or not they will take part in any war.

"The Congress demands that these war preparations be put an end to, and further declares that in the event of the British Government embarking on any warlike adventure and endeavouring to involve India in it for the furtherance of their imperialist aims, it will be the duty of the people of India to refuse to take any part in such a war or to co-operate with them in any way whatsoever."[6]

Those who have studied the history of inter-war years know that Britain and France were not plotting for any war against the Soviet Union. But they were certainly objecting to Soviet Russia's interference in their internal affairs through communist fifth-columns created by the Comintern in these countries and their colonies. It is recorded history that Soviet Russia was trying to arm the Pathan tribals on India's North-West Frontier, and let them loose on the Punjab. The preparations referred to in the resolution were

[6] All India Congress Committee, *The Background of India's Foreign Policy*, New Delhi, April 1952, pp. 46-47.

aimed at tackling the tribal uprising. Pandit Nehru had, however, already become used to looking at the world through Comintern glasses. He had been fully indoctrinated by now so far as Soviet Union's foreign policy was concerned.

He could accept the new Comintern thesis because he had already accepted the other communist lie that the "imperialists" had tried to "strangle" the Soviet Union at its very birth in 1917-18. It never occurred to him that if any Great Power in Europe or America or Japan had seriously desired to destroy the "proletarian revolution" in 1917-18, it had only to use a single battalion of trained soldiers. Even in 1927, when he was visiting the Soviet Union, the communist regime would have collapsed like nine-pins if any first class Western Power or Japan had made a move against it. But the non-communist nations at that time were too busy in quarrelling with each other to be able to conspire together against the Soviet Union. In fact, around 1928, the capitalists in Europe and America were getting ready to do business with the Red regime which in their estimation had stabilised itself in Russia.

The ideological background of this War Danger resolution was fully floodlit by a series of articles which Pandit Nehru wrote in various Indian newspapers immediately after the Madras Congress. All these articles were collected in his first book, *Soviet Russia,* published in October 1928. Herein he revealed very clearly how deeply he had been infected by the Comintern line on the world situation.

Commenting on relations between India and Soviet Russia, he wrote: "We have grown up in the tradition, carefully nurtured by England, of hostility to Russia. For long years past the bogey of a Russian invasion has been held up to us and has been made the excuse of vast expenditure on our armaments. In the days of the Tsar we were told that the imperialism of Russia was for ever driving south, coveting an outlet to the sea, or may be India itself. The Tsar has gone but the rivalry between England and Russia continues and we are now told that India is threatened by the Soviet Government."[7] He should have known that the rivalry between British imperialism and Tsarist imperialism in Central Asia, Persia, and Afghanistan was no fiction, and the British in India had to be alert.

[7] *Soviet Russia,* p. 126.

In any case, in his opinion now Soviet Russia could never want war, for: "Russia has only recently passed through a period of international war and civil war, of famine and blockade, and above everything she desires peace to consolidate her economic position and build up on a sure foundation her new order of society. She has already attained a large measure of success and is working at high pressure and with 'full steam' to develop peacefully her vast territories. War, even successful war, must put a stop to this process of consolidation and development, and is bound to delay indefinitely the full establishment of her new social order."[8] He would advance similar arguments for Red China even though the People's Army had invaded Korea and Tibet, and instigated insurrections in Indo-China. Till his own country was invaded in 1962, the real warmongers for him were the Western democracies and their allies in Asia.

The real warmonger for him in 1928 was Britain. Taking stock of Britain's post-war policy in Europe, he assured his readers: "The whole basis of this policy has been to encircle Russia by pacts and alliances, ultimately to crush her. England has worked unceasingly for this end and has made the League of Nations an instrument of her policy. Locarno was the result of this policy, and the occasional flirtations of England with Germany have also the isolation of Russia for their object... Thus it is absolutely clear from the official utterances and policy of British politicians that they eagerly desire a conflict with Russia and prepare for it and only await a suitable opportunity to wage open war."[9]

India had nothing to fear from Bolshevik Russia. According to Pandit Nehru: "It is inconceivable that Russia, in her present condition at least, and for a long time to come, will threaten India. She can desire no additional territory, and even if she did the risks are too great for her. She is still mainly an agricultural country trying to develop her industries. For this she requires capital and expert knowledge. She gets neither from India. She produces raw materials in abundance and not manufactured articles for export and dumping in foreign countries. So does India. The two countries are today too similar to be exploited by each other, and there can be no economic motive for Russia to covet India."[10]

[8] Ibid., p. 127.
[9] Ibid., pp. 129-30.
[10] Ibid., p. 131.

On the same premises, Red China had no reason to invade India. The communists in India are in fact using Pandit Nehru's logic to refute "Indian propaganda" that India has been the sinned-against. There is, however, no truth in this logic except that it is a paraphrase of Lenin's theory of imperialism which he had concocted in order to damn the capitalist countries.

The real barrier between India and Bolshevik Russia, according to Pandit Nehru, was not the latter's creed of Communism but Britain's imperialist interests. In his own words: "Ordinarily Russia and India should live as the best of neighbours with the fewest points of friction. The continual friction that we see today is between England and Russia, not between India and Russia. Is there any reason why we in India should inherit the agelong rivalry of England against Russia? That is based on the greed and covetousness of British imperialism, and our interests surely lie in ending this imperialism and not in supporting and strengthening it."[11]

Indians should, therefore, "make it clear that we shall not permit ourselves to be pawns in England's imperial game, to be moved hither and thither for her benefit. We must continually proclaim, in the words of the Madras Congress resolution, 'that in the event of the British Government embarking on any warlike adventure and endeavouring to involve India in it for the furtherance of their imperialist aims, it will be the duty of the people of India to refuse to take any part in such a war, or to co-operate with them in any way whatsoever'. And if this declaration is made repeatedly and emphatically, it may be that England may hesitate to embark on this adventure; and India and the world may be spared the horrors of another great war."[12]

Thus the real inspiration behind his resolution on War Danger presented at the Madras Congress was his eagerness to protect Soviet Russia from a war which he believed Britain was threatening. The resolution had nothing to do with India's own struggle for independence. Even its language was largely borrowed from resolutions being passed everywhere in those days by all sorts of communist fronts.

The same resolution was presented to and passed by the Calcutta Congress which met towards the end of 1928. It said: "This Congress reiterates the War Danger resolution of the Madras ses-

[11] Ibid.
[12] Ibid., pp. 131-32.

sion of the Congress, and wishes to declare that the present Government of India in no way represents the people of India, and their policy has been traditionally guided by considerations of holding India under subjection and not of protecting her frontiers. The people of India have no quarrel with the neighbouring states or the other nations of the world and they will not permit themselves to be exploited by England to further her imperialist aims."[13]

This Congress passed another resolution for participation in the League against Imperialism. The resolution said: "This Congress welcomes the Second World Congress of the League against Imperialism to be held next year and authorises the Working Committee to appoint a representative on behalf of the Congress."[14]

And with a view to colonise the Indian National Congress with Comintern agents, Pandit Nehru persuaded its Calcutta session to pass another resolution which stressed: "This Congress, being of opinion that the struggle of the Indian people for freedom is a part of the general world struggle against imperialism and its manifestations, considers it desirable that India should develop contacts with other countries and peoples who also suffer under imperialism and desire to combat it. The Congress therefore calls upon the All India Congress Committee to develop such contacts and to open a Foreign Department in this behalf."[15]

The Foreign Department could not be set up at that time because very soon the country was plunged in the Simon Commission agitation and the Salt Satyagraha. Pandit Nehru's opportunity came only in 1936 when, as President of the Congress, he created a Foreign Department and staffed it with card-carrying communists, notably Z.A. Ahmed and K.M. Ashraf.

[13] *The Background of India's Foreign Policy*, p. 48.
[14] Ibid.
[15] Ibid., p. 47.

TEN

A FELLOW-TRAVELLER OF SOVIET FOREIGN POLICY-2

Ever since Pandit Nehru visited the United States of America for the first time in 1949 and the U.S. Administration discovered that it was impossible to have a free and frank discussion with him regarding concrete policies, a horde of U.S. specialists and psychologists have been in and out of India for a "fuller understanding of Jawaharlal Nehru, India's man of destiny". They have studied his life story exhaustively and brooded for years over his least little idiosyncrasy. And, by now, they are unanimous in their "analysis" that he is an extremely touchy person who will never brook any affront to his sense of self-respect. The U.S. State Department has, therefore, been deputing its topmost experts in public relations to his court at New Delhi, and there has been no end of their kowtowing before this king of independent India. But in spite of all their endeavours, the U.S.A. has been singularly unsuccessful with him. Every now and then he gets irritated with the U.S.A. and starts shouting against U.S. policies so that even his loyal lobbymen in the U.S.A., such as Chester Bowles, Cooper, Walter Reuther etc., are shocked and have to hang their heads in a confession of defeat.

But Moscow's reading of Pandit Nehru's character has been entirely different. Moscow has never hesitated in launching vile and vicious attacks on him whenever the exigencies of India's domestic politics have forced him to stray away from the line laid down by Moscow, or whenever there has been a dramatic turn in Moscow's policies and poor Pandit Nehru has been caught napping. He on his part has not only pocketed the most puerile personal attacks on him and kept quiet, but also taken to introspection and self-criticism. His recurring reaction in the face of Moscow's fury against him has always been an effort to catch up with Moscow's new line in as short a time as his power and opportunity have allowed him.

Such an occasion came for the first time in 1930. Pandit Nehru had been faithfully following the Moscow line and injecting it into the Indian National Congress ever since he returned from Europe in 1928. But, meanwhile, Moscow's line was moving more and more left due to the struggle that was raging at that time in Germany and China between the communist conspiracy and the forces of nationalism. One fine morning towards the end of 1930, *Pravda* published an article and denounced Pandit Nehru as a "dangerous obstacle to the victory of the Indian Revolution". This article was reproduced in the Comintern weekly, *Imprecor,* under the title 'Platform of Action of the Communist Party of India'. It said: "The most harmful and dangerous obstacle to victory of the Indian Revolution is the agitation carried on by the 'left' elements of the National Congress led by Jawaharlal Nehru, Bose, Ginwala and others. Ruthless war on the 'left' national reformists is an essential condition if we are to isolate the former from the workers and the mass of peasantry and mobilise the latter under the banner of the Communist Party."

This was a signal for a spate of swearology against Pandit Nehru in the communist press inside India and abroad. All his fulminations against the Social Democrats had failed to save him from what looked like the fortuitous fury of Moscow. He was now classed with those very Social Democrats whom he hated from the core of his heart. And, soon after, he was summarily expelled from the League against Imperialism for which organisation he had worked so hard in India. But all this meant nothing to him. He was only sorry that he was not given a chance to defend himself.

Recalling his disgrace during this period he wrote later on: "The League against Imperialism veered more towards Communism in later years, though at no time, so far as I know, did it lose its individual character. I could only remain in distant touch with it by means of correspondence. In 1930, because of my part in the Delhi truce between the Congress and the Government of India, it grew exceedingly angry with me, and excommunicated me with bell, book, and candle, or to be more accurate, it expelled me by some kind of a resolution. I must confess that it had great provocation, but it might have given me some chance of explaining my position."[1] Thus in spite of this direct evidence he was not prepared to believe that the League against Imperialism was an out-and-out communist front financed by Moscow in the interests of Soviet foreign policy. And all this provocation meant nothing to him except a sense of regret that he was not given a chance of explaining his position!

Had Moscow cared to give him that chance, he would have

---

[1] *An Autobiography,* p. 164.

protested that he was opposed to the Gandhi–Irwin Pact and that as such he did not deserve that denunciation. Referring to this Pact, he had written: "There was nothing more to be said. The thing had been done, our leader had committed himself; and even if we disagreed with him, what could we do? Throw him over? Break from him? Announce our disagreement? That might bring some personal satisfaction to an individual, but it made no difference to the final decision. The Civil Disobedience movement was ended for the time being at least, and not even the Working Committee could push it on now, when the Government could declare that Mr. Gandhi had already agreed to a settlement."[2] But unfortunately for him, it has always been Moscow's method to decide matters *ex parte* and victimise people without any verification or warning given to them.

Pandit Nehru on his part has been hewed out of "bourgeois" stuff as he himself confesses in his autobiography. Moscow might have denounced him as a degenerate in so many words. But that did not mean that he would turn a traitor to Moscow. His "sense of honour" demanded that he should continue to defend and disseminate the Moscow line. So he drafted yet another resolution for the Karachi Congress of 1931. It read: "This Congress declares that the people of India have no quarrel with the countries and peoples bordering on India and desires to establish and maintain friendly relations with them. It disapproves of the so-called 'forward' policy of the British Government in India in the North-West Frontier and of all imperialist attempts to destroy the freedom of the people of the frontier. The Congress is strongly of opinion that the military and financial resources of India should not be employed in furtherance of this policy and the military occupation of the tribesmen's territory should be terminated."[3] The North-West Frontier at that time was a hotbed of communist conspiracy as the channels of contact with the communists in India ran from Kabul to Tashkent to Moscow. So that area had to be kept free from every kind of "imperialist" vigilance.

Pandit Nehru's heart had always bled for the "brave Pathans" against whom the "British imperialists were committing unprecedented crimes". Had he studied India's history in right earnest, he would have known that the problem of these frontier tribals was

[2] Ibid., p. 257.
[3] *The Background of India's Foreign Policy*, p. 111.

not new, and that every government in India had had to keep them in check lest they descended on peaceful citizens for plunder and abduction. He himself had to learn this history the hard way. As soon as he became the first Prime Minister of undivided India in September 1946, he rushed to the North-West Frontier. He had been assured by the Khan brothers that he would get a hero's welcome everywhere. Welcomed he was, but with bullets from which he escaped with an hair's breadth. Next year, the same "brave Pathans" descended on Kashmir and their brave deeds there became everybody's knowledge. He has never mentioned the "brave Pathans" again.

He did not have a chance to draft any more foreign policy resolutions because between 1931 and 1935 he was in and out of jail in connection with the Civil Disobedience Movement. But even when he was in jail, his primary preoccupation continued to be service to the communist cause. This becomes obvious when he comes to the contemporary period in his *Glimpses of World History*. On every single international issue, he takes the same stand as the communists. He denounces all those people whom the communists were denouncing and gaves his full support to all those people who happened to be Moscow's stooges at that time.

To start with, he accepts the Leninist definition of imperialism which says that any country which exports her surplus industrial production, surplus capital, and surplus population to other countries is an imperialist country. In terms of this definition, Soviet Russia which was deficient in industrial goods as well as capital, could never be called an imperialist country, although she had occupied a number of foreign lands in both Europe and Asia and was importing people from all these lands to do forced labour in her slave-labour camps. But this definition made the 'invisible empire of America' visible to Pandit Nehru. Commenting on this empire, he wrote: "The United States prevented interference in Latin America from Europe by means of the Monroe Doctrine. But as they grew wealthy they began to look outside for fresh fields for expansion. Naturally their eyes first fell on Latin America. They did not attempt to take possession of any of these countries by force in the old way of building up empires. They sent their goods there and captured their markets. They also invested their capital in railways, mines, and other undertakings in the south; they lent money to governments and sometimes arms to warring factions at times of revolution. By 'they' I mean American capitalists and bankers, but behind them and supporting them was the American Government. Gradually these bankers controlled, through the money they had lent or invested, many of the smaller South and Central American Governments."[4] This communist image of the USA has continued to haunt him.

This "new kind of empire, the modern kind of empire" was, in his opinion, more profitable and more convenient as compared to the old type of empire which the die-hard British imperialists were still practising. Drawing his daughter's attention to the subtleties of this "new imperialism", he theorised: "Most of us still think of empires of this kind, like the British in India, and we imagine that if the British were not in actual political control of India, India would be free. But this type of empire is already passing away, and giving place to a more advanced and perfected type. This latest kind of empire does not annex even the land; it only annexes the wealth or the wealth-producing elements in the country. By doing so it can exploit the country fully to its own advantage and can largely control it, and at the same time has to shoulder no responsibility for governing and repressing that country. In effect, both the land and the people living there are dominated and largely controlled with the least amount of trouble."[5]

When the cold war started between the United States and the Soviet Union immediately after the Second World War, many people wondered why Pandit Nehru was so suspicious of the United States and so consistently siding with the Soviet Union on all international issues. They had not cared to know his definition of imperialism — a definition which he had derived from communist doctrine and to which he still adheres. That is why he is still obsessed with Western colonialism, even though the Western nations have freed every enslaved nation in Asia and have, with the exception of Portugal, almost cleared out of Africa. So long as any nation imports goods and capital from a Western country, it remains for him a colony of Western imperialism unless, like India, it starts serving the Soviet Union by supporting the latter's foreign policy!

Next, he turned his attention towards the rise of Fascism. Stripped of all its superfluous slogans, Fascism was a last-bid en-

[4] *Glimpses of World History*, p. 569.
[5] Ibid., p. 570.

deavour of Italian, German and Spanish nationalism to root out the communist cancer from their countries and stop Soviet imperialism from a subversive takeover. The Fascists had to suppress and sometimes slaughter the communists and their fellow-travellers. The only alternative was to be slaughtered by the communists. That is an indispensable job which all patriots, who want to save their country's sovereignty from Moscow's strangle-hold, have to perform sooner or later whenever the communist conspiracy assumes a certain magnitude. The communists, however, have reserved the right to suppress and slaughter all opposition as their own exclusive privilege, and their term for anyone who suppresses and slaughters them is 'Fascist'.

Communists have also developed an elaborate thesis about the genesis of Fascism. They propose that Fascism is the "last desperate bid of capitalism to save itself from proletarian revolution". Pandit Nehru swallowed this thesis and wrote: "For the first ten years after the War it appeared that perhaps capitalism might recover and steady itself for another considerable period. But the next three years or so have made this very doubtful. Not only is the rivalry between capitalist States growing to dangerous dimensions, but, at the same time, within each State the conflict between classes, between the workers and the capitalist owning class which controls the government, is becoming acute. As these conditions worsen, a last desperate attempt is made by the owning class to crush the rising workers. This takes the form of fascism. Fascism appears where the conflict between the classes has become acute and the owning class is in danger of losing its privileged position."[6]

And he noted that Fascism was becoming a universal phenomenon everywhere in Europe outside the Soviet Union. He observed: "Fascism exists in varying degrees in all countries of Europe except, I suppose, Russia. Its latest triumph has been won in Germany. Even in England, fascist ideas are spreading among the ruling classes, and we see their application often enough in India. On the world-stage today fascism, the last resort of capitalism, faces communism."[7]

He spotted this "last resort of capitalism" manifesting itself in China also, although China at that time was hardly a capitalist country. In later years many people came to believe that Pandit

[6] Ibid., p. 687.
[7] Ibid., p. 826.

Nehru was a friend of Chiang Kai-shek and the Chinese Nationalists. But that was an altogether false impression. He had befriended Chiang Kai-shek from 1937 onwards when the Comintern had also befriended him. He dropped Chiang Kai-shek immediately after the communists turned against him in 1947, in which year the final struggle for power flared up in China. Thus, all along, he had toed the communist line regarding China.

In 1934, his comment on the 1926 break-up between the Nationalists and the Communists in China was as follows: "The nationalist Government, now established at Hankow or Wuhan, were faced with a difficult problem—to advance or not to advance, to take Shanghai or not to do so... Borodin [Comintern Agent sent from Moscow] advised caution and consolidation. He was of opinion that the nationalists should keep away from Shanghai and strengthen their position in the southern half of China which was already under their control, and prepare the ground in the north with propaganda. Very soon, within a year or so, he expected the whole of China to be ready to welcome a nationalist advance. That would be the time to take Shanghai, march to Peking, and face the foreign imperialist Powers. Borodin, the revolutionary, gave this cautious advice, because he was experienced in judging the various factors in a situation. The right-wing leaders of the Kuomintang, however, and especially the commander-in-chief, Chiang Kai-shek, insisted on marching to Shanghai. The real reason for this desire to take Shanghai appeared later when the Kuomintang split up into two. The growing power of the peasants' and workers' unions was not liked by these right-wing leaders. Many of the generals were themselves landlords. They had therefore decided to crush these unions, even at the cost of breaking up the party into two and weakening the nationalist cause. Shanghai was an important centre of the big Chinese 'bourgeoisie', and the right-wing generals counted upon it to help them, with money and otherwise, in their fight against the more advanced elements in their party, and especially against the communists. In such a fight they knew they could also rely on the support of the foreign bankers and industrialists in Shanghai."[8] The simple truth was that the Chinese communists were getting ready to hijack the nationalist revolution, and convert China into a Soviet colony when Chiang Kai-shek, who

[8] Ibid., pp. 831-32.

knew their game, anticipated their move and turned the tables on them.

Again: "Having rebelled against his own Government at Hankow, Chiang now made war on communists, left-wingers, and trade-unionist workers. The very workers who had made it easy for him to take Shanghai and had welcomed him joyously there were now hunted out and crushed. Large numbers of people were shot down or beheaded, thousands were arrested and imprisoned. The freedom that the nationalists were supposed to have brought to Shanghai was soon converted into a bloody terror."[9] The Government in Hankow was a self-appointed communist clique, and Chiang Kai-shek was not honour-bound to obey it. Unlike Pandit Nehru, Chiang Kai-shek was a patriot who was not prepared to see his country becoming a battleground between the Soviet fifth-column on the one hand and the Western powers on the other.

And again: "In Peking, as in Shanghai, a 'clean-up' of communists and advanced workers was carried out. The imperialist Powers of course welcomed this development, because it broke up and weakened the ranks of the Chinese nationalists. *Chiang Kai-shek sought to co-operate with the representatives of the Powers in Shanghai.*"[10] It was not for the first time that Pandit Nehru saw communist traitors as "workers' and peasants' unions". He used the same labels for them when they waged war against the government headed by him, from 1948 onwards. He himself was, of course, the "more advanced" element as compared to Sardar Patel who took care of the traitors. Sardar Patel represented the "landlord and capitalist interests" in his eyes.

Japan, too, was viewed by him through the same communist glasses. The fact that Japan at that time had very good relations with Soviet Russia did not mean anything to the Comintern. Communists have never been able to understand goodwill; they invariably interpret it as a symptom of weakness. Pandit Nehru followed the communist line and wrote: "Japan had come to terms with Russia because of her difficulties, but this did not mean approval of communism. Communism meant the end of emperor-worship, and feudalism and the exploitation of the masses by the ruling class, and indeed almost everything that the existing order stood for...

[9] Ibid., p. 832.
[10] Ibid. Italics added.
[11] Ibid., p. 836. Italics added.

But communism is the outcome of widespread misery due to social conditions, and unless these conditions are improved, mere repression can be no remedy. There is a terrible misery in Japan at present. The peasantry, as in China and India, are crushed under a tremendous burden of debt. Taxation, especially because of heavy military expenditure and war needs, is very heavy. *Reports come of starving peasants trying to live on grass and roots, and of selling even their children.* The middle classes are also in a bad way owing to unemployment and suicides have increased."[11] He was prepared to see whatever the Comintern wanted him to see, wherever. He shared the communist hatred for Japan's indigenous culture, as much as he has shared with them their hatred of everything Indian.

Nor could the Social Democrats escape his onslaught. The Comintern had dubbed them as aids and allies of capitalism in its last desperate bid to save itself. He followed suit and sobbed: "Gradually, as year followed year after the end of the World War, things appeared to settle down to some extent. The revolutionary elements were suppressed by a curious alliance of the reactionary conservatives, monarchists and feudal landlords on the one side, and the moderate socialists or social democrats on the other. This was indeed a strange alliance, for the social democrats proclaimed their faith in Marxism and a workers' government. Their ideal thus appeared to be, on the surface, the same as that of the Soviets and communists. *And yet these social democrats feared the communists more than the capitalists, and combined with the latter to crush the former.* Or it may be that they feared the capitalists so much that they did not dare to go against them; they hoped to consolidate their position by peaceful and parliamentary means, and thus bring in socialism almost imperceptibly. Whatever their motives may have been, they helped the reactionary elements to crush the revolutionary spirit, and thus actually brought about a counter-revolution in many of the European countries. This counter-revolution in its turn crushed these very social democratic parties, and new and aggressively anti-socialist forces came into Power."[12] Unfortunately for him, and unlike him, the Social Democrats were patriots who saw through the "revolutionary spirit" emanating from Moscow.

All these "counter-revolutionary" forces—the capitalists, the neo-imperialists, the fascists, and the social democrats—had, ac-

[12] Ibid., p. 787. Italics added.

cording to Pandit Nehru, forged a united front against the Soviet Union and were conspiring for a new world war for the destruction of the 'proletarian revolution'. And this "capitalist conspiracy" was really responsible for all the crimes being committed in the Soviet Union! He apologised:

"Because there can be no real peace between communism and capitalism, and the imperialist nations are very keen on suppressing communism, and manoeuvre and intrigue to that end the nerves of the Bolsheviks are always on edge and their eyes grow big at the least provocation. Often enough they have reason for anxiety and they had to meet, even internally, widespread attempts at sabotage or destruction of their factories or other big concerns.

"Nineteen-thirty-two was a very critical year for the Soviet Union. The Government took the most drastic steps against sabotage and against the stealing of communal property, which had occurred in many of the communal farms. Ordinarily there is no death penalty in Russia, but it was introduced in cases of counter-revolution. The Soviet Government decreed that the stealing of communal property is equivalent to counter-revolution, and is therefore punishable by death. For, says Stalin: 'If the capitalists have pronounced 'private' property sacred and inviolable, thus achieving in their time a strengthening of the capitalist order, then we communists must so much the more pronounce 'public' property sacred and inviolable in order thus to strengthen the new socialist forms of economy.' "[13]

Thus having denounced the whole world in terms of communist swearology, Pandit Nehru returned to the defence of the Soviet Union which was at that time using the same swearology for nailing him down as an obstacle to the "Indian Revolution". No lackey has ever provided a more glaring instance of licking the boot that kicks.

[13] Ibid., pp. 859-60. As we shall see in Volume II, he provides a similar apology for Aurangzeb's crimes. Aurangzeb, he writes, was irritated by the opposition he faced from the Rajputs, Marathas, and Sikhs. (Footnote added in 1993).

ELEVEN

A FELLOW-TRAVELLER OF SOVIET FOREIGN POLICY-3

An year or so before Sardar Patel's death in December 1950, there was a serious rift between him and Prime Minister Nehru on questions concerning the foreign policy of India. The Sardar did not like the way in which our foreign affairs were being conducted. He felt that our foreign policy was too servile to the Soviet camp in spite of the violent hostility which that camp had all along shown towards the Government of independent India. But he could not or did not review this policy in terms of any alternate international analysis of his own. Pandit Nehru, on the other hand, pointed out repeatedly that the general direction of India's foreign policy after the attainment of independence was not new but only an application of the principles enunciated in the various foreign policy resolutions which the Congress had passed in pre-independence days. The Sardar was exasperated. And he made a public statement that he had never read a single foreign policy resolution of the Congress. He added that these resolutions were passed always and unanimously more in order to avoid controversy over what was an academic issue for enslaved India than to denote any decisive national attitudes towards international politics.

Pandit Nehru was himself aware all along that his foreign policy resolutions were not being taken seriously by anyone except himself and his communist co-conspirators. He admits: "This all-round support was very gratifying, but I had an uncomfortable feeling that the resolutions were either not understood for what they were or were distorted to mean something else... These resolutions of mine were somewhat different from the usual Congress resolutions; they represented a new outlook. Many Congressmen no doubt liked them; some had a vague dislike for them, but not enough to make them oppose. Probably the latter thought that they were academic resolutions, making little difference either way, and the best way to get rid of them was to pass them and move on to something more important."[1] Yet after attainment of independence he insisted that these resolution were binding on his Party and

[1] *An Autobiography*, p. 167. Italics added.

Government! This was a typically communist operation.

At the same time, however, that confession on the part of Sardar Patel conveyed the utter poverty of that mind which views international affairs only in terms of narrow national interests, and refuses to project national principles and power into the arena of international conflicts. The indefensible indifference towards international politics which led the Congress foreign policy into the Soviet trap through the agency of Pandit Nehru is still the predominant national mood, in all circles outside the communist camp. For people who happen to be admirers of Pandit Nehru for personal or ideological reasons, the foreign policy of India is safe in his hands. The only duty they assign to themselves is to shout the slogans issued by him with ever increasing ardour, no matter what the source of these slogans is and where they are leading the nation. On the other hand, people who claim that they are opposed to Pandit Nehru's foreign policy proclaim their difference only on matters of detail, and endorse the general direction and the underlying principles of that policy.

That is the tragedy of this nation. Either we are narrow-minded nationalists who think that our quarrel with Pakistan, and Portugal, and now with communist China, constitutes the whole of our concern for foreign affairs, and that, for the rest, our policy should be 'a plague on both (or all) your houses'; or we are followers of this or that international camp; or we are empty-headed but self-righteous simpletons. There is not a single voice which proclaims that we are an ancient nation with our own *svadharma* which alone should be our touchstone for settling our attitude towards international questions. Our national *svadharma,* which lays down the lofty principle of *Vasudhaiva kuṭumbakam* (i.e., the whole world consists of my kinsmen), should be able to point out principles which can be our strength and solace in a tormented and topsy-turvy world.

A greater tragedy is that hypocrisy in certain quarters which, while they know fully well that Pandit Nehru's foreign policy has been and still remains a copy-book exercise of the turns and twists of Soviet foreign policy, yet refuse to subject that policy to a free and frank public discussion. Not only that. These quarters go out of their way to bestow fulsome praise on that foreign policy, and say that this policy has raised the prestige of the nation. Their criticism is confined to a clever footnote, namely that in spite of all its sweep and loftiness, the policy has served no "practical interests" of the nation.

The need of the hour, if it is already not too late, is first to expose Pandit Nehru's foreign policy fully and frankly for whatever it is. He should be told that he is the Prime Minister of India and not a Soviet satrap set up for superintending the interests of Soviet imperialism in Asia and the world. He becomes temperamental and difficult only when he is criticised in what he calls "a constructive" manner. The only way of dealing with him firmly is to identify him and his ideology for what they really are. Our people are still not denuded of patriotism in spite of decades of drugging by Pandit Nehru and his communist camp-followers. It was these people who rose and protested when Tibet was over-run, and when our own territory was occupied. Nor has our people's sense of moral values become blunted beyond repair in spite of a total absence of that sense in their Government. Wherever the communists have committed crimes against humanity, as in Hungary and Tibet, our people have registered a powerful protest.

So, on the balance, it is not our people who have failed their political leaders. On the contrary, it is our political leaders who have failed their people. There is so much of self-seeking or party patriotism among even the top leaders of all political parties that they have no devotion or patriotism to spare for the nation. Session after session of our Parliament has witnessed broadsides against the "betrayals by Krishna Menon". Session after session of our Parliament has seen Pandit Nehru hitting out in all directions in defence of his indefensible Defence Minister. Yet no member of Parliament has had the partiotic urge or the moral courage to stand up and point out an accusing finger at this villain of the piece. If India is ever undone, it will be because India's political leaders are more afraid of losing their leadership than of losing their country.

And in this surging sea of cowardice, cynicism, and hypocrisy, Pandit Nehru comes out easily as the only man who has had the courage of his convictions. He became a communist quite early in his political career. He stuck to that creed even when he could not have his way in the Congress. But as soon as his opportunity came, he translated his convictions into concrete actions. For others, convictions have been like cosmetics, and their brand of powder and puff has changed with the change in political fashion. Of course, the fashion has always been set by Pandit Nehru.

It may be said that courage is often combined with stupidity. Pandit Nehru may be stupid in the sense that he could never think a thought of his own all through his life. And his courage may be in a very large measure the by-product of cowardice on the part of other political leaders. He has, however, been courageous in yet another sense. Surely it requires a lot of courage to imbibe other people's ideas at short notice and proclaim them publicly without looking into the logic of one's own past pronouncements. He has always exhibited this courage whenever the call has come to him from Moscow.

We have seen how he was denouncing all the "enemies" of the Soviet Union from 1927, when he visited his Fatherland, to 1934, when he completed his exercise in world history, in spite of the fact that the Soviet press had denounced him in strong terms. He must have thought that he had caught up with the Comintern line. But, unfortunately for him, the Comintern was ahead of him once again. The Seventh Congress of the Comintern, held in Moscow during July/August 1935, proclaimed the strategy of "United Front" which meant that the communist parties everywhere were to join hands with their erstwhile enemies — the Social Democrats and the Nationalists — in order to "stem the rising tide of Fascism".

The earlier strategy of the Comintern had resulted in the victory of Nazism in Germany, and the strengthening of Japan in the Far East. Both of them now threatened the Soviet Union with containment. So the Soviet foreign policy underwent a volte-face. In May 1935, the Soviet Union signed the famous Franco-Soviet Pact. An year later, the Soviet–Czechoslovak Pact was signed. The Soviet Union was out to cooperate with the Western nations in a bid to save itself from the Frankenstein it had raised. The Comintern hammered out a new strategy suited to the new situation in which the Soviet Union now found itself.

Delivering his Main Report to the Comintern Congress, Comrade Dimitroff said: "How can fascism be prevented from coming to power and how can fascism be overthrown when it has come to power? *The first thing that must be done, the thing with which to begin, is to form a united front, to establish unity of action of the workers in every factory, in every district, in every region, in every country, all over the world.*"[2] Coming to India, he proposed: "In

[2] G. Dimitroff, *The United Front*, International Publishers, New York, 1938, pp. 30–31. Italics added.

India the communists have to support, extend and participate in all anti-imperialist mass activities, not excluding those that are under national reformist leadership."[3]

Pandit Nehru was released from jail in September 1935. He immediately went to Europe. The ostensible purpose was to attend to his sick wife. But the real purpose was to "refresh" his mind once more. And he did get "refreshed" very soon. By the time he returned to India in early 1936 to preside over the Lucknow Congress held in April that year, he was completely converted to the new Comintern line. He himself says: "I was full at the time of the idea of Popular Fronts and Joint Fronts, which were being formed in some European countries. In Europe, where class and other conflicts were acute, it had been possible for this cooperation on a common platform. In India these conflicts were still in their early stages and were completely overshadowed by the major conflict against imperialism. *The obvious course was for all anti-imperialistic forces to function together on the common platform of the Congress.*"[4]

Dr. Pattabhi Sitaramayya, the official historian of the Congress, reports: "When he had presided over the Lahore Session in 1929, he stated in his Presidential address that he was a Socialist and Republican. When seven years later he presided over the Lucknow Session (April, 1936) he reached the logical fulfilment of socialism—namely, communism."[5]

Once again he presented his famous foreign policy resolutions to the Congress. He writes: "On the eve of the Lucknow Congress we met in Working Committee, and I was pleased and gratified at the adoption by this Committee of a number of resolutions that I sponsored and which seemed to give a new tone and a more radical outlook to the Congress."[6]

The first resolution sent greetings to the World Peace Congress announced by the World Committee for the Struggle Against War and Fascism—a regular communist front. It said: "This Congress, having considered the invitation of Monsieur Romain Rolland, Honorary President of the World Committee for the Struggle Against War and Fascism, to participate in the World Congress for

[3] Ibid., p. 68.
[4] *The Unity of India*, p. 96.
[5] Pattabhi Sitaramayya, *The History of the Indian National Congress*, Padma Publications Ltd., Bombay, 1947, Vol. II, p. 8.
[6] *The Unity of India*, p. 98.

Peace to be held in Geneva in September next, conveys its greetings to the organisers of the Peace Congress and its assurances of its full sympathy and cooperation in the great work of ensuring peace in the world based on national and social freedom. The Congress is convinced that such a peace can only be established on an enduring basis when the causes of war are removed and the domination and exploitation of nation by nation is ended."[7] Krishna Menon was selected by Pandit Nehru to represent the Indian National Congress at this communist rally. Incidentally, the word "peace" means "Soviet Foreign Policy" in the *Glossary of Marxist Terms* published from Moscow.

He was also able to persuade the Lucknow session to pass a resolution for setting up a Foreign Department of the A.I.C.C The resolution read: "The Congress authorises and directs the Working Committee to organise a Foreign Department of the A.I.C.C. office to work under the general superintendence of the General Secretary and with such special staff as may be necessary, with a view to create and maintain contacts with Indians overseas, and with international, national, labour and other organisations abroad with whom co-operation is possible and is likely to help in the cause of Indian freedom."[8] The Foreign Department was immediately manned by two communist stalwarts — Z.A. Ahmed and K.M. Ashraf.

Now he could get regular communist drafts from his comrades in the Foreign Department. Next year, he was elected president of the Faizpur Congress held in December 1936. A majority of Congressmen wanted Sardar Patel to assume this office. But the Sardar had to withdraw under pressure from Gandhiji and Pandit Nehru was elected without a contest. And he continued to carry forward his communist game inside the Congress.

Resolution No. II of the Faizpur session congratulated Krishna Menon in the following words: "The Congress having considered the report of Shri V.K. Krishna Menon on the World Peace Congress, records its appreciation of the part he took in this Congress as its representative. It supports wholeheartedly the objective of the Peace Congress to ensure world peace by removing the causes of war and offers its full cooperation to it in this urgent and vital task. The National Congress will willingly associate itself with the organi-

[7] *The Background of India's Foreign Policy*, pp. 49–50.
[8] Ibid., p. 49.

zation which the Peace Congress has established in this behalf. The Congress, however, wishes to emphasise that imperialism itself is a continuing cause of war and its elimination is essential in the interests of world peace. The President is authorised and directed to take necessary steps in this behalf."[9]

Resolution No. IV toed the communist line in Spain where General Franco was putting up a heroic fight to save his country from becoming a colony of Soviet Russia. It said: "The Congress has followed with the deepest sympathy and anxiety the struggle that is going on in Spain between the people of Spain and a military group aided by foreign mercenary troops and Fascist Powers in Europe. The Congress realises that this struggle between democratic progress and Fascist reaction is of great consequence to the future of the world and will affect the future of imperialism in India. The Congress has noted without surprise that in this struggle, the policy of non-intervention followed by the British Government has been such as to hamper in many ways the Spanish Government and people in fighting the Fascist rebels, and has thus in effect aided these rebels who are being openly backed and helped by the Fascist Powers. This Congress, on behalf of the people of India, sends greetings to the Spanish people and the assurance of their solidarity with them in this great struggle for liberty."[10]

Soviet Union's single-minded policy in Europe now was to draw both France and Great Britain into an *entente* against Nazi Germany and Fascist Italy, both of which were strongly opposed to Communism. To this end, the Soviet Union was trying to precipitate "Popular Front" governments in Britain and France. The game was "dialectical" as in the case of every game the communists play. A "Popular Front" government meant a government in which the communist party of that country participated directly or which depended on communist support. Such a government was expected to become increasingly an instrument of the Soviet Government, and, at the same time, try to capture complete power in slow stages by internal subversion.

The game succeeded to quite an extent in France where Leon Blum got deeply entangled with the Communist Party of France and the Soviet Foreign Office. France was to pay dearly for this policy in 1939-40 when Stalin ganged up with Hitler and the Com-

---

[9] Ibid., p. 50.
[10] Ibid., p. 51.

munist Party of France worked actively for the defeat of French armies. But Great Britain refused to walk into the trap. There was no prospect of a "Popular Front" government in London. And Great Britain's price for a pact with Soviet Russia was that the Kremlin should withdraw her communist fifth-columns from every part of her far-flung empire. Soviet Russia felt furious. She decided to force Great Britain into a "Popular Front" government and a British–Soviet pact with the help of her communist hirelings. They were directed to agitate everywhere against the Chamberlain Government. The standard plank of this agitation was that the Chamberlain Government was conspiring with the Axis Powers — Germany, Italy, and Japan — for a war against the Soviet Union.

The Communist Party of India decided to start such an agitation in India. But, meanwhile, the Indian National Congress had formed governments in several provinces. Pandit Nehru had opposed this decision of the Congress after his return from Europe. But he could not prevail over the "reactionaries" of the Congress Right. So he consoled himself by injecting the communist line into another foreign policy resolution which was passed by the Faizpur Congress.

This resolution was the most thinly camouflaged communist pill swallowed by the Congress. It said: "The Congress has drawn repeated attention in the past to the danger of imperialist war and has declared that India can be no party to it. Since the last session of the Congress the crisis has deepened and fascist aggression has increased, the fascist powers forming an alliance and grouping themselves together for war with the intention of dominating Europe and the world and crushing political and social freedom. The Congress is fully conscious of the necessity of facing this world menace in cooperation with the progressive nations and peoples of the world, and especially with those peoples who are dominated over and exploited by imperialism and fascism. In the event of such a world war taking place, there is grave danger of Indian manpower and resources being utilised for the purposes of British imperialism, and it is therefore necessary for the Congress to warn the country against this and prepare it to resist such exploitation of India and her people. No credits must be voted for such a war and voluntary subscriptions and war loans must not be supported and all other war preparations resisted."[11]

---

[11] Ibid., pp. 51–52.

In February 1937, Pandi Nehru issued an appeal for aid to the communist armies in Spain: "We have already expressed our deep sympathy and solidarity with the Spanish people in many ways. The National Congress has given eloquent expression to the Indian people's voice and feelings. But that is not enough. We must translate our sympathy into active and material help. We are poor and hungry folk, crushed under many burdens, dominated by an arrogant imperialism, and we struggle ourselves for freedom. But even in our poverty and misery we feel for our Spanish comrades and we must give them what aid we can, however little this might be. We can help in sending them medical supplies and food. I trust it will be possible for us to arrange to send grain and other food supplies, and I appeal to those who deal in such food-stuffs for their cooperation in this matter. *In London our countrymen have formed a Spain-India Committee with Syt. V.K. Krishna Menon as chairman.* I suggest that we might send money to them for the purchase and despatch of medical supplies. I trust that contributions for this purpose will be forthcoming from all parts of the country."[12]

And, finally, at the Haripura Congress in February 1938, he repeated his lies against Great Britain in yet another resolution which read:

"In view of the grave danger of wide-spread and devastating war which overshadows the world, the Congress desires to state afresh the policy of Indian people in regard to foreign relations and war.

"The people of India desire to live in peace and friendship with their neighbours and with all other countries, and for this purpose wish to remove all causes of conflict between them. Striving for their own freedom and independence as a nation, they desire to respect the freedom of others and to build up their strength on the basis of international cooperation and goodwill. Such cooperation must be founded on a world order and a free India will gladly associate itself with such an order and stand for disarmament and collective security. But world cooperation is impossible of achievement so long as the roots of international conflict remained and one nation dominates over another and imperialism holds sway. In order, therefore, to establish world peace on an enduring basis,

[12] *The Unity of India*, pp. 266–67. Italics added.

imperialism and the exploitation of one people by another must end.

"During the past years there has been a rapid and deplorable deterioration in international relations, fascist aggression has increased and an unabashed defiance of international obligations has become the avowed policy of fascist powers. British foreign policy, in spite of its evasions and indecisions, has consistently supported the fascist powers in Germany, Spain and the Far East and must, therefore, largely shoulder the responsibility for the progressive deterioration of the world situation. The policy still seeks an arrangement with Nazi Germany and has developed closer relations with rebel Spain. It is helping in the drift to imperialist world war.

"India can be no party to such an imperialist war and will not permit her man-power and resources to be exploited in the interests of British imperialism. Nor can India join any war without the express consent of the people. The Congress, therefore, entirely disapproves of war preparations being made in India and large-scale manoeuvres and air-raid precautions by which it has been sought to spread an atmosphere of approaching war in India. In the event of an attempt being made to involve India in a war, this will be resisted."[13]

It was now fully clear what Pandit Nehru meant by what he called an "imperialist war". As a convinced communist he had come to believe that Britain was conspiring with Nazi Germany to unleash a war against the Soviet Union. But only an idiot or a communist could believe that. For, an year later, it was not Britain but Pandit Nehru's Fatherland, the Soviet Union, which signed a pact with Nazi Germany and left the latter free to unleash war in Europe.

---

[13] *The Background of India's Foreign Policy*, pp. 55–56. Leaders of the Communist Party of the Great Britain, R. Palme Dutt and Ben Bradley, had written an article, 'The Anti-Imperialist People's Front in India', in *Labour Monthly* of March 1936. Pandit Nehru's biographer, Sarvepalli Gopal, says that "this article was written after the talks with Jawaharlal at Lausanne and stated what Palme Dutt and Bradley believed to have been accepted by Jawaharlal as the common programme for which he will strive" (*Jawaharlal Nehru: A Biography*, Volume One, OUP, 1976, pp. 203-04). Pandit Nehru was in Lausanne, Switzerland, during the last days of his wife's illness. Kamala Nehru died on February 28, 1936. (Footnote added in 1993.)

Twelve

A FELLOW-TRAVELLER OF SOVIET FOREIGN POLICY-4

Shri D.G. Mohan Rao, a friend from Warrangal, who has been reading this series, writes: "There is confusion to know exactly what is Ekaki's name to write about either Shri Nehru or Krishna Menon. Ekaki collected only the 'yes' quotations of him—Nehru. But Nehru tells sometimes 'no' also about communists. The theory and the way of collecting only 'yes' quotations in Nehru's praise of communism does not underline the psychology in perfect way because there are so many other 'no' quotations also in Shri Nehru's warnings against communists."

Shri Mohan Rao has expressed a misgiving which must have arisen in many other minds. The myth that Pandit Nehru is our sole barrier against the communist flood which will otherwise inundate us, has been prevalent for such a long time in this country as well as abroad, and our press has been so tirelessly talking about his anti-communist role, that to many people it appears self-evident that he must have criticised the creed of Communism and its temple in the Soviet Union systematically and strongly. If, therefore, you inform these people that in the mountainous mass of verbiage which he has produced in his speeches and writings all along these thirty and more years, there has never been even a mild criticism of Communism or of the Soviet Union, they are most likely to dismiss you as a mad man.

It is true that in recent years Pandit Nehru has occasionally pointed out that much of Marxism is out of date due to developments that have taken place after Marx's death. But that is quite in the line of orthodox communist thinking. Lenin, the hallowed theoretician of Communism, had stated quite clearly, and as early as 1916, that Marx had thought and written in an age when capitalism had not yet become "monopoly capitalism" and a "single chain of world imperialism", and that, therefore, Marx's strategy of creating (or predicting, if you please) the first proletarian revolutions in the metropolitan countries of Europe such as England, France and Germany was no more suited to the new stage in human history. The later-day theoreticians of Marxism-Leninism such as Stalin, Mao Tse-tung and Khrushchev, have also claimed that they have developed the original doctrine of Marx in the light of changing world conditions. Even a petty communist like S.A. Dange said the other day that much of Marx was already out of date.

As regards the Soviet Union, we have seen how Pandit Nehru has all along apologised for its outrageous aspects and praised those of its aspects which in his opinion are supposed to be beyond any blame. A man who could survive the shock of destalinisation and remain an ardent admirer of the Soviet Union which Stalin had created, cannot be expected to show any critical faculty when faced with that monolithic monster of modern materialism. The recent triumphs of what the communists describe as Soviet science such as the hydrogen bomb and the space rockets, have cleared his mind of whatever doubts he might have occasionally entertained about the Soviet Union's sacred character in moments of extreme pressure from an outraged public opinion.

There are, of course, on record a few "strong" statements from Pandit Nehru in criticism of the Communist Party of India—statements which Minoo Masani's publicity appratus has been quite dishonestly displaying in order to deceive the devoted followers of the Prime Minister. But all these statements taken together boil down to two very petty and pointless polemics against the Communist Party. Firstly, Pandit Nehru has occasionally objected that communists do not relate their means to their ends and that, being hot-headed and impatient, they easily take resort to violence. Secondly, in his moments of exasperation against communist hooliganism during his mass meetings or his election campaigns for the Congress Party, he has hinted that communists are inspired from abroad and that they do not have their roots in the Indian soil.

Now, the charge that communists specialise in violence is absolutely spurious. If there is anything in which the communists specialise, it is in serving the Soviet Union which is their one and only Fatherland and source of inspiration. If the Soviet Union orders the communists to create violence in a particular country or all over the world, they can become a pack of wild wolves as they did during 1948-50 all over South-East Asia: But if the Soviet Union orders them to be sweet to a particular regime, they are quite capable of behaving like sheep as they did from 1942 to the end of 1944 in their relations with the British Government of India.

Pandit Nehru's complaint that communists often fail to relate their means to their ends sounds more fundamental to certain people who fancy themselves as "philosophically inclined". But a clearer and closer analysis of this problem of ends and means will reveal to any logical mind that, at its best, it is no better than an endless exercise in the crudest type of casuistry. A choice regarding means appears to arise only so long as the end is defined "vaguely and generally", to use one of Pandit Nehru's favourite phrases. But as soon as the end, and the circumstances in which that end is to be achieved, are defined precisely and concretely, one's sense of choice regarding means evaporates, and one is left with a single and straight road on which one may or may not have the guts to travel.

But the communist fraternity has never defined its aim "vaguely and generally". If there is any word in human language to which communists are particularly addicted, it is the word 'concrete'. Their definition of their goal is concrete, and their estimation of the circumstances in which they have to achieve that goal is also always concrete, no matter how technical and specialised the language in which they love to talk. Communists may be a pack of traitors but no one can accuse them of not being realists in the game of power politics. And it is quite another matter that the exigencies of Soviet foreign policy seldom allow the communist parties in non-communist countries to play their political game in a simple and straight manner.

In post-Gandhian India, an endless discussion about means and ends has acquired the proportions of a national epidemic. Quite a few of our politicians who either do not know what they want or who do not have the guts to struggle and fight for what they want, waste their entire time in spinning soap-bubbles about ends and means and, in the process, become monuments of self-righteous stupidity. Their only positive role is that they serve the communist cause by *violently* objecting against everyone who tries to expose the communist game and isolate the Communist Partyof India. Their standard charge against anti-communists is that the latter are using "communist means" in a bid to stop the spread of Communism. But they fail to point out or demonstrate the other sort of means which can be employed to oppose the communist game.

We have to think seriously some day as to what is so monstrously wrong with communist means. In general, they have been using the standard methods of modern political warfare with a few minor additions of their own. And if anyone ever really wants to defeat the communists, he would have to turn most of these methods back on them. The true distinction between communists and anti-communists is that the two are aspiring for diametrically opposite ends. Communists want to turn every independent country into a satellite of the Soviet Union. Anti-communists, on the other hand, are proud patriots. It is the character of these ends that should distinguish the two, unless one believes that there is no difference between a buffalo and a bonafide Gandhian because both of them are vegetarians!

In the context of Pandit Nehru, however, even this philosophical exercise is not pertinent. We have seen how he distinguishes between "capitalist violence", which he considers wasteful, and "communist violence", which in his opinion serves the perfect purpose of bringing about a new and better world order. We have also seen how he has apologised for or justified every instance of Soviet violence at home and abroad. It is, therefore, not for him to raise an accusing finger against the Communist Party of India committing violence under orders from his dreamland, the Soviet Union.

And accusing the Communist Party of India of having no roots in the soil is like accusing a hare of having no horns on its head. No communist theoretician has ever claimed that communists care for normal nationalism or ordinary patriotism, both of which are for them symptoms of a "bourgeois disease". Communists have always taken intense pride in what they describe as proletarian internationalism. Pandit Nehru can read with profit that small pamphlet, *Patriotism and Internationalism,* already referred to.

Or he can have read a speech which Comrade Georgi Dimitroff, General Secretary of the Comintern, delivered in 1935. Speaking to the May First Delegation of Foreign Workers visiting Moscow, he said: "When the reactionary Social Democratic leaders say and write — 'we do not want to receive orders from Moscow', they only prove that they are against the State of the proletariat.... To every sincere worker in France or England, America or Australia, Germany or Spain, China or Japan, the Balkan countries or the Canary Islands—to every sincere worker, Moscow is his own Moscow, the Soviet Union is his own State. *Our opponents very often set up a howl about 'orders from Moscow'. To receive orders from Moscow means salvation to the world proletariat.*"[1]

---

[1] *The United Front,* p. 143. Italics added.

A communist is a communist simply because he places the interests of the Soviet Union above even the most vital interests of the country which gave him birth and provided the wherewithal for his upbringing. The mere belief in Marxism-Leninism does not make anyone a communist. If a theoretical adherence to the Marxist-Leninist platform could create communists, then the overwhelming majority of socialists and leftists in general would fall in the communist camp. But we find that the various other socialists and leftists are quite often at daggers drawn with the communists. The one criterion that divides them decisively is the question of loyalty to Moscow. To blame the Communist Party of India for its devotion to Moscow is like blaming an animal for breathing.

Apart from these petty and pointless criticisms of the Communist Party, I am not aware of any serious anti-communist utterances on the part of Pandit Nehru. If, however, Shri D.G. Mohan Rao or any other reader of this series is aware of any profounder pronouncements against Communism emanating from him, I shall heartily welcome the relevant references, withdraw my charge against him, and apologise for having sinned against an innocent man.

Incidentally, Shri Mohan Rao has also raised a standard but meaningless slogan of our present-day politics. He writes: "Therefore is it positive to think that Ekaki is writing only just before General Elections to create anti-atmosphere against Nehru while keeping silence till now? How people's suspicion, thinking that this is a political stunt, will be cleared? This is the big psychology of the people now a days."

The author of this series has always failed to understand certain words of everyday use in our politics, and the word 'stunt' is one of them. To a certain type of mind (or absence of mind), whenever a political party says something against its opponents, it is indulging in stunts. Now, winning the General Elections is quite a legitimate end as laid down in our Constitution. If someone wants to influence public opinion in a certain direction by opposing and exposing people who are opposed to that direction, it does not add up to anything more than a normal use of a democratic right. If an exercise of this democratic right is a stunt, then this series is surely a stunt. But at this point the word stunt ceases to have any meaning because there is no politician or party who is not doing so, every minute and every day.

Or, perhaps, Shri Mohan Rao means by the word 'stunt' what in everyday language we mean by the word 'lie'. In that case, this series cannot be described as a 'stunt' by any stretch of imagination. If there are any stunts in our present-day political life, they are the speeches of Prime Minister Nehru who goes on raising the bogey of "communalism" and "reaction" whenever and wherever he sees genuine Indian nationalism raising its head and making its power felt in the political arena. If the most mendacious lies that the Prime Minister tells about the patriotic opposition parties, day in and day out, are not stunts, then this telling of the truth and nothing but the truth about him should not be taken as a stunt by any sober or serious man. And it is Shri Mohan Rao's lack of information which leads him to believe that Pandit Nehru is being exposed as a communist only now. There have been repeated attempts on the part of informed people to warn the country against this Moscow patriot masquerading as a martyr in the cause of Indian freedom. A recent and excellent example is Shri C. Parameshwaran's book, *Nehru's Foreign Policy X-Rayed,* published as early as August 1954 when Pandit Nehru started preaching his *Panchashila* in the face of communist occupation of Tibet. Mr. Philip Spratt's *Blowing up India* was a better and more authentic attempt in the middle of 1955.

But, unfortunately, our intelligentsia has been drugged with categories of communists thought so thoroughly that it is not prepared to accept any criticism of Pandit Nehru unless it comes from communist quarters. This intelligentsia could believe that Pandit Nehru was "the Chiang Kai-shek of India" and a "running dog of American imperialism" when Moscow and Peking said so during 1948-52. But if anybody points out that Pandit Nehru is a crypto-communist, his loyalty to the country becomes suspect. Courtier journalists like Prem Bhatia start seeing American agents and MacCarthies all around if anyone expresses doubts regarding even the Prime Minister's foreign policy. And no popular paper or journal in this country is prepared to publish even a small letter from such "American agents".

Even now it is not due to any reawakening on the part of our intelligentsia that this exposure has become possible. It is the shock of Red China's outrages against Tibet and our own country that has made a certain section of our public opinion sit up and look deeper into the sources of these disasters. Top leaders like

C. Rajagopalachariar knew all the time that Pandit Nehru is a communist. But it was the Chinese action which finally emboldened Rajaji to say that the Communist Party of India was functioning through the Congress Government of Pandit Nehru. Being a mature or practical politician, Rajaji had to take care of his reputation and wait for a proper oppurtunity in order to state the truth.

And now, to get back to our main story of Pandit Nehru's unceasing solicitude for the interests of the Soviet Union, let us return to June 1938 when the Comintern network took him out once again for a guided tour of Europe. He writes: "Subhash Bose was elected President of the next Congress session which was held at Haripura, and soon afterwards I decided to go to Europe. *I wanted to see my daughter, but the real reason was to freshen my tired and puzzled mind*."[2] The mind of this man is so constituted that it can get freshened or cleared only by trips to Europe! But to continue: "It was the Europe of 1938 with Mr. Neville Chamberlain's appeasement in full swing and marching over the bodies of nations, betrayed and crushed, to the final scene that was staged at Munich. There I entered into this Europe of conflict by flying straight to Barcelona. There I remained for five days and watched the bombs fall nightly from the air. *There I saw much else that impressed me powerfully; and there, in the midst of want and destruction and ever-impending disaster, I felt more at peace with myself than anywhere else in Europe.* There was light there, the light of courage and determination and of doing something worthwhile."[3] So only a civil war created by Communism, such as he witnessed in Spain, could soothe his shattered nerves. Poor India at that time happened to be too non-violent to present him with such a spiritually satisfying spectacle.

In July 1938, he presided over a communist rally in London, the so-called Conference on Peace and Empire, organised by Krishna Menon's India League and the London Federation of Peace Councils, a regular Red Front. In his presidential address, he said:

"In Europe and the West, where progressive groups have a longer history and different background, you have both advantages and disadvantages. But in Asia, where such groups have recently come into existence, the issue is often clouded by the nationalist issue, and one cannot think of it so easily in terms of international-

---

[2] *An Autobiography*, p. 604. Italics added.
[3] Ibid., p. 605. Italics added.

ism, obviously because we have to think first of all in terms of national political feeling.

"Even so, these modern developments, and especially what has happened in Abyssinia, in Spain and in China, have now forced people to think in terms of internationalism. *We find a remarkable change in some of these countries of Asia, for even though we were engrossed in our struggles, we began to think more and more of the social struggles in other parts of the world, and to feel more and more that they affected the entire world.*"[4]

This was of course pure nonsense. There was no section in India or any other enslaved country of Asia at that time which bothered about international issues except in so much as they affected the immediate imperialist enemy. The Indian people in general were full of admiration for Hitler and Mussolini and Fascism and Nazism because they were giving hard knocks to the national enemy — Britain. People swearing by "proletarian internationalism" could be found only on the fringes, unless it managed to rope in a popular leader like Pandit Nehru. Even such popular leaders had to function on false pretensions, that is, as champions of nationalism.

A few days later, he represented the Indian National Congress at another communist rally, this time in Paris. He said: "I have to convey to this great gathering the greetings and the assurances of full support in the cause of peace of the Indian National Congress representing the people of India. I do not speak on behalf of kings and queens or princes, but I do claim to speak for hundreds of millions of my countrymen. We have associated ourselves with this work of peace most willingly because of the vital urgency of the problem. Also because, in any event, our past background, and our civilisation, would have urged us to do so. For, the spirit of India for long ages past, like that of our great sister nation, China, has been a spirit of peace. Even in our national struggle for independence, we have always kept this ideal before us and adopted peaceful methods. So we gladly pledge ourselves to labour for peace."[5] And peace in the mind of Pandit Nehru as in the mind of any convinced communist has always meant that the Soviet Union and its hirelings should be allowed to slaughter whomsoever they will. Whenever someone tries to resist this sort of slaughter or refuses to approve of it, he immediately becomes a threat to peace!

[4] *The Unity of India*, pp. 270-71. Italics added.
[5] Ibid., pp. 278-79.

Commenting on Mr. Chamberlain's intended visit to Munich for meeting Hitler and Mussolini, he now wrote: "And yet, what of Czechoslovakia, what of democracy and freedom? Was there going to be another betrayal, the final murder of that nation? *This sinister gathering of four at Munich was the prelude to the Four-Power-Pact of Fascism-cum-Imperialism to isolate Russia, to end Spain finally, and to crush all progressive elements?* Mr. Chamberlain's past record inevitably makes one think so."[6] He forgot to remember on mention that Czechoslovakia at that time had a mutual defence pact with the Soviet Union. It was certainly an inconvenient thought for him that Stalin had not raised even his little finger in support of a solemn treaty. Nor did he think it fit to mention that Czechoslovakia under his prototype, Benes, was being taken over by Soviet Russia. That was normal for him. He started weeping over Czechoslovakia's fate only when Hitler defeated the Soviet game and took over Czechoslovakia for Germany. He did not say a word when the Soviet Union took over Czechoslovakia in 1948, and forced Benes to commit suicide.

After the Munich Agreement he wrote: "This act of gross betrayal and dishonour did not even bring peace, but has brought us to the threshold of war. *Yet peace was to be had for the asking by building up a joint peace front between England, France, Russia and other Powers, which would have been too powerful for Nazi Germany to dare to challenge. The British Government refused to line up with Russia and made Hitler believe that he could deal with Czechoslovakia singly, with England and other Powers looking on.* They ignored Russia in all their negotiations and worked in alliance with Hitler for the crushing of Czechoslovakia. They preferred the risk of making Hitler dominant in Europe to cooperation with Russia in the cause of peace. *Their class feeling and hatred of the new order in Russia were so great that everything else was subordinated to it.* They gladly agreed, at the bidding of Hitler, to the termination of the alliance between Russia and Czechoslovakia, and thus sought to isolate Russia. *The next obvious step was a Four Power Pact between England, France, Germany, and Italy, and alliance between imperialism and fascism in order to make the world safe for reaction and for the crushing of the progressive elements all over the world.*"[7] How wild and vicious was this charge

---

[6] Ibid., pp. 292-93. Italics added.
[7] Ibid., p. 296. Italics added.

was proved next year when Stalin ganged up with Hitler for a joint rape of poor Poland and world peace. France and England were to prove that they had been only trying to salvage peace, even though their methods were half-hearted and self-defeating.

Pandit Nehru's visit to Europe brought him still closer to the communist creed. On his return to India, therefore, he felt still more maladjusted with his own country and his colleagues in the Congress. He wrote: "I returned from Europe sad at heart with many illusions shattered... In India the old problems and conflicts continued and I had to face the old difficulty of how to fit in with my colleagues. It distressed me to see that on the eve of a world upheaval many Congressmen were wrapped up in these petty rivalries."[8]

He could never understand or adjust himself with an organisation the policies and internal struggles of which were divorced from devotion to the Soviet Union. This became more than clear when he made common cause with the communists against Subhas Chandra Bose, President of the Indian National Congress in two successive sessions, Haripura and Tripuri. Bose had placed India's struggle against British imperialism on top in his list of priorities. But Pandit Nehru's interest in the struggle against British imperialism was only a byproduct of his solicitude for the Soviet Union, as we shall see later in this series.

---

[8] *An Autobiography*, p. 605.

THIRTEEN

A FELLOW-TRAVELLER OF SOVIET FOREIGN POLICY-5

Subhas Chandra Bose and Jawaharlal Nehru have always been associated in our intelligentsia's mind as leftists and socialists who are supposed to have stood for the same sort of ideals during the days of our struggle against foreign rule or at least upto 1939 when Bose was ousted from the Indian National Congress by "Sardar Patel's rightist clique". The intelligentsia is also aware that at no time did Pandit Nehru have a soft corner for Bose whom he increasingly came to suspect as a sympathiser of Fascism and Nazism. And it is also widely known that Bose had nothing but contempt for Pandit Nehru whom he saw as a spineless soap-box orator.

But no one has as yet seriously tried to resolve the mystery of this mutual distrust and discord between two "anti-imperialist leaders with identical ideological inclinations". The explanation which has found favour whenever this issue has been raised is that the two of them were temperamentally different. In this explanation, Subhas Bose is presented as a rash and impatient and hot-headed young man. Pandit Nehru, on the other hand, is acclaimed as a mature and cool-headed and patient person who did not have Subhas Bose's dash — an explanation which Pandit Nehru, who even in his dotage struts about as a youthful revolutionary, must strongly detest. What, then, was the real difference and the cause of this discord?

A study of Subhas Bose's writings as well as the course of his political career till he disappeared from the stage, leaves no doubt that to him the cause of India's freedom from British imperialism was sacred above all other causes, and that he analysed all international alignments from that point of view alone. He, therefore, welcomed every weakening of British power, whether as a result of the rise of powerful enemies who challenged Britain's domination over a large part of the world, or as the outcome of a World War in which British power would be shaken to its very foundations. It was, therefore, natural for him that, when he saw the Second World War taking shape in Europe, he gave a call to this country to get ready for exploiting the opportunity and achieving its independence. The slogan coined by him in early 1939 was — "Britain's difficulty is India's opportunity". As President of the Indian National Congress, he wanted this organization to give six month's ultimatum to Britain for quitting India, failing which the nation was to struggle in all possible ways in order to free itself from foreign bondage.

Pandit Nehru, on the other hand, has never been able to see the good of India from a purely patriotic point of view. To him, the good of India has always been identical with the good of the Soviet Union. It was, therefore, natural for him to take the Soviet line on the eve of the Second World War. The Soviet Union, as we have seen, was trying frantically to whip up an anti-Chamberlain campaign inside Britain as well as in the British colonies, of which India was the most strategic, in order to force the existing British Government to sign a defence pact with the Soviet Union or get out in favour of a "Popular Front" Government *a la* France. The Comintern boss, Dimitroff, had advised the Communist Party of Great Britain that "at the present stage, fighting the Fascist danger in Great Britain means fighting the 'National Government' and its reactionary measures."[1]

Inside India, the Communist Party came out in support of Subhas Bose and against what the Party called the "right reaction" inside the Congress simply because Bose stood for an immediate struggle against Britain. But the nature of this support to Bose was limited and geared to the achievement of a limited end. The Communist Party of India received its mandate from a British boss in the following words: "The policy of Popular Front in the Western Democracies and Peace Alliance between the Western Democracies and the Soviet Union are merely the Western and world equivalents of what is taking place in India. *You, our Indian comrades, know that in the world of today patriotism is not enough and that our creed of brotherhood of man requires a new and deeper and tragically urgent significance that part of the mission of a free India will be to join hands with us in the West in building up a World Peace Union strong enough to end the existing aggression and to arrest a drift to war.*"[2] It may be mentioned that till 1947, the Kremlin channelled its instructions to communist parties in the colonies through the communist parties of the imperial

[1] *National Front*, March 12, 1939, article by "Vigilante". Italics added.
[2] Ibid., article by Ben Bradley. Italics added.

country concerned. In the case of the Communist Party of India, the instructions came through the Communist Party of Great Britain.

Another British boss of the Communist Party of India wrote:

"In England today we believe that Chamberlain and his fascist friends can be swept aside by the formation of a people's front against fascism and reaction. What does this defence of democracy in England mean to India? The Communist Party has been accused of advocating some sort of neo-imperialism, of asking the colonial people to fight for the Popular Front in defence of democracy in England but without any guarantee of the grant of democracy and freedom to India. We are accused of advocating some sort of liberal imperialism, a better and a more humane exploitation of the colonies.

"Frankly, we do not expect a popular government to come to power on a programme of complete socialism or the grant of independence to the colonies. It would be absurd, however, to regard the defence of democracy as an isolated struggle, something that was entirely unconnected with the other vital struggles taking place in England and the Empire. In order to develop the true democratic forces we are prepared, on conditions, to support a real popular front: in order to develop the same forces it is the duty of the Indian people to carry forward their struggle for democratic liberty. *In this process it is not simply possible, but certain, that such immediate and important reforms could be at once gained by India and the colonial people as would enormously strengthen their position and weaken that of the Imperialists. This is of immense importance not as an alternative to freedom but as an armoury to win it.*

"We believe that in the course of this struggle against Fascism and the dangerous situation created by it, it would be possible to convince all sections of anti-fascists of the necessity of granting democratic rights to the colonies and India as bulwark against Fascism. *As far as the Communists are concerned, this would be the maximum concession attainable at the particular moment without disruption of the popular front.* The Indian people are merely asked to consider whether the development of this objective situation is not one that is more advantageous to them than the supposed weakening of imperialism under Chamberlain."[3]

[3] Ibid., article by Harry Politt.

An Indian communist also wrote an article along the same lines:

"The great decision we are about to take at Tripuri has to be reviewed against the background of the maturing world war crisis. India's struggle for freedom cannot be viewed in isolation. It is a part of the great fight which the peoples of the world are beginning to wage against war and fascist aggression. *The slogan 'Britain's difficulty is India's opportunity' is no longer enough to indicate the interconnection of our national struggle with world politics.* There is a tendency to oversimplify the relation between our struggle for freedom and the coming war crisis in Europe. It is argued that what is happening after all is the sharpening of the inter-imperialist conflict between two groups of world monopoly capital. In this conflict the USSR would have to take sides as determined by the need of self-preservation, but that would not alter the character of the war. What India should be concerned about is how to take advantage of the war situation and the difficulties of Britain.

"This is what we would call banal analysis which entirely ignores the changes that have taken place in the world since 1917. We have, firstly, the emergence of the mighty socialist State of the U.S.S.R. which is on the one hand a powerful factor for peace. Secondly, we have a giant proletarian movement in the colonies and the subject nations fighting for freedom and democracy against their imperialist rulers.

"Significant developments followed as a reaction to the rise of Hitler. First, the people's counter-offensive against Fascism in France and Spain and, second, the Franco-Soviet Pact together with other peace pacts aimed against Hitler's aggression. Against the peace system of the U.S.S.R. and rise of the Popular Movement in France and Spain, Britain has pursued the policy of siding with Hitler and Mussolini, of conniving at Japanese aggression against China. The aim of this policy is to direct German aggression against the Soviet.

"The democratic peoples of the world and the forces of anti-fascist unity cannot afford to wait till war actually breaks out. They have to act here and now and prevent the rulers of their own countries from pursuing the ruinous policy which promotes fascist aggression and brings war nearer. *The fight for peace demands a frontal attack upon Chamberlain. If we in India deliver the blow now, we facilitate a similar action on the part of the people of Brit-*

ain. British imperialism is more vulnerable in India than it is in England. A struggle in India in the present situation would give a push to the world forces of peace and democracy and be the signal for the overthrow of Chamberlain."[4]

Thus, so far as the Communist Party of India was concerned, the anti-imperialist struggle in India was to be a mere appendix of the Communist Party of Great Britain's struggle against the Chamberlain Government. It was understood that if the Chamberlain Government was overthrown and replaced by a "Popular Front" Government willing to sign a pact with the Soviet Union or if the Chamberlain Government persuaded itself under pressure from public opinion to enter into an alliance with the Soviet Union, the Communist Party of India would give up the anti-imperialists struggle in India. And this was not only a logical deduction. This was what actually happened in the French colonies as soon as there was a "Popular Front" Government in France.

George Padmore, the Negro leader of French colonies in Africa and a Comintern executive since 1934, was to write later on: "I was at the time the Secretary of the International Trade Union Committee of Negro Workers, the anti-imperialist centre of the African liberation movement. I continued to carry on my work from Paris, but the Comintern, having decided to change its line in conformity with the foreign policy of the U.S.S.R., instructed me to change my attitude in relation to France — *I was told to boost the League of Nations and to stop all criticism of French Imperialism, especially its militarisation of subject peoples.* I declined to agree to this betrayal of my people and requested that a delegation of Negro communist leaders should be received by the Comintern in order to present our views on this new policy. The Comintern declined and I had no alternative to resignation. Immediately, the usual campaign of slander began in which the communists characterised me as a disruptive element and an agent of British Imperialism!"[5]

In India, too, the same logic worked itself out at a later stage. In 1942, when the Soviet Union was invaded by the German armies and Britain became an ally of the Soviet Union, the Communist Party of India came out immediately in support of the British Government of India which it now described as "British bureaucracy".

---

[4] Ibid., article by S.V. Ghate. Italics added.

[5] Quoted by Ram Swarup, *Russian Imperialism: How to Stop it,* Prachi Prakashan, Calcutta, 1950, pp. 27-28. Italics added.

But with that phase we shall deal later. Our intention in quoting at length from communist sources at this stage is to point out that Pandit Nehru's hue and cry against the Chamberlain Government was dictated not by the needs of India's struggle for independence but by the needs of the Soviet Union which felt threatened by the alliance among Germany, Japan, and Italy — the Axis Powers — and which was seeking an alliance with Britain and France.

Subhas Bose's fight against British imperialism was, on the other hand, of a much more fundamental character. He refused to concede that formation of a "Popular Front" Government in Britain would make a material difference to the colonial status of his own motherland. He was not interested in obtaining concessions of a secondary character from the British Government, which was all that even the inclusion of the Labour Party of Britain and its crypto-communist left faction could have secured at the utmost. He wanted to see India free, and at the earliest. So he staked his hopes on an all-out struggle against Britain at a time when Britain found herself hard-pressed elsewhere.

Moreover, he was not interested in preventing a world war by a collective security agreement between the Western Democracies and the Soviet Union. What would that mean to India, he asked? A stalemate and a status quo. To hell with collective security in that case, he said. A world war in which India could strike for her freedom was welcomed by him. A peacemonger who wanted to prevent such a war was, in his opinion, an enemy of India's independence. There could be nothing more ridiculous than an enslaved nation passing resolutions in support of world peace. Subhas Bose had no use for such pompous piety.

Nor did he believe for a moment that the alliance of a "progressive" Soviet Union with an "imperialist" Britain would "release powerful pressures and advance the cause of India". He knew the Soviet Union and its "progressive" character too well to be hoodwinked by any such vague hopes. And he was entirely correct in this analysis. An alliance between the Soviet Union and Britain did materialise a few years later when Hitler and Stalin came to blows. Instead of getting any concessions from Britain, India was forced to launch a direct struggle for defence of her elementary right to protest that she had been unwillingly yoked to a war which was not of own seeking. But the "progressive" Soviet Union did not utter a word against British repression, either in public or in private. And

Soviet Union's hirelings in India worked as spies for the British police. The only world leader who sympathised with Indian aspirations at that time was Chiang Kai-shek of China whom Pandit Nehru had denounced as a reactionary tool of Western imperialism only a few years earlier.

Years later, Pandit Nehru himself recorded as follows: "In 1938 the Congress sent a medical unit consisting of a number of doctors and necessary equipment and material to China. For several years this unit did good work there. When this was organised, Subhas Bose was President of the Congress. He did not approve of any step being taken by the Congress which was anti-Japanese or anti-German or anti-Italian. And yet such was the feeling in the Congress and the country that he did not oppose this or many other manifestations of Congress sympathy with China and the victims of fascist and Nazi aggression. We passed many resolutions and organized many demonstrations of which he did not approve during the period of his presidentship, but he submitted to them without protest because he realized the strength of feeling behind them. There was a big difference in outlook between him and others in the Congress Executive, both in regard to foreign and internal matters, and this led to a break early in 1939."[6]

It is, of course, not true that Pandit Nehru's brand of "internationalism" had much support in the Congress organisation or in the country at large. The effective power over both was in the hands of Mahatma Gandhi who was personally enamoured of Pandit Nehru and who had borrowed the latter's ideas about the international situation almost A to Z. Pandit Nehru could, therefore, always throw Gandhiji's weight in the balance. And Subhas Bose was not in a position to challenge or negate that weight. He, therefore, did not actively oppose the activities and resolutions of Pandit Nehru's communist clique before his own strength in the Congress and the country was sufficiently consolidated.

Had there been a straight contest between Subhas Chandra Bose and Jawaharlal Nehru, the latter would have been worsted any number of times. But, as in his contest with Sardar Patel, Pandit Nehru always took shelter under the Mahatma's all-protecting mantle. The Mahatma was too keen to reconcile his social thinking with the prevalent socialist thought to disown Pandit Nehru and his

---

[6] *Discovery of India*, p. 508.

communist crowd. Had the Mahatma not protected Pandit Nehru in the latter's pro-communist pre-occupations, Pandit Nehru would not have been able to write the following lines: "It is surprising how internationally minded we grew in spite of our intense nationalism. No other nationalist movement of a subject country came anywhere near this, and the general tendency in such other countries was to keep clear of international commitments. In India also there were those who objected to our lining up with republican Spain and China, Abyssinia and Czechoslovakia. Why antagonize powerful nations like Italy, Germany and Japan, they said; every enemy of Britain should be treated as a friend; idealism has no place in politics, which concerns itself with power and the opportune use of it. But these objectors were overwhelmed by the mass sentiment the Congress had created and hardly ever gave public expression to their views."[7]

Subsequent history is a witness that this summing up of the situation by Pandit Nehru was no more than a projection of his subjective state of mind with no reference to the objective atmosphere. The politicians and the people in India were all through this period one in wishing a victory to the Axis Powers. The press in India pretended to be anti-Axis only because of the Defence of India rules. The atmosphere in the country was so much surcharged with pro-Axis sentiments, particularly after Japan entered the War in December 1941 and gave some very hard blows to British power all over Far and South-East Asia, that if the Congress had collaborated with the British Government of India it would not have been able to do much better than the British Government did on its own. Sympathy with the Soviet Union, on the other hand, was confined only to the small communist and fellow-travelling fraternity which had Pandit Nehru as its most outstanding leader and lawyer.

It was indeed very difficult for Subhas Bose to swallow the big lie that the defence of the Soviet Union meant the defence of "freedom and democracy" in the world, as Pandit Nehru started saying day in and day out as soon as he received the ukase from Moscow. He knew that the Stalinist regime in Russia was several shades worse than the Nazi regime in Germany so far as "freedom and democracy" were concerned. He did not want to be hysterical

[7] Ibid.

in defence of a regime which had committed the worst possible crimes in human history, and against a regime the strengthening of which could only mean relief to his own motherland.

The way of Subhas Bose was the way of a straight patriot. And he stuck to that way to the bitter end. He did not change his way when he was thrown out of the Congress by a curious combination of Rightists and Leftists. He did not change his way when he was completely isolated in the country. It was while walking on that way that he went out of the country, organized the Azad Hind Fauj, forged national unity on a bloody battlefield, and, wrecked the morale of the British Indian Army which (and not the resolutions and jail journeys of the Khaddar-clad crowd, as we are now officially asked to believe) forced the British to quit India.

Meanwhile, our Don Quixote of "world peace" continued to compose one resolution after another. He composed angry resolutions against "British imperialism" when the communists were campaigning against an "imperialist war". He composed pathetic resolutions in favour of "peaceful negotiations" when the communists re-characterised the war as a "people's war". And his highest achievement during all these eventful years was to spend three years in jail where he paraphrased the communist lore in yet another book.

Pandit Nehru practised the most shameful type of opportunism vis-a-vis Subhas Bose. So long as the war continued and whenever he had an opportunity to make an oration, he described Bose's way as the wrong way and occasionally threatened "to go to the front to fight against Japan's fifth-column if it tried to march into India". That other "progressive" politician of the Congress, Maulana Azad, also echoed Pandit Nehru in his fits of fervour for "democracy and peace". But as soon as the war was over and Netaji's name started reverberating through the length and breadth of India, Pandit Nehru was the first to jump on the bandwagon. How could he do otherwise? Weren't his communist comrades ahead of everybody else in defending the Azad Hind prisoners and leading out violent processions wherever they could? The situation had changed again. Soviet Union's hireling were once again on the warpath against British imperialism because Stalin had sent the signal.

And Bose's tragedy came to serve this turncoat in yet another context. He hated India's hallowed national battle-cry, *Vande Mataram*. It was couched in Sanskrit which he had never understood and never honoured. But worst of all, it offended the Muslims whom he wanted to please and pit against "Hindu communalism". So, while the name of Netaji was still stirring the people, he pleaded that *Vande Mataram* should be replaced by *Jai Hind*, a cocktail phrase hurriedly coined by the Azad Hind leaders in the heat of an emergency. I myself heard him, in several crowded meetings, asking his audience to shout *Jai Hind* more loudly than they had done. He himself gave the lead by raising his voice to the highest pitch. I also heard him singing *qadam qadam baḍhāyē jā*, the marching song of the Azad Hind Fauj, and expressing dissatisfaction when people failed to repeat the refrain in the right tune. He suffered from no qualms in fattening himself on the fame of a "fascist".

But we are running ahead of our story. The details of Pandit Nehru's dancing to the Kremlin tune during the period when Subhas Bose was making history, have yet to be filled up.

FOURTEEN

A FELLOW-TRAVELLER OF SOVIET FOREIGN POLICY-6

The main plank of Congress propaganda after independence has been that it drove out the British by means of non-violent non-cooperation and brought freedom to the country. The Congress refers with particular pride to the policies it pursued during the Second World War period, particularly after the Quit India Resolution was passed in Bombay in August 1942. To put it simply, we are asked to believe that British imperialism in India got frightened because some Congressmen in some parts of the country pulled down some telephone poles and broke a number of letter-boxes before they were herded into British jails.

But this is one of the big lies known to human history. And deep down in his own mind every Congressman knows that he is telling a lie. For, whatever might have been the merit or demerit of Congress policies before the Second World War broke out, the policies which the Congress pursued during the War period were singularly barren and bankrupt. If these policies succeeded in achieving anything, it was the partition of the country and the planting of the communist Trojan horse squarely in our midst.

As regards independence, it came because the War reduced Britain to a bankrupt power, because the morale of the British Indian Army was broken by Subhas Bose's Azad Hind Fauj, and because the British Labour Party, in spite of Pandit Nehru's malicious insinuations against it in all his books, really believed in the slogans it had raised. It is quite another matter that the Congress inherited the power which the British were in a hurry to part with. That does not prove that power came to the Congress as a result of its own efforts, or that the Congress was qualified to use that power in terms of its inner cohesion or intrinsic character. The only thing it proves is that the departing British had retained a sufficient measure of confidence in the Congress organisation. The British believed that the Congress would be able to prolong the life of that political system which they had imposed on India, and which they regarded as the *sine qua non* of civilized life.

Let us look into this matter a little more closely. Even a novice in politics comes to know pretty soon that every politics is ultimately a balance between the moral merits of a case and the disposition of power in support of that case. Projection of pure power without any moral merit in the case concerned is bound to be defeated in the long run. And mere moral merit without any disposition of power to back it up is never able to convince the adversary. It is only when the two are combined that a politics becomes operative and capable of achieving something in the end.

Now, the cause of Indian freedom had become an excellent moral case by the time the Second World War broke out. The sacrifices of several generations in the service of that cause had created an atmosphere in which the justice of that cause had come to be conceded by everybody except the die-hard imperialists. Even the British establishment in India was committed to India's freedom, at least in its public pronouncements. That was a commitment which Britain's democratic conscience or, if you please, pretensions could not refuse to make.

And the Indian National Congress, which represented India's aspiration for freedom above every other organisation in the country, had also become a power to be reckoned with. A series of struggles since the Swadeshi Movement of 1905-09 had awakened the broad masses of India, and the main current of power produced by that awakening had got channelled into the Congress organisation. The fact that the British conceded to the Congress the control of a considerable part of public administration in seven or eight of the eleven Provinces during 1937-39, was proof positive that the British were quite conscious of the scale of Congress power.

But as soon as the Second World War broke out, the Congress started frittering away the moral merits of its case as well as the unparalleled power it had accumulated over the years. The nation at large expected the Congress to play some courageous and concrete role in the midst of that unprecedented opportunity. But the Congress did absolutely nothing beyond passing one routine resolution after another. And when, in due course, the country had become fully frustrated, the Congress led it into a most inopportune adventure — the Quit India Movement of 1942. The British broke the back of Congress hooliganism in less than a month and extended all its patronage to the Muslim League and the Communist Party of India. These two organisations monopolised the political field for three long years and emerged at the end as powers to be reckoned with.

When the War broke out, the Congress had two courses of action open before it. One course of action was that which had been pointed out by Subhas Bose, namely to use Britain's difficulty as India's opportunity. The situation in the country as well as in the world at large was quite favourable for that course of action. The support which Bose had received in two successive contests for Congress presidentship had revealed a radical mood in the nation. And the British power was very soon shown to be utterly bankrupt by the severe reverses it suffered in Europe. Had the Congress gone in for an all-out offensive during 1939-40, the chances were that the British would have surrendered virtual control of the country to the Congress. The Muslim League was as yet too weak and diffident to have come in the way of such a revolutionary seizure of power. The Communist Party of India was nowhere on the scene except in the slogans of the Congress Left led by Pandit Nehru.

But this course of action did not square with Mahatma Gandhi's moral principles. And, fortunately or unfortunately, the Mahatma meant the Congress in those days. Nor did this course of action square with past Congress declarations vis-a-vis the international situation. The Congress had pronounced its opposition to Fascism in so many of its foreign policy resolutions. It had accused the Chamberlain Government of appeasing Fascism and plotting war against the Soviet Union. The foreign policy resolution which Pandit Nehru had presented to the Tripuri session of the Congress after Bose had been worsted by Mahatma Gandhi and deserted by his leftist supporters, had the most unmistakable anti-fascist ring.

That resolution, which was passed unanimously, had said: "The Congress records its entire disapproval of British Foreign Policy culminating in the Munich Pact, the Anglo-Italian Agreement and the recognition of rebel Spain. This policy has been one of deliberate betrayal of democracy, repeated breach of pledges, the ending of the system of collective security and cooperation with governments which are avowed enemies of democracy and freedom. As a result of this policy, the world is being reduced to a state of international anarchy where brutal violence triumphs and flourishes unchecked and decides the fate of nations, and in the name of peace stupendous preparations are being made for the most terrible of wars. International morality has sunk so low in Central and South-Western Europe that the world has witnessed with horror the organised terrorism of the Nazi Government against people of the Jewish race and the continuous bombing from the air by rebel forces of cities and civilian inhabitants and helpless refugees in Spain. The Congress dissociates itself entirely from British foreign policy which has consistently aided the Fascist Powers and helped in the destruction of democratic countries. The Congress is opposed to imperialism and fascism alike and is convinced that world peace and progress require the ending of both these. In the opinion of the Congress, it is urgently necessary for India to direct her own foreign policy as an independent nation, thereby keeping aloof from both imperialism and fascism, and pursuing her path of peace and freedom."[1]

This resolution did not have a word to say about India's status vis-a-vis a very serious world situation. It had merely paraphrased the Comintern pronouncements current in those days. Providing the background of this resolution, Pandit Nehru wrote the following words just after Tripuri: "Our problems fill our minds. Yet the problem of problems today, overshadowing all else, is the growth of gangsterism in international affairs. The lights go out in Europe and elsewhere, the shadows increase, and in the darkness freedom is butchered and brutal violence reigns... Spain of the Republic and freedom is no more, only the bright and imperishable memory of her glorious struggle remains. Czechoslovakia used to be on the map of Europe; it is no more, and Herr Hitler's minions trample on her brave children, betrayed so shamefully by England and France. From day to day we await in suspense what this dictator or that says, anxiously we wonder what the next aggression will be. How does all this affect India? Dare we ignore these tremendous happenings in Europe? India's freedom will not be worth many days' purchase if Fascism and Nazism dominate the world. Our own existence is bound up with the fate of freedom and democracy in the world. *Only a union of freedom-loving peoples and their mutual cooperation can avert the common peril. For that union India must stand.*"[2]

It could, therefore, be logically expected that once Britain and France made up their mind to fight the Fascist Powers, the Congress would be prepared to cooperate with them. In fact, Mahatma Gandhi drew this conclusion when, immediately after the Second

[1] *The Background of India's Foreign Policy*, p. 58.
[2] *The Unity of India*, pp. 148-50. Italics added.

World War broke out in Europe, he advised the Congress to give unconditional moral support to the British Government of India. Writes Dr. Pattabhi Sitarammaya: "Gandhi was of the view that we must offer our moral support, allow the ministries to function and he had the confidence that through the ministries, he could manoeuvre a declaration of Poorna Swaraja or Dominion Status."[3]

But Mahatma Gandhi was not aware that Pandit Nehru had committed the Congress to an anti-fascist faith not because he linked prospects of India's freedom with that faith but because his Soviet mentors had at that time laid the line that way. Had the Soviet Union joined the anti-fascist war against the Fascist Powers, he would have felt no difficulty in advocating cooperation with her British ally, as he did at a later date. But the Soviet Union was now an ally of Nazi Germany, and the Comintern apparatus everywhere had characterised the War as an "Imperialist War". The Comintern had also invited the "people" in Western countries as well as in the colonies of those countries to convert the "imperialist war" into a "civil war" or a "war of liberation" on the pattern advocated by Lenin in 1914-18. It was, therefore, not at all possible for Pandit Nehru to advocate cooperation with the British Government of India.

Pandit Nehru, however, could not straight-away ask the Congress to give up its anti-fascist stand without at the same time exposing the character of his own brand of anti-fascism. There was, therefore, an acute *impasse*. Such an *impasse* is created for every "bourgeois" organisation which permits its own inborn attitudes to be supplanted by a communist clique working inside it. It is easy for a communist party to stage an overnight somersault simply because a communist party is indoctrinated from the beginning to place the interests of the Soviet Union above every other interest. But a "bourgeois" organisation cannot stage such a somersault without losing credibility. Nor can the communist clique inside the "bourgeois" organisation push it beyond a certain point without exposing itself. The next best thing is to paralyse the "bourgeois" organisation and prevent it from following any of its own characteristic courses of action.

And that is exactly what Pandit Nehru, aided by his communist clique in the Congress, did in September 1939 when the Congress

[3] *The History of the Indian National Congress*, Vol. II, p. 130.

was called upon to define its attitude towards the war crisis in Europe. The Congress Right including Mahatma Gandhi was in favour of continuing in the Provincial Ministries and bargaining for more power by means of cooperation and in a constitutional manner. But that course was contrary to Pandit Nehru's communist commitment. And he was by now a power to be reckoned with inside the Congress High Command. The Mahatma could resist everyone else, but he never liked to counter Jawaharlal. So Pandit Nehru had his way and the Working Committee at Wardha came out with the clumsiest resolution on Congress record till that date.

To start with, the resolution repeated its earlier slogans against Fascism. "The Congress," it said, "has repeatedly declared its entire disapproval of the ideology and practice of Fascism and Nazism and their glorification of war and violence and the suppression of the human spirit. It has condemned the aggression in which they have repeatedly indulged and their sweeping away of well-established principles and recognised standards of civilized behaviour. It has seen in Fascism and Nazism the intensification of the principles of imperialism against which the Indian people have struggled for many years. The Working Committee must therefore unhesitatingly condemn the latest aggression of the Nazi Government in Germany against Poland and sympathise with those who resist it."[4]

Next, the resolution expressed its hostility towards Britain and France in the current communist fashion. That hostility could not be hinged upon the current policies of these nations because they had at last come out against Fascist aggression. So the resolution denounced these nations for their past failures, and said: "The Committee are aware that the Governments of Great Britain and France have declared that they are fighting for democracy and freedom and to put an end to aggression. But the history of the recent past is full of examples showing the constant divergence between the spoken word, the ideals proclaimed and the real motives and objectives. During the war of 1914-18, the declared war aims were preservation of democracy, self-determination and the freedom of small nations, and yet the very Governments which solemnly proclaimed these aims entered into secret treaties embodying imperialist designs for the carving up of the Ottomon Empire. While stating that they did not want any acquisition of terri-

[4] *The Background of India's Foreign Policy*, p. 62.

tory, the victorious Powers added largely to their colonial domains. The present European war itself signifies the abject failure of the Treaty of Versailles and of its makers who broke their pledged word and imposed an imperialist peace on the defeated nations. The one hopeful outcome of that Treaty, the League of Nations, was muzzled and strangled at the outset and later killed by its parent States. Subsequent history has demonstrated afresh how even a seemingly fervent declaration of faith may be followed by an ignoble desertion. In Manchuria the British Government connived at aggression, in Abyssinia they acquiesced in it. In Czechoslovakia and Spain democracy was in peril and it was deliberately betrayed, and the whole system of collective security was sabotaged by the very powers who had previously declared their firm faith in it."[5] It may be mentioned that when the Soviet Union was invaded by Nazi Germany at a later stage, and Pandit Nehru proclaimed that the conflict had become a "People's War", the sin of the Soviet Union in signing the Stalin-Hitler Pact in 1939, was never mentioned by him.

Then the resolution characterised the War as an "imperialist war" in the current communist terminology. It said: "As the Working Committee view past events in Europe, Africa and Asia, and more particularly past and present occurrences in India, they fail to find any attempt to advance the cause of democracy or self-determination or any evidence that the present war declarations of the British Government are being, or are going to be, acted upon. The true measure of democracy is the ending of imperialism and fascism alike and the aggression that has accompanied them in the past and the present. Only on that basis can a new order be built up. In the struggle for that new world order, the Committee are eager and desirous to help in every way. *But the Committee cannot associate themselves or offer any cooperation in a war which is conducted on imperialist lines and which is meant to consolidate imperialism in India and elsewhere.*"[6]

The rest of the resolution extended an invitation to the British Government to declare its war aims and to implement its defence of democracy etc. in India. But in its sum total the resolution was a bundle of contradictions. Pandit Nehru was himself quite conscious of these contradictions contained in his resolution. He was to write

[5] Ibid., p. 63.
[6] Ibid., p. 65. Italics added.

later on: "Thus the Congress laid down and frequently repeated a dual policy in regard to War. There was, on the one hand, opposition to fascism, nazism and Japanese militarism both because of their internal policies and their aggression in other countries... On the other hand, there was emphasis on the freedom of India, not only because that was our fundamental objective for which we have continously laboured but also especially in relation to a possible War... *The two parts of this dual policy did not automatically fit into each other; there was an element of mutual contradiction in them.* But that contradiction was not of our creation; it was inherent in the circumstances and was inevitably mirrored in any policy that arose from circumstances."[7]

The imbecility exhibited in this statement can hardly find a match in normal political pronouncements. Politics is never and in no sense a passive portrait of existing circumstances. It is, on the contrary, an active exercise of will to overcome the circumstances and change them. The powerful Congress organisation in 1939 was not expected to merely register a pathetic protest against a world that had gone out of joint and thus humbug a whole nation. The nation had put its faith in the Congress. It was, therefore, the duty of the Congress to give a clear call for action, whatever the path the logic of that action pointed out.

But the Congress had promoted an incurable Soviet-addict to positions of power in its highest organs, and had permitted him to become its sole spokesman on foreign policy as well as its second best mass leader. The Congress had to pay the price. It had to remain in a state of paralysis from September 1939 to August 1942. The only action taken by the Congress during this period was the resignation of its Provincial Ministries under direction from another resolution drafted by Pandit Nehru and passed by the Congress Working Committee in October 1939. All its other attempts at political action, whether it was an attempt at cooperation with the British Government under the lead given by Rajaji in early 1940 or an attempt at direct action through individual civil disobedience, were half-hearted hazards devoid of all sense of self-confidence.

And the Congress frittered away its moral reputation as an organisation of fighters for human freedom when it refused to say even a single word of protest against the Stalin–Hitler Pact, against

[7] *Discovery of India*, pp. 509-10. Italics added.

the invasion of Poland and Finland by the Soviet Red Army, and against the incorporation of half of Poland and three independent Baltic States — Latvia, Lithuania, Estonia — in the Soviet Slave Empire. The foreign policy resolutions of the Congress subsequent to the lead given by Pandit Nehru in September 1939 and till November 1940 when he was sent to jail, were only full of sound and fury but devoid of any significant political content.

P.C. Joshi, General Secretary of the Communist Party of India till 1947, was to identify the inspiration behind these resolutions passed by the Congress during what he called the "Imperialist Phase of the War", when he reviewed them in November 1945. He observed:

"Among the national organisations of suppressed colonial peoples, the Indian National Congress is not only the oldest but also the greatest. It is the pride of our ancient and freedom-loving people. *On the initiative of Pandit Jawaharlal Nehru and supported by younger progressive elements within it all its declarations of international policy have been based on and have popularised the following ideas:*

"World Imperialism as a whole is one oppressive system of enslavers and aggressors.

"World peoples form another camp of peace, freedom and democracy. The Congress has always identified its ideas with this camp and also recognised and welcomed the existence of the Socialist Soviet Union."[8]

Here was a testimonial, if a testimonial was at all needed, in appreciation of Pandit Nehru's services to the Soviet brand of Western imperialism.[9] His stand in the subsequent period, when the Soviet Union got involved in the Second World War, supplied further evidence as to where his real loyalties lay at that time.

---

[8] Cited in *Communist Reply to Congress Working Committee Charges*, People's Publishing House, Bombay, 1945, pp. 22-23. Italics added.

[9] In a letter dated January 24, 1940 which Pandit Nehru wrote to Mahatma Gandhi, he justified the Stalin-Hitler Pact and characterised the war as an imperialist war (*A Bunch of Old Letters*, OUP, 1990, pp. 424-25). Footnote added in 1993.

FIFTEEN

A FELLOW-TRAVELLER OF SOVIET FOREIGN POLICY-7

Hitler got defeated in the Second World War. Therefore, everyone can now shout: "Hell, thy name is Hitler." So if anyone says today that at least in so far as Hitler's relations with the Soviet Union were concerned after Molotov signed a Non-Aggression Pact with Ribbentrop in August 1939, his record was absolutely unimpeachable, he should be committing the most horrible crime. For, the Soviet Union won the War along with her Western allies. And no sane person is supposed to find faults with those who are successful. After all, the one sure sign of insanity is that one refuses to swallow the current surges of public opinion without a fistful of salt.

But the truth must be faced unless one is prepared to believe with Schopenhauer that every page in every book of history is as infested with lies as a public woman with syphilis. Even today, the truth is waiting for anyone who honestly seeks it — in the published records of the German Foreign Department.

Communist propaganda wants us to believe that Hitler's aggression against the Soviet Union was wanton and unprovoked. But the talks that took place in a Berlin bunker between a bull-headed Molotov and a patiently persuasive Hitler, tell a different story. And that story had a still more shady start. For, the Hitler–Stalin Pact of August 1939 was not a mere diplomatic manoeuvre on the part of Stalin to break through a deadlock with Britain and France, or to turn the Nazi wolves against "their own kinsmen", as Pandit Nehru would have us believe, or to gain time for getting ready to face a war with Germany which seemed inevitable to Stalin. These versions of the Hitler–Stalin Pact are pure fabrications retailed by the communist apparatus as well as its aids and allies like Jawaharlal Nehru.

The records of the Pact leave no doubt that the Pact was a cold and calculated move on the part of Stalin to divide the spoils of war with a victorious Nazi Germany. According to the Pact, kept secret at that time, Hitler had insisted and Stalin had agreed that after Poland had been partitioned, the small Baltic States gobbled up by the Soviet Union, and adjustments of the Soviet border made with Rumania etc., the interests of the Soviet Union lay towards the South and East of that sprawling giant, that is, in the general direction of the Persian Gulf and the Indian Ocean. The Balkans and Asia Minor and Africa had been reserved by Hitler and conceded by Stalin as Germany's legitimate sphere of expansion. Hitler's scheme for the rest of Europe, the British Empire and the Americas was neither broached by the Soviet Union, nor discussed at the conference table.

In all the developments that took place after the War broke out and till the German armies occupied the Balkans, Hitler adhered to this Pact scrupulously and both in letter and spirit. The invasion of Finland by the Soviet armies and the subsequent concessions which that small country was forced to make to the Soviet Union, were breaches of that Pact on the part of Stalin. But Hitler kept on looking the other way without registering even a protest. Perhaps that was the German mistake which whetted Stalin's appetite for further acts of bad faith, and which made Molotov adamant on a revision of the earlier agreement during fresh Nazi–Soviet talks in the later half of 1940.

Molotov kept on bludgeoning Ribbentrop in his characteristically bull-headed manner that the Soviet Union's interests in the Balkans as well as in the Straits should be redefined. Ribbentrop reminded him repeatedly that a solemn agreement signed by both the parties in respect of those areas was already in existence, and that it was not proper on part of the Soviet Union to reopen that question. But Molotov was Molotov. His master in the Kremlin had ordered him to be obstinate. Even Hitler's intervention in those tiresome talks could not convince Molotov that the Soviet Union did not have a solid case on her side.

Hitler now felt convinced that the Soviet Union wanted to bully the Germans into a surrender of German interests in the Balkans and the Straits. The talks broke down, and Molotov departed from Berlin a morose man wearing the mask of a martyr. Hitler now knew that Stalin was out for mischief. The movements of Soviet armies all along the common frontiers were clearly calculated to convey that message to the German Chancellory. And Hitler made up his mind at last. The letter he wrote to Mussolini after he had ordered the German General Staff to prepare for invasion of the Soviet Union reveals the stress which Stalin's breach of faith had created in Hitler's mind.

Western historians and journalists, who have never failed to find an apology for Soviet crimes, have tried to justify Stalin's breach of faith in terms of the "legitimate" fears which the Soviet Union came to entertain when the Western defences collapsed speedily before the German onslaught, and Germany became a colossus which Stalin had never expected it to be. But that justification lies in the region of *realpolitik*. In terms of *realpolitik*, perhaps it was right for Stalin to kick up trouble with Germany while the West was still alive and in a fighting mood. A fully worsted West would have left the Germans free to pounce upon the Soviet Union. But all that does not add up to any moral right on the part of Stalin to go back on a solemn agreement which he had signed only an year earlier. Nor does it prove that Hitler's attack on the Soviet Union was wanton and unprovoked. Hitler had only forestalled Stalin's stab in his back.

Pandit Nehru was in jail along with other Congress leaders when this nemesis fell upon his Soviet Fatherland. The war on the Russian Front had released Britain from that powerful German pressure which had almost pulverised her after the fall of France. Britain, therefore, saw no immediate reason to seek a settlement with the Congress. It was Pearl Harbour and the swift Japanese victories that followed everywhere in the Far East which sent a signal that a settlement in India was the need of the hour. The Congress leadership was brought out of jail, and a hint was given that Britain was ready for a real bargain.

But the Congress mood had considerably stiffened by this time. Frustration in their earlier attempts at settlement had made them bitter against Britain. And the growing menace from Japan seemed to guarantee that the Congress could get a good bargain this time. Had the Congress leadership shown cohesion and determination, there was every chance that Britain would have parted with the substance of power. But once again, communist mischief played through the medium of Pandit Nehru created a breach in the Congress leadership. And the British turned the scales against the Congress once more after a brief pretence at negotiations.

Pandit Nehru's anti-fascism had been in abeyance between August 1939 and June 1941, simply because the Soviet Union did not sanction it during that period. But now that the Kremlin was crying for help against the "Nazi hordes", he immediately resurrected his old roar against Fascism. That roar could not reach the world outside because this "lion of Indian progressivism" was behind prison bars since November 1940 on account of his protest against the British war effort in India. But as soon as he came out of prison on December 4, 1941, in the wake of Pearl Harbour and the entry of Japan and America into the arena of world conflict, he held a press conference in Lucknow and said: "In the grouping of powers struggling for the mastery of the world, on either side, there seem to be dreams entertained by Governments for world domination. Undoubtedly this is so on the part of Hitler. It is not proclaimed as such on the other part... Still, I think that in the grouping that exists, there is also no doubt that progressive forces of the world are aligned with the group represented by Russia, China, America and England."[1]

Thus, so far as Pandit Nehru was concerned, the character of the war had changed simply because Britain had now the high honour of being an ally of the Soviet Union. The Working Committee of the Congress was called into session at Bardoli and it passed a new resolution on December 30. Reviewing the world situation once again through the eyes of Pandit Nehru, the Working Committee now resolved that "while there has been no change in Britain's policy towards India, the Working Committee must nevertheless take into full consideration the *new world situation* that has arisen by the development of the war into a world conflict and its approach to India."[2] The real reason for reviewing the world situation was kept camouflaged in this resolution.

That reason, however, became manifest when, Pandit Nehru further persuaded the Working Committee to pronounce as follows: "*The Soviet Union has stood for certain human, cultural and social values which are of great importance to the growth and progress of humanity.* The Working Committee considers that it would be a tragedy if the cataclysm of war involved the destruction of this endeavour and achievement. They have admired the astonishing self-sacrifice and heroic courage of the Soviet people in defence of their country and freedom and send to them their warm sympathy."[3]

Nobody seemed to remember that hardly two years had

---

[1] Cited in *Communist Reply to Congress Working Committee Charges*, People's Publishing House, Bombay, 1945, p. 43. Italica added.

[2] *The History of the Indian National Congress*, Vol. II, p. 292.

[3] *The Background of India's Foreign Policy*, p. 85, Italics added.

elapsed since the same Soviet Union had stabbed Poland in the back after signing a secret pact with Nazi Germany. Nobody seemed to bother that the same Soviet Union had forced Finland into surrendering some of her most valuable sovereign rights. It seemed nobody's business to point out that the same Soviet Union had only yesterday eaten away three independent Baltic States. An impression was abroad that the Congress Working Committee as a whole was weeping over the woes of the Soviet Union.

But that was a false impression. Early in January 1942, it became widely known that Sardar Patel, Dr. Rajendra Prasad, Acharya Kripalani and Dr. Prafulla Ghosh were opposed to this Bardoli stand, and that Pandit Nehru, who was supported by Maulana Azad, Pandit Pant and Mr. Asaf Ali, got away with the resolution because the Mahatma intervened in his favour at the last moment. The Mahatma was still writing in his weekly paper in support of the Bardoli resolution. But in spite of his stand, Sardar Patel and Dr. Rajendra Prasad issued a press statement appealing to Congressmen not to pass the Bardoli resolution at the forthcoming AICC session. Once more, the Congress was seriously split. Only the factions had changed sides.

In the AICC session at Wardha, the two groups joined issues once again. Knowing that the Mahatma was on his side, Pandit Nehru fretted and fumed at everybody who was not in agreement with him. Dr. Sitarammaya records:

"Replying to the debate at the meeting of the AICC, Pandit Jawaharlal Nehru criticised the tendency to be carried away by slogans and catchwords. So far as he could see, Communists, Socialists and Gandhites were equally victims of that tendency. Socialism or Communism never meant the application of abstract theories based on experiences of Western countries without regard to conditions in India. The suggestion of Congress Socialists to convene a Constituent Assembly was, in his opinion, impracticable at this juncture, although he believed that, ultimately, a Constituent Assembly alone could decide the fate of India.

"Nehru added that he failed to understand the attitude of those who talked of 'hundred per cent non-violence', but tolerated the present economic and social structure based on violence and injustice, and who hoped to build up a new structure by means of bringing about a mental change amongst the capitalist and propertied classes. He expressed disagreement with Rajendra Prasad and his friends who said that they did not consider the freedom which countries like England and America enjoyed worth acceptance. He for one would any day accept that type of freedom, imperfect though it was, and would then try to remedy the defects and build up a new structure of society, which would be free from periodical wars and the use of violence."[4]

And once again, the Mahatma urged his genuine desciples like Sardar Patel and Dr. Rajendra Prasad to submit to Pandit Nehru's nonsense.

The knowledge that Pandit Nehru was likely to prevail in the Congress organisation provided a clue to the British Government which was finalising the terms for a settlement in India. Had the Congress presented a united front in favour of supporting the war effort only if the British parted with the substance of power, the terms which Stafford Cripps brought to India would not have been such a swindle, and the British side would have behaved much better during the course of those negotiations. But Pandit Nehru's larynx had now got fully loosened, and he was daily lashing out at those who "continued to think in the old and out-moded manner".

Cripps came. The Mahatma saw his proposals and went away to his *ashrama* next day. He was reported to have said that the Cripps' proposals amounted to a postdated cheque on a bank that was crashing. But Maulana Azad, prompted by Pandit Nehru, prolonged the negotiations which finally failed without producing any worthwhile result. The country became still more bitter against the British. The fate of Burma and Malaya was a grim reminder that the British could not defend India if and when the Japanese made a determined bid to cross her borders. Either the British parted with power or there had to be some understanding with the Japanese—that was the prevailing national mood.

But Pandit Nehru was now no more a part of the nation. As soon as the Cripps Mission failed, he rushed to panic-stricken Bengal and pronounced: "The fundamental fact is not what the British do to us or what we do to them, although that governs much of what we do; the fundamental fact is the peril to India and what we are going to do about it. *Therefore, certainly, in spite of all that has happened, we are not going to embarrass the British war effort in India or the effort of our American friends who may come here.*

[4] *The History of the Indian National Congress,* Vol. II, pp. 295-96.

We want production to go at full speed ahead. We want people to hold on to their jobs and not run away from them."[5]

On April 13, 1945, he went further and said; "The issues before the country are so grave that no responsible person can talk lightly about them in terms of bitter reaction to events. We cannot afford to be bitter because bitterness clouds the mind and affects judgement in a grave crisis. It is our duty, the Congressmen's duty and the duty of other persons to carry out the programme of self-protection and self-sufficiency to the utmost. It may be we would have to take up guerrilla warfare. I don't know what the Congress will decide. But it is the foundation, and this organisation that we are building up will ultimately help us to meet the situation. My general advice is: Do not submit or surrender, do not give supplies, non-cooperate with the aggressor, embarrass him in every way. Fighting will be done by the armed forces."[6]

And, finally, on April 16, he declared: "During the last three or four months we have been fighting a definite pro-Japanese feeling in the country which is not pro-Japanese essentially but is so anti-British that it leans over to the Japanese side. We do not wish India to lapse into a feeling of passivity. It is fantastic to talk of peace with Japan."[7]

What was really fantastic in the whole situation was this Don Quixote of the Soviet Union. All through his life he had learnt nothing except going to jail properly garlanded and coming out of jail properly garlanded. But he had the cheek to ask a disarmed and downtrodden nation to fight in defence of a cause which now sounded criminal to most of his countrymen. No one in the Soviet Union or her vast Comintern network had said a word in support of the case for India's independence.

Pandit Nehru was now completely isolated in the country. His age-old allies, the Congress Socialists, parted company with him because their nationalism was too strong to be deluged by their devotion to the Soviet Union. The only Congressman who kept company with Jawaharlal was Maulana Azad. Of course, the communist crowd which had been brought out of jails and provided by the British with propaganda facilities, was constantly quoting

---

[5] Quoted in *Forward Bloc and Its Allies Versus Communists*, People's Publishing House, Bombay, 1945, pp. 1-2. Italics added.

[6] Quoted in *Communist Reply to Congress Working Committee Charges*, pp. 73-74.

[7] Ibid., p. 82.

Pandit Nehru while it vehemently criticised all other Congress leaders and groups. But the Mahatma's mood was changing. His Quit India articles were taking shape in his sensitive mind. And a lonely Pandit Nehru wept loudly on April 18, 1942: "I do not know what to do, but am moving about impelled by a sense of restlessness, feeling oppressed with the idea that while India is being attacked by an enemy and America and Britain and other countries are taking part, I myself feel helpless."[8]

The Congress Working Committee met at Allahabad from April 27 to May 1, 1942 to consider a Draft Resolution for the next session of the AICC. According to the proceedings of the Congress Working Committee meeting:

"Gandhiji was not present at the meeting (at Allahabad from April 27 to May 1) of the Working Committee. But he sent from Wardha a Draft (Resolution) for the consideration of the Committee. Miraben, who brought the draft, explained how Gandhiji's mind was working along the lines sketched in it.

"The draft contained the following points: (i) A demand to the British Government to clear out, (ii) India is a zone of war as a result of British Imperialism, (iii) No foreign assistance needed for the freedom of this country, (iv) India has no quarrel with any country, (v) If Japan invaded India it shall meet with non-violent resistance, (vi) Form of non-cooperation laid down, and (vii) Foreign soldiers a great menace to Indian freedom.

"JAWAHARLALJI: Gandhiji's draft is an approach which needs careful consideration. Independence means amongst other things the withdrawal of British troops. *It is proper; but has it any meaning, our demanding withdrawal?* Nor can they reasonably do it even if they recognise independence. Withdrawal of troops and the whole apparatus of civil administration will create a vacuum which cannot be filled up immediately.

"If we said to Japan that her fight was with British Imperialism and not us, she would say: 'We are glad the British Army is withdrawn; we recognise your independence. But we want certain facilities now. We shall defend you against aggression. We want aerodromes, freedom to pass our troops through your country. This is necessary in self-defence.' They might seize strategic points and proceed to Iraq, etc. The masses wont be touched if only the strate-

---

[8] Ibid., p. 83.

gic points are captured. Japan is an imperialist country. Conquest of India is in their plan. *If Bapu's (Gandhiji's) approach is accepted we become passive partners of the Axis Powers. This approach is contrary to the Congress policy for the last two years and a half. The Allied countries will have a feeling that we are their enemies.*

"MAULANA SAHIB: What is our position? Shall we tell the British Government to go and allow the Japanese and Germans to come, or do we want the British Government to stay and stem the new aggression?

"PANTJI: I want the right of self-government and we shall exercise it as we like. If the British troops and the rest must withdraw let them do so by all means and we shall shift for ourselves...

"JAWAHARLALJI: A draft like this weakens their (the British Government's) position. They will treat India as an enemy country and reduce it to dust and ashes...

"ASAF ALI: The draft asks us to accept non-violence for all time.

"ACHYUT PATWARDHAN: It (the question of non-violence for all time) was put to Gandhiji. He said that the Congress can take the stand that under existing circumstances non-violence was the best policy.

"JAWAHARLALJI: The whole background of the draft is one which will inevitably make the world think that we are passively lining up with the Axis Powers. The British are asked to withdraw. After the withdrawal we are to negotiate with Japan and possibly come to some terms with her. These terms may include a large measure of civil control by us, to a certain measure of military control by them, passage of armies through India, etc.

"KRIPALANIJI: Why should it mean passage of armies through India, etc.? Just as we call upon the British and the Americans to withdraw their armies, so also we ask others to keep out of our frontiers. If they do not, we fight.

"JAWAHARLALJI: Whether you will like it or not, the exigencies of the war situation will compel them to make India a battleground. In sheer self-defence they cannot afford to keep out. They will walk through the country. You cannot stop it by non-violent non-cooperation. Most of the population will not be affected by the march. Individuals may resist in a symbolic way. *The Japanese armies will go to Iraq, Persia etc., throttle China and make the Russian situation more difficult.*

"The British will refuse our demand for military reasons apart from others. They cannot allow India to be used by Japan against them. Our reaction in the event of refusal will be a passive theoretical lining up with the Axis Powers. Japan may have an excuse for attack. We get involved in a hopeless logical quandary. We get hostility from every other element outside the Axis Powers. Japan will occupy strategic points. We get no chance for mass civil disobedience. Our policy of sympathy with one group is completely changed.

"So far as the main action is concerned, there is no difficulty about Bapu's draft. *But the whole thought and background of the draft is one of favouring Japan.* It may not be conscious. Three factors influence our decisions in the present emergency: (i) Indian freedom, (ii) sympathy for certain larger causes, (iii) probable outcome of the war: who is going to win? *It is Gandhiji's feeling that Japan and Germany will win. This feeling unconsciously governs his decision. The approach in the draft is different from mine.*

"RAJENDRA BABU: We cannot produce the proper atmosphere unless we adopt Bapu's draft. The Government has closed the door on armed resistance. We have only unarmed resistance to offer. We have therefore to strengthen Bapu's hands.

"GOVIND VALLABH PANT: There is no difference of opinion so far as non-violence is concerned. There may be two opinions as to its effectiveness...

"JAWAHARLALJI: It (Babu Rajendra Prasad's amendment) retains the approach in Bapu's original draft. The approach is a variation from the attitude we have taken up about the Allies. *At least I have committed myself to that sympathy 100 per cent.* It would be dishonourable for me to resign from that position. There is no reason why that choice should arise. But it has arisen somewhat in the approach. The position of the draft about resistance has some substance. The positions about minorities, Princes are unrealistic. We go on thinking in terms of what was and not what is, and that is a dangerous thing in a rapidly changing situation. There is no difference among us about (i) our reaction to Government and (ii) our total inability to cooperate with the Government. Our problem of self-sufficiency and self-protection helps the Government but that cannot be helped, and (iii) we do not embarrass the British war efforts because that in itself would mean aid to the invader. We agree on these points but we have different ways of getting at them. It is true that since my approach is different my emphasis too would be different.

"ASAF ALI: The draft will not make any effective appeal to the Axis Powers. Telling the British to withdraw will do nobody any good.

"BHULABHAI DESAI: No resolution is called for. We passed at Wardha one which expressed our definite position. This resolution is made in an unreal way. It is inconsistent with our previous stand. We have said that if offered an opportunity we shall side with the Allies.

"RAJAJI: I do not think the changed draft is different from the original. We appeal to Britain and Japan. The appeal to Britain will fail but certain tangible results will follow. The entire policy of the Congress will be reinterpreted and new interpretations will go terribly against us. Japan will say 'excellent'.

"I do not agree that if Britain goes away India will have some scope for organising itself even if Japan should make some headway...

"ACHYUT PATWARDHAN: I am in general agreement with the draft. The open door policy is at an end. The resolution emphasizes a factor which has been emphasized by every intelligent man, i.e. the war is lost unless the people are in it. The war is an imperialist war. Our policy can be that we take no sides. I would consider the position if the Allies could defeat the Axis. But I see clearly that Britain is going towards the deep...

"SARDAR PATEL: I see that there are two distinct opinions in the Committee. We have ever since the outbreak of war tried to pull together. But it may not be possible on this occasion. Gandhiji has taken a definite stand. If his background is unacceptable to some members of the Committee, there is the other background which is unsuitable to us. The first four or five paragraphs of the draft are a reply to the Cripps Mission. Cripps is a clever fellow. *He has gone about saying that his mission has not been a failure*. The draft is a perfect reply to his propaganda.

"I am not in favour of making any approach to Jinnah. We have made repeated attempts and courted many insults. The Congress today is reeling under two blows, one Cripps' and the other Rajaji's resolution, which have done us enormous harm. I have placed myself in the hands of Gandhiji. I feel that he is instinctively right, the lead he gives in all critical situations. In Bombay, at the time of the AICC meeting, there was a difference in approach but the door to negotiations was not closed. In Bardoli it was made clear that the door was still open and our sympathies were with the Allies. It is time the door is finally closed after the repeated insults heaped upon us. I agree with the draft before us. If there is any pro-Fascist hint in the draft let it be removed.

"ACHARYA NARENDRA DEO: I do not agree with the view that the war is one and indivisible. The aims of Russia and China are not identical with those of Britain and America. If it is one we should join the war and side with Britain. Our position has not been that we want power because without it we cannot kindle the national spirit. Our position has been that if the war was a people's war and there was proof of it in action we are willing to throw in our weight on the side of democracy... I am not interested in defeating Hitlerite Germany. I am more interested in war aims and peace aims.

"MAULANA SAHIB: The discussion has been useful...Cripps was a great hope. He came here with the reputation of a radical. But he proved a great disappointment... Great Britain has made it impossible for us to defend our country. But we have something to do with the Japanese aggression. It is my firm belief that nationalism is the only religion for a subject nation. If I felt that Japan was better than Britain and her invasion for the good of India, I would have said so in public. But that is not so. Gandhiji's prescription is the only alternative, though I doubt its effectiveness.."[9]

Pandit Nehru, now that he knew that the Mahatma was no more on his side, was in a very meek mood. He emphasized the points of agreement between the two sections of the Working Committee. But Sardar Patel emphasized the points of difference which were fundamental. Thus, the only thing which Pandit Nehru could now do was to insert some pro-Soviet paras in the main resolution which finally came before the fateful AICC meeting at Bombay in August 1942. But thanks to him, the British now had a propaganda handle and they felt self-righteous enough to suppress the national movement with a strong hand. Sir Stafford Cripps, Sir Girija Shankar Bajpai, and the communist network were broadcasting Pandit Nehru's words all over the world, particularly to the United States of America where he became popular in inverse pro-

[9] Published by the British Government of India in an official document and quoted in *Nehru's Foreign Policy X-Rayed*, pp. 9-14. Italics added.

portion to the rising tide of unpopularity which was the share of the Congress. That popularity was to serve him at a later date. For the time being, however, he joined his Congress colleagues inside the jails. That was the only thread of loyalty left between him and his party organisation.

It was not an accident that in the volumes of the communist war-time weekly, *People's War,* there was not a word of criticism against Pandit Nehru while Mahatma Gandhi and other Congress leaders were wildly abused. The weekly cartooned Subhas Bose as a donkey and a dog and a rat and a rogue in fascist employ. The Communist Party of India denounced the Congress Socialists and Forward Blocists as agents of German-Japanese imperialism and regularly informed the British police about their activities. But all through this period Pandit Nehru and Maulana Azad were selected by the communists for fulsome praise. The communists have never failed to stand by their fellow-travellers which is in direct contrast to the bourgeois mores which are supposed to be at their best when one has publicly denounced every friend whose sacrifices serve one's best interests.[10]

---

[10] This conclusion has since been borne out by subsequent events.

SIXTEEN

A FELLOW-TRAVELLER OF SOVIET FOREIGN POLICY-8

As I draw towards the end of this series, I have a second letter saying that I have not at all succeeded in establishing my case about Prime Minister Nehru's communist leanings. Mr. Tolo Panjabi from Bombay thinks that the "tone and trend" of my arguments is "most regrettable and deliberately misleading", and that my description of Fascism as the "last-ditch battle of nationalism against communism" shows where my "sympathies are". He refers to the imperialist record of Fascist Italy in Africa to prove his point. And then in a bid to defend Pandit Nehru, he goes on, "I wonder how he would explain the policy of Mr. Nehru on such matters as Goa, Kashmir, Algeria, and *de jure* transfer of French occupied territories in India. Let him not tell us that a conflict between India and Portugal will not embarrass Western countries and delight Russia, or the occupation of a part of Kashmir and establishment of American bases there serves the interests of Russia. Certainly, the Russians are not such naive goblins as would allow such a thing to happen through one of their stooges. I dare him to analyse Mr. Nehru's role in Belgrade in the light of his far-fetched arguments."

Before I present my defence against Mr. Panjabi's observations, let me confess that I have also received, quite frequently, some very laudatory letters from the readers of these articles. People who have spotted me behind the mask of my pseudonym have also spoken or written to me personally some very warm words of appreciation. If I have so far refrained from referring to this side of the picture, it is partly because I feel embarrassed whenever I am praised, and partly because, having known that the overwhelming majority of my countrymen are quite capable of siding with truth whenever it gets known to them, I am not surprised by such a positive response.

What surprises me is that there should be some patriotic people in my country whom no amount of objective evidence or straight logic seems to satisfy. I can understand a communist when he shows contempt for such "flimsy things" as facts or when he cold-shoulders "bourgeois logic" in favour of "proletarian dialectics". For, the major premise of Marxism is that "all philosophy is partisan". But Mr. Panjabi does not seem to be a communist for the simple reason that he has not been able to see any Anglo-American inspiration behind these articles. I, therefore, take Mr. Panjabi seriously and am overlooking his insinuation that I have been deliberately trying to mislead my readers.

As regards Mr. Panjabi's charge that I sympathise with Fascism, let me inform him that being a conscious and convinced Hindu by faith I look at all these "isms" from the West as mere variations on the single sinful theme of modern materialism. I see no merit either in capitalism with its paraphernalia of parliamentary democracy, or in Fascism with its cant about the corporate State, or in Socialism of any variety with its witchcraft about social welfare. I stand solidly and without any doubt whatsoever for the Hindu concept of *Dharma-rajya* as detailed in our appropriate *Shastras* and as practised by our great monarchies and republics in the past.

But whenever I discuss the Western world, I do make distinctions between one ideology and another. I do choose parliamentary democracy wherever it has not yet become an ally of communism as it had in pre-Fascist Italy, Weimer Germany, Republican Spain and France of the Popular Front days. As a student of history, however, I know that parliamentary democracy has not suited and will not suit any people outside the Anglo-Saxon peoples and a few small countries like Sweden, Norway, Denmark and Switzerland, etc. Everywhere else, parliamentary democracy has, sooner or later, broken the bounds of national unity and become an instrument of Communism.

And strong maladies always suggest equally strong remedies. Nationalism must take the form of Fascism wherever the communist cancer eats into the vitals of a nation. That is why I have described Fascism as the *last-ditch* battle of nationalism against Communism. Surely, such a transformation of nationalism must leave a bad taste in the mouth of everyone who cares for certain basic human values. But it is a million times better for a nation to go Fascist than surrender its body and soul to Communism. For, Communism means not only the end of all civil liberties but also the end of national independence and the destruction of all national culture.

It is, of course, a false generalisation to say that Fascism must inevitably erupt into predatory imperialism. Except in the case of Mussolini's Italy and Hitler's Germany, Fascism has been mostly content with its "achievements" at home. Nor has any variety of Fascism committed the crimes in which Communism takes particular pride—forced starvation and plunder of the peasantry; mass murder of the intelligentsia; brain-washing and a total extinction of all higher aspirations of the human mind and spirit. Fascism at its worst has been physically cruel and politically oppressive. But it has never attempted to rob every single human being of his soul, and convert him into a mere moron caught in the matrix of a monolithic materialism.

Next, Pandit Nehru's stand vis-a-vis Goa, Kashmir, Algeria and the *de jure* transfer of French possessions in India proves to my mind the opposite of what Mr. Panjabi concludes from these cases. Pandit Nehru is not an ardent admirer of Algerian nationalism simply because that nationalism still looks towards Nasser and has not yet become a stooge of Soviet imperialism. He was very much fascinated by Nasser so long as Nasser looked like an ally of the communist camp. But as soon as Nasser came out as an Arab nationalist, first and last, Pandit Nehru visibly turned cold towards him. Let the Algerians import Soviet arms and Soviet military advisers and we shall see Pandit Nehru putting on quite another colour.

And the fact that Pandit Nehru has not ordered the Indian Army to march into Goa nor amalgamated the French possessions into the Indian Union without further reference to France, is also a positive proof that he is not an Indian patriot. I am convinced that not a fly will flutter in France if the French possessions are integrated forthwith into India. Portugal will most probably put up a fight over Goa. But, again, I am sure that no other Western nation will show her much sympathy or give her any support. Goa under the Portugese and the French possessions without a *de jure* transfer are only convenient excuses for Pandit Nehru in his communist game of perverting Indian nationalism and setting it up against the Western camp. If Goa and the French possessions are taken by India, he will not know how to harangue against the North Atlantic Alliance, day in and day out.

The question of Kashmir is a little more complicated. For, it is a question with a very complicated history. Perhaps Mr. Panjabi does not know that Pandit Nehru had befriended Shaikh Abdullah simply because the latter was also, and for a long time, a Soviet-addict like him. I have in my possession several pamphlets published by the People's Publishing House in praise of the *Sher-e-Kashmir.*

Pandit Nehru dropped Shaikh Abdullah primarily because the Shaikh picked up a quarrel with Sadiq & Co., the communist clique in Kashmir. Shaikh Abdullah proved to be a traitor to India. But we could not catch him as such. We had to invent an American conspiracy and brand the Shaikh as an American agent before we could arrest and arraign him. That is the measure of perversion suffered by our nationalism under the leadership of a communist camp follower like Pandit Nehru.

Also, Mr. Panjabi does not seem to know why Pandit Nehru promised a plebiscite in Kashmir without consulting any of his cabinet colleagues or even Mahatma Gandhi. I refer him to the *Memorandum* which the CPI had submitted to the British Cabinet Mission and in which Kashmir was described as a separate nationality which should be given the right of self-determination to the point of becoming a sovereign State. The CPI had denounced Kashmir's accession to India as an imperialist annexation in early 1948. The Indian army in Kashmir had been described as an army of occupation in all official Soviet publications at that time. So Pandit Nehru's communist conscience suffered persistent pricks. He not only promised a plebiscite but also ordered the Indian Army to stop its triumphant march into Pakistan-occupied Kashmir. He changed his stand on a plebiscite in Kashmir only when the Soviet Union and the CPI had changed their stand and come out in support of the Indian case in Kashmir after Pakistan entered into an alliance with America. And he let loose a lying campaign against the West which was only reminding him half-heartedly of the plebiscite promise he had himself made earlier.

Of course, the establishment of American bases in Pakistan-occupied Kashmir does not serve the interests of Soviet Russia. But was it Pandit Nehru who invited the Americans to establish those bases there? He has registered only resentment against those bases and encouraged all sorts of communist fronts in India to raise a continuous hue and cry on that score. What more can he do? Go to war with Pakistan? I am sure the Soviet Union will not relish that so long as it involves the possibility of a World War. It is significant that-up to date no communist platform or publication has invited India to wage a war with Pakistan over the issue of Kashmir. The USA is sure to intervene on the side of Pakistan if such a war arises. The Soviet Union will have to come to the aid of India unless she is prepared for a loss of prestige in the eyes of her own satellites, actual and potential. So it is better to keep the Kashmir kettle boiling and woo Indian nationalism over to the Soviet side. Does Mao Tse-tung cease to be a communist because he has done nothing about American bases in Formosa?

Look at the altogether different attitude of Pandit Nehru in the face of Chinese occupation of Indian territory. He refuses to enter into any negotiations with Pakistan unless Pakistan changes her foreign policy. Taking the excuse of Pakistan's membership, he has attacked, again and again, the whole system of Western alliances in Europe, the Middle East and South East Asia. But he has been more than willing to negotiate with China without raising any accusing finger against China's foreign policy. He is not tired of sounding China secretly and through all sorts of diplomatic channels in spite of an overwhelming national demand that no talks with the aggressor should be held unless aggression is first vacated. And he has never uttered a word against the Sino-Soviet military alliance under which China is getting arms aid which may be eventually used against India.

As regards Pandit Nehru's role at Belgrade, Mr. Panjabi has readily believed the stories spread by a section of the Western press about "Nehru, the pro-Western and moderate neutralist" on the eve of the Conference. Since then the Conference has issued a declaration repeating all the age-old communist slogans and attacking every Western position everywhere in the world. And the disappointed Western world is already shedding tears regarding the role of their knight errant. His role at Belgrade was particularly pernicious because he would not let the Conference go into particular instances of right and wrong, and urged it all along to confine itself to pious proclamations about world peace — a theme so dear to Soviet hearts if only it is played without reference to Soviet imperialism and the Soviet stockpile of nuclear bombs. The subsequent satisfaction expressed by Comrade Khrushchev and the Soviet press is proof positive that the Conference which accepted Pandit Nehru's suggestion after initial hesitations has only served the cause of the Soviet Slave Empire.

And, now, I must get back to my analysis of Pandit Nehru's foreign policy till today. We have seen, in the foregoing articles, how he followed, till 1942, every twist and turn of Soviet foreign policy with the tenacity of a trained communist. Since then we see a noticeable change in the mode and method of his presentation of his foreign policy. He always makes out a plausible case without direct reference to the source of his inspiration. But amidst all the conflicting and contradictory justifications given by him about the different positions taken at different occasions vis-a-vis the international scene, we see a consistent pro-Soviet pattern running all through the theme. In all its essentials, the foreign policy pursued by him as the Prime Minister of independent India has closely followed the Soviet lead.

Let us contemplate this foreign policy against the background of the world situation as it has emerged after the Second World War in order to realise the full horror and shame implied in it. The Western nations have, in most cases, peacefully liquidated their vast empires. Today only a few pin-points like Hong Kong, Macao, Goa, Aden, and West Irian are all that is left of Western imperialism in Asia.[1] The vast continent of Africa is fast becoming free in an orderly manner. From Latin America, too, the last vestiges of Western imperialism are in the process of vanishing.

The Soviet Union, on the other hand, has enslaved vast areas and populations in East and West. The three Baltic States—Latvia, Lithuania, Estonia—have once again disappeared from the map and into the belly of the Russian Bear. Poland, Hungary, Czechoslovakia, Bulgaria, Rumania and Albania are being ruled by Soviet satraps sustained by Soviet bayonets. Parts of Finland, Germany, Korea, Vietnam and Laos are under Soviet armed occupation. Mongolia, China and Tibet have been overrun by traitorous gangs armed by the Soviet Union. And the totalitarian terror of Soviet imperialism that now prevails in all these lands has had no parallel in the whole of human history.

Yet, there is not a single resolution of the Indian National Congress or a single statement by any Indian Government spokesman which either appreciates the change of heart among the western nations, or denounces the dirty deeds of the Soviet warlords. On the contrary, India has joined her voice to every tirade which the communist parties and fronts have launched against Western "colonialism". And India has patronised persistently and painstakingly the puppet regimes which the Soviet Union has set up in so many countries. It was only the other day that the Prime Minister of India declared in broad daylight that the East European Satellites of the Soviet Union were fully sovereign nations!

[1] Goa and West Irian, too, have since been freed from Western colonialism.

Similarly, India has been on the Soviet side in every single international tangle since the Second World War—Palestine, Korea, Tibet, Viet Nam, Hungary, Cuba, Berlin. And India has never failed to denounce whatever measures of self-defence the Western nations have adopted against the communist menace. All that has happened while the West has honestly tried to understand, appreciate, and accomodate our point of view and while the Soviet camp has heaped foul abuse and slander upon us whenever we have strayed away from its stand even by an hair's breadth.

Pandit Nehru made known to the whole world on December 4, 1947 the path he was going to follow in the field of foreign policy. Speaking before the Constituent Assembly, he said: "But talking about foreign policies the house must remember that these are not just empty struggles on a chess board. Behind them lie all manner of things. *Ultimately, foreign policy is the outcome of economic policy, and until India has properly evolved her economic policy, her foreign policy will be rather vague, rather inchoate, and will be groping.* It is well for us to say that we stand for peace and freedom and yet that does not convey much to anybody, except a pious hope. We do stand for peace and freedom. I think there is something to be said for it. There is some meaning when we say that we stand for the freedom of Asian countries and for the elimination of imperialistic control over them. There is some meaning in that. Undoubtedly it has some substance, but a vague statement that we stand for peace and freedom by itself has no particular meaning, because every country is prepared to say the same thing, whether it means it or not. What then do we stand for? Well, you have to develop this argument in the economic field. As it happens today, in spite of the fact that we have been for sometime in authority as a Government, I regret that we have not produced any constructive economic scheme or economic policy so far. Again, my excuse is that we have been going through such taxing times which have taken up all our energy and attention that it was difficult to do so. *Nevertheless, we shall have to do so and when we do so, that will govern our foreign policy, more than all the speeches in this House.*"[2]

This was the forecast of Avadi when India under Pandit Nehru's lead adopted the "socialistic pattern of society", and openly

[2] *Jawaharlal Nehru's Speeches, 1946-53*, p. 203. Italics added.

moved into the "international socialist camp". The communist camp admits in so many words that India under Pandit Nehru stands on their side. The Vijaywada thesis of the CPI says: "The interest of the Indian nation demands a continuation of the present foreign policy. *Nehru, who has been the main architect of this policy, has shown no inclination to abandon it.* India stands in the camp of peace and anti-colonialism, against war and for disarmament."[3]

Comrade Ajoy Ghose, General Secretary of the CPI, proclaimed as follows before the Vijaywada Congress of the Party: *"It is a matter of great joy that relations between our country and the Soviet Union have become more friendly than ever.* This relationship is not only a big factor in advancing the struggle for world peace but also, as the Political Resolution adopted by the National Council stresses, helps us to strengthen our national economy and thereby consolidate our national freedom. *The sentiment of friendship towards the Soviet Union has steadily grown and is shared today by people from all walks of life and following diverse political parties."*[4]

He added in the same speech: "*Conditions in India are in many respects extremely favourable for the development of a powerful mass movement for peace, against colonialism, for Afro-Asian solidarity.* Peace is essential for our national reconstruction and we have long traditions of anti-imperialist struggle. Sentiments of friendship for the USSR, sentiments of solidarity with Afro-Asian countries are strong among our people. *The Government of India generally takes a position which helps the cause of peace and national liberation.*"[5]

As regards the arguments advanced in defence of this foreign policy, Pandit Nehru clarified his position on March 8, 1948. Speaking again before the Constituent Assembly, he said: "Naturally we cannot as a Government go as far as we might have done as a non-official organisation in which we can express our opinions as frankly and as aggressively as possible. Speaking as a Government we have to moderate our language. We have sometimes to stop doing things which we might otherwise do. Nevertheless, the

---

[3] *New Age*, May 7, 1961, p. 14. Italics added.

[4] *New Situation and Our Tasks*, Communist Party Publication, New Delhi, p. 4. Italics added.

[5] Ibid., p. 7. Italics added.

fundamental thing is whether we sympathise and openly sympathise with a country like Indonesia in her struggle for freedom, or not. That applies not to Indonesia only, but to several other countries. In each case, we have to face the passive hostility of various interests, not only the direct interests involved, but also the indirect interests involved, because the direct and the indirect interests hang together in such matters...We have either to pursue our policy generally within limitations—because we cannot pursue it wholeheartedly, nevertheless openly—or give it up. *I do not think that anything could be more injurious to us from any point of view, certainly from an idealistic and high moral point of view, but equally so from the point of view of opportunism and national interest in the narrowest sense of the word than for us to give up the policies that we have pursued, namely those of standing up for certain ideals in regard to the oppressed nations, and try to align ourselves with this great power or that and become its camp followers in the hope that some crumbs might fall from their table.*"[6]

There was in this statement a dig against anyone attempting to revise India's foreign policy in the light of Soviet hostility to independent India, and Soviet encouragement of internal subversion through the Communist Party of India. Zhdanov divided the world into two irreconcilable camps in September 1947. India had been placed squarely in the "imperialist camp" and Pandit Nehru himself described as an "agent of American imperialism". The Ranadive Resolution had been passed in the Second Congress of the CPI a few months later. But all that was of no consequence to Pandit Nehru. He was out to prove that he was a "man of honour" vis-a-vis the Soviet Union, and that no amount of dollars would ever delude him.

The Soviet Union recognised after a few years that Pandit Nehru had stood the severest test and rather very well. From then onwards Krishna Menon became a bright star in the international firmament. From being a peon of Pandit Nehru he became a world figure in no time. The scent of his sinister schemes very soon sent a wave of misgiving in most Indian minds. But Pandit Nehru staked all his personal prestige in a bid to protect his protege. Speaking on January 31, 1957 before a mass meeting in Madras, he said: "There are some people in this country and some people in other coun-

[6] *Jawaharlal Nehru's Speeches, 1946-53*, pp. 214-15. Italics added.

tries whose job in life appears to be to try to run down Krishna Menon, *because he is far cleverer than they are, because his record of service for Indian freedom is far longer than theirs, and because he has worn himself out in the service of India.* It is not necessary for them or for me or for you to agree with Krishna Menon in everything, although he is my close colleague. I do not agree with T.T. Krishnamachari, although he is a close colleague. We do not agree with each other in everything. *But we do agree in our broad approach to problems, and we do believe in each other's bonafides and integrity. Otherwise, we cannot cooperate.* But this kind of repeated and persistent attempt to undermine our policy by throwing mud at a colleague of ours seems to me not very desirable or proper. It is because of this, I want to tell you, that though Krishna Menon is a member of the Rajyasabha, and it was not necessary for him to seek election, yet we have agreed to his seeking election from the city of Bombay, for Bombay is a cosmopolitan city and we want our foreign policy to be voted upon in Bombay. It is for the people to say whether they agree with our foreign policy or not. *It is our challenge to those who disagree with our foreign policy.* We do not run away from criticism."[7] He should have added that he was planning to send the Indian Army into Goa so that Krishna Menon scored over Acharya Kripalani.

That is the whole story in which every strand says unmistakably that Pandit Nehru and not Krishna Menon is the real culprit in the context of our foreign policy failures. If we want to get rid of Krishna Menon and all that he symbolises, let us make up our minds to see that Pandit Nehru is swept out of power as soon as possible. We must mobilise the whole country against Pandit Nehru after educating our people about the true character of this Soviet stooge hiding under a Gandhi cap. If we do not do that, we should be prepared to see a Nehru–Communist coalition installed at New Delhi in the course of the next few years. The next article of this series will reveal how Pandit Nehru's collaboration with the Soviet Union in the field of foreign policy has been accompanied by a similar collaboration with the Communist Party of India in India's domestic politics.

---

[7] *Jawaharlal Nehru's Speeches, 1947-57,* p. 228. Italics added.

SEVENTEEN

A PROMOTER OF THE COMMUNIST PARTY

When the Soviet Union denounced Pandit Nehru in 1948 as a puppet whom "American imperialism" was trying to prop up in place of the old "paper tiger", President Chiang Kai-shek of China, the Western nations, particularly the United States of America, had proclaimed immediately that Pandit Nehru was the "bulwark of democracy in Asia". But the Korean War was hardly half through when it was widely realised in the West that at least in the field of international politics Pandit Nehru was no friend of the West, and that his sympathies, whenever and wherever they became mainfest, were always and all along with the communist camp. The West has, however, been bewitched by Pandit Nehru on another count. He seems to it to be the "only person who understands the dynamics of the modern world" in a "surging sea of superstition and primitivism that is India". Western statesmen and scribes have floated another myth also about him, namely that whatever the policies he pursues in the sphere of international politics, "at least inside India he is not prepared to tolerate Communism", and that "he is fighting the Communist Party of India tooth and nail". And in support of this new illusion, Western writers have been quoting his record of resistance to communist violence during 1948-50.

But if we examine Pandit Nehru's statements and behaviour all through this period, we find no evidence in support of this belief. In fact, all available evidence goes against any such supposition. We have seen how he was worshipping the Soviet Union and adhering to Soviet foreign policy all through this period. He never reacted against all that foul abuse which was heaped upon him by the Soviet camp without any provocation whatsoever on his part. He had not a word to say in condemnation of the Soviet grab in Eastern Europe and China, or against the Zhdanov line which neatly divided the world into two uncompromisingly hostile camps — the "camp of socialism and peace led by the Soviet Union", and the "camp of imperialism and war led by the United States of America".

Nearer home, he never saw eye to eye with Sardar Patel who as Home Minister in the Government of India and the strong man of the Congress Party, was the real author of that suppression of communist violence which saved India from becoming a prototype of Burma, Malaya and Indo-China in 1948-50. In fact, he never relished the strength shown by the Sardar during those fateful years. He said repeatedly that the real problem was not Communism but poverty and socio-political backwardness of the Indian masses. In his opinion, it was useless to try to suppress the communist movement so long as the economic and social problems of India were not solved. The differences that thus arose between him and Sardar Patel at that time assumed serious proportions and at one stage he almost decided to quit the Congress Party in order to form a platform of his own in collaboration with various leftist and crypto-communist elements and some disgruntled Gandhians. That was the genesis of the Democratic Front organised by Acharya Kripalani and Rafi Ahmad Kidwai, both of whom had left the Congress at his behest.

But, fortunately for Panndit Nehru and unfortunately for India, Sardar Patel died in December 1950, and the "Congress Right" which the Sardar had consolidated against Pandit Nehru before and after the election of Purushottama Das Tandon to the presidentship of the Congress, was left leaderless. The other stalwarts of the Sardar's camp turned out to be men of straw whose first preference was saving their personal position and power rather than doing service to their country. The only man, D.P. Mishra of Madhya Pradesh, who came out publicly against Pandit Nehru's swift shift of Congress policies towards Communism, was left in the lurch by this crowd of self-seekers and job-hunters, and hounded out of the Congress. And six months had hardly passed since the Sardar's death when the communist criminals, who had indulged in widespread arson and murder against the innocent peasantry in several parts of India, were brought out of jails like martyrs in the cause of humanism, and given a signal to get ready for the forthcoming First General Elections. Small wonder that they were soon to win unexpected victories.

This instance of Nehru–Communist collaboration in the domestic politics of India was neither the first nor the foremost of its kind. It was only a link in that long chain which was forged immediately after Pandit Nehru's first pilgrimage to the Soviet Union in 1927, and which is now leading the country blindfold into an inevitable Nehru–Communist coalition at the Centre in the next few years to come. Pandit Nehru has always nursed the Communist Party of India with the fondness of an old woman who gave birth to her first and only child at an advanced age. And if India allows him to wield power for a few more years, he will see to it that the Communist Party of India is safely installed in power. The pattern of Congress–Communist collaboration which is to emerge in due course has already been blueprinted by the Vijaywada Congress of the CPI held early this year (1961), and initially experimented with during the recent mid-term elections in Orissa.

Getting back to Pandit Nehru and his age-old collaboration with communism, we find that as soon as he returned from the Soviet Union at the end of 1927 he propounded the thesis that the Indian National Congress was a "party of the Indian bourgeoisie" and as such inevitably "bound to become an instrument of imperialism" if it was not "radicalised" by bringing into it "the revolutionary labour and peasant movements". It was another way of saying that the Communist Party of India, which was at that time the leader of whatever "revolutionary labour and peasantry" had raised their heads in India, should be brought into the Congress organisation. So he started courting the Communist Party which was at that time keeping away from the Congress and trying to build its own independent organisation.

He attended a session of the All India Trade Union Congress (AITUC) held at Jharia in Bihar a few days before the Calcutta Session of the Congress in 1928. And he was immediately elected President of the AITUC against a worker candidate put up by the communist group. His own name had been proposed by the non-communist section of the AITUC. He regretted this "infancy and weakness" of the Trade Union Movement in the following words: "It was my first Trade Union Congress and I was practically an outsider, though my activities amongst the peasantry, and lately amongst the workers, had gained for me a measure of popularity with the masses. *I found the old tussle going on between the reformists and the more advanced and revolutionary elements. The main points at issue were the question of affiliation to one of the Internationals, as well as to the League against Imperialism and the Pan-Pacific Union, and the desirability of sending representatives to the International Labour Office Conference at Geneva.* More important than these questions was the vast difference in outlook between the two sections of the Congress. There was the old trade union group, moderate in politics and indeed distrusting the intrusion of politics in industrial matters. They believed in industrial action only and that, too, of a cautious character, and aimed at the gradual betterment of worker's conditions... The other group was more militant, believed in political action, and openly proclaimed its revolutionary outlook. It was influenced, though by no means controlled, by some communists and near-communists... *My own sympathies at Jharia were with the advanced group but, being a newcomer, I felt a little at sea in these domestic conflicts of the TUC and I decided to keep aloof from them.* After I had left Jharia and annual TUC elections took place, I learnt at Calcutta that I had been elected President for the next year. I had been put forward by the moderate group, probably because they felt that I stood the best chance of defeating the other candidate who was an actual worker (on the railways) and who had been put forward by the radical group. *If I had been present at Jharia on the day of the election I am sure that I would have withdrawn in favour of the worker candidate.* It seemed to me positively indecent that a newcomer and a non-worker should be suddenly thrust into the presidentship. This was in itself a measure of the infancy and weakness of the trade union movement in India". [1]

But the communist group was rather happy at this turn of events. Philip Spratt, who was leader of the CPI at that time, writes: "My recollection is that though the communist group put up a worker, or rather a railway clerk, against him, we were not displeased at his election. *We did not regard him as one of us, but we recognised him as one who could be useful. The term was not yet current, or we should have called him a fellow-traveller.*"[2]

They had reason to be happy. Next year, Pandit Nehru was elected president of the Indian National Congress as well. And he used his position to "radicalise the Congress". He himself writes: "During these final weeks prior to the Lahore Congress I had to attend to important work in another field. The All India Trade Union Congress was meeting at Nagpur and, as president for the year, I had to preside over it. It was very unusual for the same person to preside over both the National Congress and the Trade Union Congress within a few weeks of each other. *I had hoped that I might be a link between the two and bring them closer to each*

---

[1] *An Autobiography*, pp. 186-87. Italics added. Pandit Nehru means communists whenever he uses the expression "more advanced" section, or group, or elements.

[2] *Blowing Up India*, p. 109. Italics added.

other—the National Congress to become more socialistic, more proletarian and organised Labour to join the national struggle. It was, perhaps, a vain hope, for nationalism can only go far in a socialistic or proletarian direction by ceasing to be nationalism. Yet I felt that, bourgeois as the outlook of the National Congress was, it did represent the only effective revolutionary force in the country. As such, Labour ought to help it and cooperate with it and influence it, keeping, however, its own identity and ideology distinct and intact. And I hoped that the course of events and the participation in direct action would inevitably drive the Congress to a more radical ideology and to face social and economic issues... The advanced sections of Labour, however, fought shy of the National Congress. They mistrusted its leaders, and considered its ideology bourgeois and reactionary, *which indeed it was,* from the Labour point of view. The Congress was, as its very name implied, a nationalist organisation. Throughout 1929, Trade Unions in India were agitated over a new issue—the appointment of a Royal Commission on Labour in India, known as the Whitley Commission. The Left Wing was in favour of a boycott of the Commission, the Right Wing in favour of cooperation, and the personal factor came in, as some of the Right Wing leaders were offered membership of the Commission. *In this matter, as in many others, my sympathies were with the Left.*"[3]

His efforts towards "radicalising the Congress" met with considerable success, mainly because the international communist line underwent a change in 1935 after a violent swing to the left in 1931-33. The new line, however, required the Communist Party of India to cooperate with the Congress. So a communist platform was crystallised inside the Congress. It was named Congress Socialist Party. Pandit Nehru was its leader for all practical purposes. He, however, never lent his name officially to this old model of the new Ginger Group. That was profitable for him as well as the Party because he could pass before the country as a non-factious leader, while all his power and prestige thus acquired came to the succour of the pro-Soviet forces. It was at the climax of this conspiracy that he paid his second visit to Europe in order to renew his direct contacts with international Communism. And when he came back to become President of the Indian National Congress for the second

[3] *An Autobiography,* pp. 197-98. Italics added.

time in 1936, he made a definite bid to push the Congress in a communist direction.

Dr. Sitaramayya writes: "*Jawaharlal came to India full of communistic and marxian ideas. The achievements of the Congress disappointed him*. He found himself as one against the world. The resolution on the agrarian programme was an apology for an ambitious scheme of social upheaval which he had been ardently hoping to commit the nation to. He made the best of the situation by taking three ardent socialists into the Working Committee—Shri Jayaprakash Narain, Narendra Deo and Achyut Patwardhan; even Sarojini Devi was cut out from the Committee not without some internal commotion and had to be called back only in the middle of the year when a casual vacancy arose. The spirit that prevailed in the Lucknow session could be judged from the omission of any resolution on the Constructive Programme. It may be remembered that it was only lately, that is, in Bombay(1934 October) that the resolution on A.I.V.I.A. (All India Village Industries' Association) was passed and one should have expected some reference to it somewhere. No, not that no one thought about the matter, but that when a draft was prepared and placed before the Working Committee, it did not find favour with it and it was dropped at the Allahabad meeting of the Working Committee shortly before the Lucknow Session."[4]

Again: "There was, however, a fundamental difficulty in the progress of events. The President was out of tune with the majority of the Working Committee....On the one hand, there was his presidential address which was not meant to be a mere thesis but a programme of action. On the other, there was Gandhi with his following of ten members in the Working Committee thinking and acting as a solid block...*The address pleaded for pure communism in a country which had had its own traditions built up through at least a hundred and thirty centuries of progress,* and a social structure which had, through these long ages, withstood the buffets of time and circumstances and which had worked itself into the life of the nation—religious, economic and ethical."[5]

But the majority of the Congress leadership was opposed to these foreign ideas. Pandit Nehru says: "For a short while I seemed to carry the Congress in the direction I wanted it to go. But I

[4] *The History of the Indian National Congress,* Vol. II, p. 11. Italics added.
[5] Ibid., p. 13. Italics added.

realised soon that the conflict was deep-rooted and it was not so easy to charm away the suspicion of each other and the bitterness that had grown in our ranks. I thought seriously of resigning from the presidentship but, realising that this would only make matters worse, I refrained... Again and again, during the next few months, I considered this question of resignation. *I found it difficult to work smoothly with my own colleagues in the Congress executive, and it became clear to me that they viewed my activities with apprehension.* It was not so much that they objected to any specific act but they disliked the general trend and direction. They had justification for this as my outlook was different. I was completely loyal to Congress decisions but I emphasised certain aspects of them, while my colleagues emphasised other aspects. I decided finally to resign and I informed Gandhiji of my decision."[6]

He has always been in the habit of threatening to resign. So far he has never resigned from any position of privilege and power, even if he feels baulked and ideologically circumvented. Like every true communist, he sticks to power and waits for his opportunity. As ever, in 1936 also he found an excuse for withdrawing his resignation. He writes: "Soon afterwards a far-away occurrence, unconnected with India, affected me greatly and made me change my decision. *This was the news of General Franco's revolt in Spain.* I saw this rising, with its background of German and Italian assistance, developing into a European or even a world conflict. India was bound to be drawn into that and I could not afford to weaken our organisation and create an internal crisis by resigning just when it was essential for us to pull together."[7] What an excuse for staying in power!

Not only that. He readily agreed to become President of the Congress at the next session held in December 1937 at Faizpur. A majority of the Congressmen wanted Sardar Patel to preside over this session. But the Sardar had to withdraw under orders from Gandhiji and Pandit Nehru got in without a contest. And once again he played the communist game in the foreign policy resolutions of the Congress. The communists he had planted in the Foreign Department of the All India Congress Committee (AICC) were ready by now to supply the necessary drafts paraphrased from Comintern resolutions.

---

[6] *An Autobiography*, pp. 600-01. Italics added.
[7] Ibid., p. 601. Italics added.

The year 1937 proved to be an year of torment for Pandit Nehru. The Congress had accepted office in several Provinces. But his communist friends in India and abroad wanted the Congress to fight the British Government in India so that the British Government in England may be pressed into forming a "Popular Front Government" on the French pattern. The Communist Party of India was leading labour strikes and peasant agitations, particularly in Bombay and U.P. He was in sympathy with these communist moves, and felt angry with the Congress Ministries which were trying to keep law and order in the face of increasing communist violence. He writes: "This dissatisfaction found expression in the Congress itself and the *more advanced elements* grew restive. I was myself unhappy at the trend of events as I noticed that our fine fighting organisation was being converted gradually into just an electioneering organisation. A struggle for independence seemed to be inevitable and this phase of provincial autonomy was just a passing one. In April 1938 I wrote to Gandhiji expressing my dissatisfaction at the work of the Congress Ministries. 'They are trying to adapt themselves far too much to the old order and trying to justify it. But all this, bad as it is, might be tolerated. What is far worse is that we are losing the high position that we have built up, with so much labour, in the hearts of the people. We are sinking to the level of ordinary politicians'."[8]

Again: "So conflict grew within the Congress between the more moderate and the *more advanced sections*. The first organised expression of this took place in a meeting of the All India Congress Committee in October 1937. This distressed Gandhiji greatly and he expressed himself strongly in private. Subsequently he wrote an article in which he disapproved of some action I had taken as President.......*I felt that I could not longer carry on as a responsible member of the Executive but I decided not to do anything to precipitate a crisis*. My term of office as Congress President was drawing to an end and I could drop out quietly then. I had been President for two successive years and three times in all. There was some talk of my being elected for another term but I was quite clear in my own mind that I should not stand."[9]

The first time he ever resigned from a position in the Congress was when, in spite of his public protests, Subhas Chandra Bose

---

[8] Ibid., p. 603. Italics added.
[9] Ibid., p. 604. Italics added.

decided to contest presidential election, and defeated his close companion, Maulana Azad. He now feared that the Congress was in danger of becoming a "fascist organisation". He resigned from the Working Committee and issued a public statement on February 22, 1938: "In spite of my long association with the Congress I have never been closely associated with any particular group in it, though I have had the privilege of cooperating with all kinds of people. *I have been an individual in this great organisation and that is always a difficult task. Often I have felt that I was a square peg in a round hole.* During the years of my office I have frequently been on the verge of resigning because I felt that I could serve the Congress better if I did not have the responsibility of office. But I refrained from doing so, as I was firmly convinced that in the dynamic and critical times we live in we must present a united front and subordinate our individual opinions where these tended to impair that front. I have been and am a convinced socialist and a believer in democracy, and have at the same time accepted wholeheartedly the peaceful technique of non-violent action which Gandhiji has practised so successfully during the past twenty years. I am convinced that strength can only come to us from the masses, but that strength either for struggle or for the great work of building a new world must be a disciplined and orderly strength. It is not out of chaos or the encouragement of chaotic forces that we can fashion the India of our dreams. It is true that sometimes even chaos has given birth to a dancing star, but its usual progeny are suffering and degradation and internecine conflict and reaction."[10] He was talking as if his continuous hobnobbing with the paid agents of a foreign power was unknown to his colleagues and regarded by them as a perfect path towards order and peace.

But the Bose episode next year helped him to get sobered considerably in relation to Mahatma Gandhi of whom he had been becoming increasingly critical because he had come to believe that the Mahatma stood solidly in the way of the communists capturing complete power inside the Congress. Now he knew that but for the Mahatma's "magnetic personality" the Congress had almost been captured by a "band of fascists". So, sometime in the month of March 1939, he confessed: "In trying to analyse the various elements in the Congress, the dominating position of Gandhiji must

[10] *The Unity of India*, pp. 134-35. Italics added.

always be remembered. He dominates to some extent the Congress, but far more so he dominates the masses. He does not easily fall in any group and is much bigger than the so-called Gandhian group. That is one of the basic factors of the situation. *The conscious and thinking Leftists in the country recognise it and, whatever their ideological or temperamental differences with him, have tried to avoid anything approaching a split. Their attempt has been to leave the Congress under its present leadership, which means under Gandhiji's guidance, and at the same time to push it as far as they could more to the left to radicalise it, and to spread their own ideology.*"[11]

The shelter that he thus took under the Mahatma's mantle lasted till the Mahatma was murdered in 1948. There was during this period no major crisis inside the Congress organisation which was all along keyed up towards developments in the international situation. The brief isolation which he suffered in 1942 was ended by the turn-out of the Second World War. He, of course, did not relish the expulsion of the Communist Party of India from the national organisation in 1945 for its traitorous role during 1942-45. But he was helpless because on this question even his followers in the Congress Socialist Party were united with Sardar Patel's "rightist faction". Nor did he relish, as we have already pointed out, Sardar Patel's suppression of the communist insurrection during 1948-50. This time he almost jeopardised his own position as leader of the Congress Party and the Prime Minister of India. The situation was saved for him only by Sardar Patel's death.

Now he had an unbridled opportunity to patronise the Communist Party of India. We need not go into the details of his policies and pronouncements between 1951 and 1961. The statistics of Communist Party membership speak for themselves. The Party had only 9,000 members when it was legalised for the first time in 1942. The membership had risen to about 89,000 when the Party tried to create a "proletarian revolution" in 1948-50. But as a result of Sardar Patel's statesmanship the Party strength was reduced to 20,000 by the beginning of 1951. Since then the Party membership has been registering a rapid progress, rising to 75,000 in 1954, 125,000 in 1956, and 250,000 in 1958 when the Party decided to become a mass party. Today, the Party membership should be

[11] Ibid., p. 122. Italics added.

more than 300,000 in spite of the shock of destalinisation, Hungary, Tibet and Red China's encroachments in India, which episodes should have sharply reduced the strength of the Party had India been inspired by a healthy sense of human values and nurtured the natural vigour of home-grown nationalism. The Party which does not believe in parliamentary democracy and which is pledged to destroy democratic institutions as and when it has the power to do, has been permitted to wield governmental power in Kerala. The precedent has encouraged Ajoy Ghose to declare that the Party looked forward to a coalition at the Centre after winning power in a few more States.

Pandit Nehru's patronage has led the Communist Party of India to plead for a "National Democratic Front for National Democratic Tasks" in its recent Party Congress at Vijaywada. The Party now advocates "that in order to defend India's foreign policy, the public sector and the parliamentary system, in order to wage an effective battle against communalism, it is necessary that we forge links with Congressmen". The Political Resolution of the Party says: "Such a policy can alter the correlation of forces in our country *in favour of democratic forces and lead to a situation when it will become a practical policy to raise the slogan of a Government of the National Democratic Front... Conditions for such an advance are more favourable today than ever before.*"[12] Some Congressmen of long standing like B. Shiva Rao have already warned the country that after the Third General Elections we may have a Government which shall be Congress in name but Communist in content.

Soviet Russia is, in fact, urging upon Pandit Nehru to set up a real "anti-imperialist Government" in India if he wants a settlement with Red China which will vacate the territories she has occupied as soon as she is assured that India is no more in danger of becoming "a base of American imperialism". He cannot stand this pressure which is coupled with a threat to unleash a civil war in India with the help of the CPI whom the Soviet Slave Empire can now directly aid and arm across our northern borders that have been ripped open. Had Pandit Nehru been a patriot and a man of courage, he would have taken the country into confidence and tried to wipe out the Communist Party of India in a bid to meet the Chinese threat militarily. But being a communist and a coward, he

---

[12] *New Age*, May 7, 1961. Italics added.

will readily succumb to Sino-Soviet machinations and hand over his country to Soviet imperialism, as his prototype and predecessor, Benes of Czechoslovakia, did in February 1948.

In the next and the last article of this series, we shall discuss why this country and the Western world at large continue to believe that Pandit Nehru is an anti-communist in whose hands India's independence and democracy are safe. It is as big and dangerous a delusion as the one about Mao Tse-tung who was publicised and patronised by the Americans as an "agrarian reformer" till he kicked them in the pants, and took his country on the road to cannibalism.

Postscript (1993)

The Communist Party of India (CPI) passed a resolution in June 1947, asking all "progressive" Congressmen to rally round Pandit Nehru. On June 21, 1947, Pandit Nehru wrote to P. Subbarayan, Premier of Madras, asking the latter to "consider if you cannot tone down your policy in regard to keeping a considerable number of communists under detention". He thought that "the Communist Party is trying to change its policy towards the Congress and the Congress Governments", and that "a gesture on your part might be a good policy".[13] He did not care that the CPI was carrying on, at that very time, a virulent campaign against the "reactionary" Congressmen led by Sardar Patel, a stalwart of the Congress Party and Home Minister in the Government headed by him. All that he cared was that the CPI had become soft towards "progressives" like him. Significantly, he did not write similar letters to Home Ministers in the rest of the Provinces ruled by the Congress Party at that time. The reason was simple. These other Congress Governments were dominated by what the CPI regarded as "reactionary" Congressmen. P. Subbarayan, it seems, was the only "progressive" Premier. He was the father of Mohan Kumaramangalam and Parvati Krishnan, the famous communist leaders from the South, and apparently in sympathy with them.

Pandit Nehru was, however, disillusioned very soon. The CPI changed its line in the next few months. P.C. Joshi, the General Secretary of the CPI, was replaced by B.T. Ranadive who placed the Congress Government led by Pandit Nehru squarely in the

---

[13] *Selected Works of Jawaharlal Nehru*, Second Series, Volume 3, p. 237.

camp of "Anglo-American imperialists and warmongers" in January 1948. He now shared his woes with his sister, Mrs. Vijayalakshmi Pandit, who was India's Ambassador in Moscow at that time. He wrote to her in a letter dated January 23, 1948 that "the Communist Party of India has recently changed its policy again and is now against the Government which is dubbed as just a camp-follower of Anglo-Americans". And he believed that "many people in Russia may form their opinions from reports of the Communist Party of India".[14] He was, however, to admit the truth a few months later, namely that it was not the CPI which was misleading Moscow, but Moscow which was directing the CPI to become hostile to the Congress Party and India's new government.

All the same, he was dead against any action being taken against the CPI, which several Provincial Governments were forced to do in view of increasing communist violence. In a Circular Letter dated March 17, 1948, he wrote to the Premiers of all Provinces regretting that "the West Bengal Government had banned the Communist Party" without reference to Government of India, and informing them that Government of India had "no intention of banning the Communist Party or indeed of large-scale arrests".[15] He forgot that law and order was a Provincial subject, and Provincial Governments were the best judges of how to meet situations created by criminals. At the same time, he tried to see that there was no "misunderstanding in Moscow". He cabled to Mrs. Pandit on March 31, 1948, conveying that the Government of West Bengal had acted without consulting the Government of India, and that "it is not our intention to ban Communist Party in other parts of India".[16]

The Government of East Punjab had been forced to arrest a large number a communists in order to forestall violence by them. Pandit Nehru felt annoyed. In a letter dated May 3, 1948, he asked Dr. Gopichand Bhargava, the Premier of East Punjab, why "the number of arrests in the Punjab had been by far the greatest" when "in most provinces only a few persons have been arrested". He protested that "our actions in this respect had repercussions all over the world and... our reputation has suffered". He also informed Bhargava that "our ambassadors have received deputations and I

[14] Ibid., p. 541.
[15] Ibid., pp. 339-40.
[16] Ibid., pp. 349-50.

have received numerous messages from other parts of the world". On the same day he wrote a similar letter to C.M. Trivedi, Governor of East Punjab.[17]

Incidentally, he used these letters to the Premier and the Governor of East Punjab to chide them for allowing the RSS people to "function again in public under different disguises" and "to spread their poisonous propaganda".[18] The fact that the RSS had been placed under an all-India ban for a single crime committed by an individual who was not even a member of the RSS, did not bother him. Nor did the fact that the RSS was protesting peacefully against the ban, carry any weight with him. He did not notice at all that the communists were functioning from many fronts, all of them wedded to violence. The only thing that mattered to him was that, unlike the communists, the RSS people had no paymasters abroad, and no foreigners were protesting against what was being done to them.

There had been large-scale witch-hunting against the RSS all over the country, particularly in Maharashtra where some Brahmanas had been killed, many others molested, and their houses and establishments burnt down. Pandit Nehru did not even notice the persecution, not to speak of protesting against it. But he at once imagined a great persecution when communist violence was denounced in some places. In a letter dated May 29, 1948 to Govind Ballabh Pant, the Premier of UP, he saw "all manner of reactionary elements taking refuge in the cry of 'down with communism'..."[19] That leaves little doubt that, for him, the people who committed violence against innocent Brahmanas in Maharashtra were "progressive elements".

One of the leading communists arrested in Bihar was Habib Mahmud, son of Pandit Nehru's close friend, Syed Mahmud. In fact, most of his close friends in the Congress and elsewhere had sons or daughters or other relatives who were members of the CPI or its fronts. He was flooded with protests from these friends or their families. Habib Mahmud had another plus point in his favour. Besides being a communist, he was a Muslim as well. He wrote a letter to Pandit Nehru who forwarded it to Sri Krishna Sinha, the Premier of Bihar, with a covering note dated June 8, 1948 stating

[17] Ibid., Volume 6, pp. 388-90.
[18] Ibid., pp. 389-90.
[19] Ibid., p. 439.

that he was "surprised at the kind of charges that are being brought in justification of this internment". He thought that the "charges are entirely vague" and protested that "we have been very much criticized in foreign countries on this subject".[20]

By now he was finding it impossible to ignore the truth about CPI's source of inspiration. In a letter dated June 26, 1948, he complained to Krishna Menon, Moscow's man stationed as India's High Commissioner in London at that time, that (i) "The Russian attitude to India has become one of condemnation and running down the Government of India", (ii) "Articles in some Russian periodicals contain bitter criticism and we are continually referred to as some kind of stooges of the Anglo-American bloc", and (iii) "the Communist Party of India, which presumably will never go against the main trend of Russian foreign policy, has been adopting not only a hostile attitude but a rebellious attitude".[21] He was hoping that Krishna Menon might be able to soften Moscow. So he took no one else in confidence, nor stated the truth about the CPI publicly at that time or ever. The people of India did not deserve his confidence, nor did they need the correct information. And he continued to be grieved over the steps which Sardar Patel and the Provincial Governments had taken in order to counter communist violence and subversion.

In September 1948, he had gone to London in order to attend a Commonwealth Conference. On his return, he wrote a letter dated October 10, 1948 to Sardar Patel, stating that "we are criticized considerably for our detention without trial and other repressive activities of the state, in so far as trade unions and labour people and the like are concerned", that "even Lady Mountbatten told me that she was worried about it", and that "Members of Parliament also spoke about it".[22] Not many people in India knew at that time, or know even now, that Edwina Mountbatten was a whore who had slept with every communist intellectual within her reach, including Pandit Nehru. Nor did Pandit Nehru name the Members of Parliament who had protested to him. They were only a few and famous fellow-travellers. And he presented the communist criminals as trade unionists and labour leaders. He was setting the precedent which latter-day champions of human rights would

[20] Ibid., p. 392 and fn.
[21] Ibid., pp. 463-64.
[22] Ibid., Volume 8, p. 287.

follow in the face of terrorism in the Punjab and Kashmir. For the likes of Pandit Nehru, victims of violence have no rights.

Incidentally again, in the same letter he conveyed to Sardar Patel that "Regarding RSS, there is a widespread impression in England that they are Fascist, communal-minded people", and that "If at this juncture we remove the ban on the RSS... this will be widely interpreted as encouraging certain Fascist elements in India".[23] Poor RSS being a patriotic organization had no patrons abroad, and opinion within the country or even inside the Congress Party had no meaning for Pandit Nehru.

Edwina Mountbatten had also spoken to him, while he was in London, "about a proposal to hold a Conference in Calcutta under the auspices of the Women's International Democratic Federation".[24] He referred the matter to the Home Ministry which sent to him a detailed note prepared by H.V.R. Iengar, Secretary of the Ministry, about the character of this Federation and the consequence bound to follow from its conference in Calcutta. Pandit Nehru felt helpless, and forwarded the Home Ministry's note with a long letter he wrote to the "Lady" on November 11, 1948. He reminded her of his past services to the cause of Communism and apologised for his failure in the present instance. He said:

"In this note a reference is made to the South East Asia Students' Conference that was held in Calcutta early this year... I remember that the Conference was objected, at the time, but I was against prohibiting it... It was largely due to me that the Conference was held and any delegates coming to it from abroad were supplied with visas... It is now a recognized fact by all well-informed persons that this Conference immediately led to what happened soon after in Burma, Malaya, India and to some extent in Siam.[25]

"A delegation from the Women's International Democratic Federation visited India sometime back... The delegation produced subsequently a report which was a very bad one from our point of view... I might mention that that delegation also came here because I interested myself in having visas issued to them.[26]

"*You know that I have had strong leanings towards Communism and have many friends among Communists.*"[27]

---

[23] Ibid.
[24] Ibid., p. 301.
[25] Ibid.
[26] Ibid., p. 302.
[27] Ibid. Italics added.

In December 1948, the Home Ministry had deputed one of its intelligence officers, Sanjeevi, to visit Britain and some other countries in Europe in order to survey the state of India's intelligence organisation abroad, and suggest steps for its improvement. His visit had been cleared by Pandit Nehru to whom the matter had been referred by the Home Ministry. But Krishna Menon reacted violently to Sanjeevi's visit to London and said that the officer had been sent by Sardar Patel to spy on him. In his talks to Sanjeevi, he "condemned the policy of the Government of India, and particularly of the Home Ministry regarding the Communists in India which he termed as 'barbarous and inhuman'..., refused to believe that the Communists of India were resorting to violence, and justified the criticism in the British Press of the Government of India's action against the Communists".[28]

The incident created a furore in the Home Ministry when, on his return to India, Sanjeevi reported verbally to Sardar Patel the substance of what Krishna Menon had said. The Sardar advised him to talk to Pandit Nehru who suggested to him to submit a written report. At the same time, Pandit Nehru wrote a letter dated January 5, 1949 to Krishna Menon, warning him that Sardar Patel was upset, and asking him to tell "what exactly happened". A written report dated January 6, 1949 was submitted by Sanjeevi to the Home Ministry. On the same day, Sardar Patel forwarded the report to Pandit Nehru stating that he was "very distressed about it and deeply pained to find Krishna Menon adopting the attitude and views which he expressed in his interview with Sanjeevi".[29]

Pandit Nehru wrote back to Sardar Patel expressing amazement "how and why Krishna Menon should have talked in this way". He offered a defence of his minion. "I can only explain," he said, "and excuse it to some extent by imagining that he was under some deep mental strain and consequently completely upset. He is often rather ill and sometimes his nerves give way when he is unwell."[30]

By all normal rules of policy and administration, Krishna Menon should have been sacked immediately. He was not only hostile to the Government of India which he was supposed to represent, but also a sick man, physically as well as mentally. But

[28] Ibid., Volume 9, p. 385.
[29] Ibid., p. 386 and fn.
[30] Ibid., p. 386.

the problem was that Pandit Nehru was extremely fond of his spokesman in London, and shared the views the latter had expressed. In fact, he needed Krishna Menon for planting in the British press stories which could be relayed back to India.

C. Rajagopalachari who was in New Delhi during those days, waiting for a ministerial job, had also been taken into confidence by Sardar Patel. He wrote to Pandit Nehru on January 11, 1949, advising the latter that Krishna Menon should "write a letter acknowledging his error and expressing regret for his remarks about Vallabhbhai Patel to Sanjeevi".[31] Pandit replied to him on the same day stating that Krishna Menon "is an extraordinary nervous individual, and sometimes gets completely upset by rather trivial happenings." At the same time, he proclaimed that Krishna Menon's "work at the India has been first-rate", and that he "is greatly popular and his staff works harder under him than it had previously done".[32]

But Pandit Nehru was really perturbed. He wrote to Krishna Menon on January 11, 1949, doubting whether Sanjeevi's report "is strictly accurate or not", showing understanding for Krishna Menon's "feelings about certain matters in India", and admonishing him that he should have expressed to a mere officer his opinion about policies which had been laid down by the Home Ministry.[33] Krishna Menon replied on January 16, 1948, and "accused Sanjeevi of reporting a conversation which Menon had assumed to be unofficial, charged him with 'drawing him out' under false pretences, and of being an 'agent provocateur'."[34] He did not deny that he said all that he was reported to have said to Sanjeevi. But in a subsequent letter dated January 20, 1949, he authorised Pandit Nehru "to deal with this matter and its implications in anyway you wish".[35]

Pandit Nehru was busy at that time with the Conference on Indonesia as he informed Krishna Menon by a letter dated January 24, 1949.[36] But he found time on January 26, 1949 to write a long letter to Krishna Menon after consultations with Rajagopalachari. He explained to Krishna Menon at length why Sanjeevi had been sent out, assured him that Sardar Patel appreciated his work, and

---

[31] Ibid., p. 386fn.
[32] Ibid., p. 387.
[33] Ibid.
[34] Ibid., p. 385fn.
[35] Ibid., p. 389fn.
[36] Ibid., p. 389.

enclosed the draft of a letter to be sent by him to Sardar Patel.[37] The draft shows the level to which Pandit Nehru could sink for protecting his protege. He advised Krishna Menon to say that i) "I have not seen the report and I have no notes of the conversation"; ii) "I do not think I said anything of this kind"; iii) "what I told him was about reactions in England about Indian affairs"; iv) "It is possible that Mr. Sanjeevi did not quite follow what I was talking about"; and v) "I should like to express my deep regret to you for any annoyance caused to you".[38] One wonders whether Krishna Menon relished the words put into his mouth. He was a self-righteous man who seldom felt or expressed regret for his words, while he went about abusing and insulting people who could not hit back.

Pandit Nehru admitted in his Circular Letter dated April 16, 1949 addressed to the Premiers that "No one is in doubt about the highly injurious activities of the Communist Party of India". But he advised them that "the Cabinet was of the opinion that any step in the nature of banning the Communist Party of India should be avoided at present". For, "if we ban the Party the aspect of sabotage and terrorism, will rather fade out from people's mind and it will be thought that the banning was due to ideological reason".[39] Whatever the facts, his conclusions were always the same. He was always out to protect the CPI.

Next day, he wrote to B.G. Kher, the Premier of Bombay: "I have received telegrams from well-known writers informing that Bombay Government has seized their passports and prevented their departure for Paris to attend some Peace Conference. I have also received protests from Professor Joliot Curie, an eminent scientist of Paris. Could you kindly look into the matter as prominent men are involved."[40] He did not mention the fact that the "well-known writers" and the "eminent scientist" were famous communists and fellow-travellers.

He made his own position pretty clear in a Press Conference held in New Delhi on August 8, 1949. He was asked if he would "seek the cooperation of the RSS for fighting what is generally known as the communist menace". He said that "we frankly do not trust the RSS very much and we shall keep a very vigilant outlook

[37] Ibid., pp. 391-93.
[38] Ibid., p. 393.
[39] Ibid., Volume 10, p. 320.
[40] Ibid., pp. 372-73.

in regard to it". He did not say in so many words that he regarded the RSS as fascist, but that was what he meant, as was obvious from his reply to the next question. He was asked, "You made a statement some time in 1932 or 1934 that as between fascism and Communism your heed was for the latter. What is your view now?" Pat came the reply, "Still the same."[41]

Around the same time Edwina Mountbatten had written to him protesting "why leaders of communal parties should be released, when others are not". She was annoyed at the release of some RSS leaders with whom the Government of India wanted to have talks. Of course, by "others" she meant the communists. He wrote back to her on September 19, 1949 that it was difficult to detain people who disavowed violence, though "their presence is certainly an incitement to trouble". That was about the RSS. Coming to the communists, he pleaded helplessness because "they go on advocating something in the nature of violent rebellion and sabotage and indulge in it, whenever opportunity offers". He admitted that communist activity was "in the nature of a war". But at the same time, he conveyed to the "Lady" that "many people take advantage of the Communist cloak to carry out acts of private vengeance", and thus attributed to common criminals rather than the communists the "large number of murders" that the latter had committed.[42]

Finally, in a Circular Letter dated October 2, 1949 addressed to the Premiers, he informed them that the Government of Madras had banned the Communist Party of India with the approval of the Government of India, and that the public had welcomed the step. But at the same time, he warned them that this banning 'has nothing to with ideology or theory" of Communism. And he blamed the widespread communist violence in Hyderabad on "the very backward land tenure system".[43]

Thus it is a myth that Pandit Nehru approved of the steps which Sardar Patel and the Provincial Governments led by the latter took against the communist insurrection in 1948-49. It is quite another matter that he could not save the situation for the communists in spite of his best efforts.

---

[41] Ibid., Volume 12, p. 14.
[42] Ibid., Volume 13, p. 172.
[43] Ibid., p. 206.

EIGHTEEN

SAPPERS AND MINERS OF COMMUNISM

An ideology can be taken to have triumphed when those whom it declares to be its enemies start speaking its language. Communism has already passed that test and arrived at a stage when its thought-categories have acquired an almost universal adherence. Let us sample some of the more basic communist slogans and see how strongly and systematically they have seeped into the thought and language of the present-day intelligentsia in every corner of the world. In the process, we shall also discover how the human mind can be manipulated to a point where any amount of objective data fails to have any impact on it, and where superstitions of the silliest sort become its entire stock-in-trade.

Karl Marx had propounded and his followers have propagated ever since that the poor and the downtrodden people are inevitably bound to become the core of the communist movement and the vanguard of the "proletarian revolution". The whole history of the communist movement, however, leaves not a shadow of doubt that it is exactly the poor and the downtrodden people who have all along kept away from the communist parties which have been, by and large, strongholds of the intelligentsia indoctrinated in communist ideology. In Asia, Africa and Latin America, this communist intelligentsia has been derived overwhelmingly from the uppermost strata of society to whom alone education in modern universities has been accessible. Yet, a belief is abroad that the communist movement is everywhere constituted of the poor and the downtrodden people, with the result that whenever communism wins a victory it is supposed to be a victory of the poor and the downtrodden. And almost everybody who considers himself an intelligent opponent of communism goes on repeating ad nauseum that the only sure way of stopping Communism is to abolish poverty and class oppression.

Similarly, Karl Marx had propounded and his followers have propagated ever since that the capitalists everywhere are inevitably bound to oppose the communist movement. The whole history of capitalism since the rise of the communist movement, however, leaves not a shadow of doubt that the capitalists have not only financed the communist parties and competed with each other to secure business deals with communist countries, but have also packed the press they have owned with communist editors and scribes, with the result that the capitalist press has been the largest and the most powerful agency of communist propaganda. In Asia, Africa and Latin America, an average capitalist cannot tell a communist from a crab and he wholeheartedly cooperates with the communist movement which has come to represent power, prestige and pugnacity in all these three continents. Yet, a universal belief is abroad that wherever and whenever the communist movement has come up against opposition, it has always been due to capitalist inspiration and capitalist money. And almost everyone who considers himself an opponent of Communism looks to the capitalists for providing the finances he needs for his politics and gets angry because he finds the capitalists either indifferent to him or actually cooperating with the communists.

Another silly superstition which has become widespread after the Second World War is that the United States of America has always been and remains today the main bulwark of anti-communism. An examination of U.S. record vis-a-vis world communism before and after the Second World War, however, leaves not a shadow of doubt that outside the Soviet Union the United States of America has been the biggest single propagator of communist ideology and the foremost financier of the world communist movement. In Asia, Africa and Latin America, a convinced anti-communist discovers in no time that almost all serious U.S. publications, almost all outstanding U.S. scholars and scribes, almost the entire U.S. diplomatic apparatus, and almost all U.S. Foundations dread and despise a convinced anti-communist as a demon, and fawn upon communists and fellow-travellers as leaders of "the renaissance that should revitalise these backward continents". The only basis for a widespread belief in the U.S.A.'s anti-communist role is ultimately to be found in Comrade Zhdanov's celebrated speech in September 1947 in course of which he described the U.S.A. as the "leader of the camp of imperialism and war" as against the "camp of socialism and peace led by the Soviet Union".

To prove our point, let us look at a fat and high-priced book, *Communism in India,*[1] which has just come out of the U.S.A. and which the United States Information Service is distributing freely all

[1] Gene D. Overstreet and Marshall Windmiller, *Communism in India*, reprinted in India by The Perennial Press, Bombay, 1960.

over India. This precious piece of "research", undertaken by two State Department scholars, has been sponsored by the Centre for South Asian Studies, Institute of International Studies, University of California, which is headed by Dr. Richard L. Park who has spent many years in India as a student of India's foreign policy. The two "scholars" themselves spent several years in India, travelling from one end of the country to another, meeting all sorts of intellectuals and politicians and collecting a vast amount of reference material. The book is a thoroughly documented work of more than six hundred pages. And the whole project must have cost the U.S.A. several million dollars.

But this book could have as well been produced and printed in Moscow. Here are its main conclusions:

1. Moscow has always found it difficult to control the Communist Party of India which has always been fighting a bitter battle against the Kremlin bosses.
2. The Communist Party of India has always found it difficult to control its provincial units which control most of the finances and which can, therefore, defy the Party bosses with impunity.
3. The Communist Party of India has always suffered from a paucity of means and its financial resources have all along been rather meagre.
4. The only channel through which foreign money flows to the Communist Party of India is the import of foreign communist literature, but the low prices of this literature coupled with the high costs incurred on selling it, leave the Party actually in loss.
5. The Communist Party of India has increasingly come to accept the constitutional path to power under the impact of Gandhian ideology, experience of parliamentary democracy since the dawn of independence, and the taste of power through the parliamentary path in Kerala.
6. The communist fronts in India have been so thoroughly infiltrated by Congressmen as to make them useless for the Communist Party of India for all practical purposes.
7. R.K. Karanjia's weekly *Blitz* from Bombay, is the best and the most well brought-out periodical in India, and its editor is so clever that in spite of his communist leanings he has been very successful with anti-communist Prime Minister Nehru.

8. Some of the fellow-travellers of the Communist Party of India, notably Khwaja Ahmed Abbas, have come to wield so much influence in international communist counsels that sometimes they have been able to lead a change in the international communist line.

Small wonder that this book, freely acquired from the USIS, is being sold at all communist bookshops and recommended by all communist circles. An official history of the Communist Party of India was badly needed by the Party bosses. The U.S. "scholars" have done the job free of cost, and on a scale which might not have been possible for the Party for a long time to come.

But what is the truth about Communism in India as every Indian, who has watched and studied it first-hand, knows it for sure? It is just the opposite of what these U.S. "scholars" say. We know that

1. The Communist Party of India has always been and remains a paid puppet of Moscow, and has often staged overnight somersaults on orders from Moscow.
2. The Communist Party of India can create and dissolve and take any other disciplinary action against any of its provincial units without creating the slightest stir because the Party bosses pay almost every penny which the provincial units spend.
3. The Communist Party of India is the richest political party in India, not excluding the ruling Congress Party, and spends something like 30 to 40 crore rupees every year on its apparatus and activities.[2]
4. The real channels through which this huge foreign finance flows to the Communist Party of India reach out into gigantic business and banking operations carried out and controlled by what is called the underground Tech of the Party.
5. The Communist Party of India has accepted the constitutional path only provisionally because, according to its own proclamations, India under Pandit Nehru offers immense opportunities of seizing power through the parliamentary path, and the Party will resort to violent methods whenever it finds that its way to power is blocked.
6. The communist fronts in India provide platforms to those

[2] That was in 1962. The Party became richer in subsequent years.

Congressmen and others who see eye to eye with the Communist Party of India on most matters, but who are not prepared, for one reason or the other, to be known as communists.

7. The weekly *Blitz* is the shoddiest specimen of yellow journalism at its worst and R.K. Karanjia has succeeded with Pandit Nehru simply because the latter believes in the communist lies which the former sells.
8. Most fellow-travellers of the Communist Party of India, notably Khwaja Ahmed Abbas, are only paid pipers who play the tune which their paymaster calls, and so far as the international communist movement is concerned they cannot compete even with the passive pieces of paper on which the Kremlin bosses write their diktats.

It is, therefore, not surprising that the U.S.A. has never been able to understand Pandit Nehru even though the latter has never tried to hide his basic beliefs from anybody. The U.S. writers have written several biographies of "the great man" but none of them has brought out his true character as a consistent communist in thought and action. They have spread, in their own country and elsewhere, the superstition that he and he alone stands between India and the inevitable communist flood. A few years back, the present writer tried to convey the truth about Pandit Nehru to the U.S. public and politicians through the medium of some "reactionary" U.S. newspapers. But every newspaper he approached came out with the stock reply that it was too late in the day to try the "Indian brand of MacCarthyism" in the U.S.A. when U.S.A.'s own native brand had been long out of the market. One sympathetic editor, who knew the truth but did not dare publicise it in the U.S.A., wrote: "If you say that Nehru is Jesus Christ himself just descended on earth, every American will hug you to his heart. But if you want to say something different you better seek some other country and some other press."

Inside India itself, however, everyone except our Americanised intelligentsia, knows and says that Pandit Nehru is a communist. The common man is not in a position to evaluate the communist creed in terms of any moral or political values because all that he hears from all quarters is in favour of Communism. But he knows and says loudly that Pandit Nehru is on the side of the Soviet Union in the latter's quarrel with America. The author of these articles has been warned by so many of his "illiterate"cousins from the countryside not to oppose Communism because it means opposing Pandit Nehru who is all powerful and can harm people with whom he may get displeased. In fact, his own mother who is also totally "illetrate" and knows no politics, keeps on worrying about her son coming to harm because of his attitude towards "that powerful man (*ṭhāḍā māṇas)*". It is only the Indian intelligentsia which, like its U.S. mentor and counterpart, reacts negatively if someone says that Pandit Nehru is a communist. Their stock argument is that even the anti-communist U.S.A. which suspected Pandit Nehru of communist sympathies at one time, has realised its mistake and has come out in support of his policies.

For, inside India, Pandit Nehru's conscious and careful cultivation of the Communist Party in independent India's courtyard is only one side of the painful picture. On the other side, we have his proclaimed and manifest hostility towards any effort to expose and isolate the communist movement in India. Here we shall quote only one notable instance out of the many of which we have personal knowledge. That instance is connected with an effort on the part of some courageous patriots belonging to all national political parties to forestall Chinese designs against this country. Pandit Nehru and his henchmen did not allow this effort to succeed and as a result we have the Chinese Reds sitting on several thousand miles of our soil.

When Tibet was invaded by the Chinese Red Army in October 1950, the explanation which Peking put forward was: "Anglo-American imperialism and their running dog Nehru were plotting a coup for the annexation of Tibet." The only reaction from Pandit Nehru was to start apologising for Peking immediately. Talking to Reuter's Diplomatic Correspondent in Srinagar a week or two later, he said: "The current Chinese policy is perhaps partly attributable to the fact that although Peking's policy may not be dictated by Moscow, much of the information upon which this policy is based comes through Soviet sources. For instance, Moscow has repeatedly said that Anglo-American intrigues in Tibet aim at bringing that country into an anti-communist bloc or sphere of influence. However unfounded these accusations may be, I wonder whether they have not influenced the Chinese decision to move into Tibet...The apprehension in Peking that the United States was bent on the destruction of the new regime is, rightly or wrongly, very real."[3]

But public opinion in India was exercised about Chinese occupation of Tibet as it meant a threat to India's own security, apart from suppression of Tibetan freedom. Nothing could be done immediately to mobilise public opinion and put pressure on the Government of India to change its China policy. It was only on August 22, 1953 that a meeting of leaders from various patriotic political parties, including Members of Parliament, decided to raise unofficial India's voice of protest against the continued occupation of Tibet. The meeting set up a Tibet Committee and announced a Tibet Day to be observed in September. But as soon as the news of this idea being mooted appeared in the press, the Prime Minister came out against it in a public statement issued the very next day. According to *Hindustan Times* dated August 26, "He referred to a report that some persons proposed to hold a Tibet Day. He thought that it was ill-advised and asked members not to take any interest in it." The meeting on August 22 had set up a Tibet Day Committee under the Chairmanship of Shri Gurupadaswami who was a Praja Socialist Party (PSP) Member of Parliament at that time. But another MP on the Committee, Prof N.G. Ranga, had to tender his resignation from the Committee on August 28 under pressure from the Prime Minister with whose party he was at that time negotiating the merger of his own provincial Krishakar Lok Party in Andhra Pradesh.

The Committee, however, did its duty by the country and the cause of human freedom in Tibet. More than eighty persons marched to the Chinese Embassy in New Delhi carrying placards and raising slogans asking Red China to vacate Tibet. Later on, a meeting was held in New Delhi Town Hall and addressed, among others by Shri Gurupadaswamy, Shri V.P. Joshi of the Jana Sangh and Munshi Ahmed Deen of the Praja Socialist Party.

The Prime Minister felt annoyed with this effort. He put pressure on the press in New Delhi not to publish news of the Tibet Day demonstration and meeting. It became widely known in journalist circles those days that Feroze Gandhi, the son-in-law of the Prime Minister and a Director of the Express Group of newspapers at that time, explicitly ordered his chain everywhere not to report these events in the Capital.

---

[3] Quoted in the Editorial of *Mother India*, Bombay, November 11, 1950.

A few days later, the Prime Minister did something infinitely worse. Speaking on Foreign Affairs in the Rajya Sabha on September 23, he denounced and threatened the organisers of the Tibet Day in a language which was wild. He said: "Sometimes—not often, I am glad to say—some exuberant people organise some demonstration or other against friendly countries... Being a gallant band of three or four they demonstrate their wishes in this manner. Sometimes they demonstrate, at any rate they did a few days ago, against what they did not like, against the Chinese Government. Now, it is a trivial matter but I mention it because a member of this honourable House apparently, I believe, associated himself with this matter...They proclaim a Tibet Day. Why anyone should proclaim a Tibet Day passes my comperhension, more especially at this juncture. Who the genius was who suggested it or whose bright idea it was, I do not know. But anyhow here was this Tibet Day about ten days ago—nobody has noticed it—but a dozen to two dozen persons marched through the streets of Delhi to proclaim their love of Tibet and marched to the Chinese Embassy and demonstrated in front of it with loud cries. Well, it is rather childish, all this and extraordinary that grown up persons should behave in this way and show up, because if a couple of dozen persons do this it does not indicate, if I may say so, any powerful body of opinion. In fact, it indicates their own smallness and folly. I mention this because it is perfectly ridiculous. I don't mind if anybody thinks so and wants to oppose us, not in argument or debate or even in public streets. Well, if he goes beyond a certain limit, any Government will have to take action. We don't take any action normally speaking. We have not, but what I want this House to consider is the extreme, well I use the word 'folly', of such activities. Members of this House do not attach any importance to it, I know. But there is the rest of the world which exaggerates and which may be interested in exaggerating these incidents which come at a moment when we seek help in delicate matters in developing a spirit of friendly cooperation and tries to create trouble."

This statement was full of insinuations. Here was the Prime Minister of a democratic country showing extreme intolerance for, and interfering publicly with other people's freedom to think and express opinion about matters which concerned the security of the nation. The Communist Party of India and its fronts had built up before his own eyes a formidable apparatus which was leading demonstrations, every now and then, against this or that foreign embassy, and heaping the foulest possible abuse on several friendly countries. The Prime Minister has, to this day, never uttered a word against even acts of hooliganism enacted by the communists outside those embassies — burning cars, stoning, and manhandling office staff. But a small and dignified protest on the part of some patriots to draw the attention of their people and Government to the threat posed by China's illegal invasion of a buffer State, made the Prime Minister furious and robbed him of all sense of proportion and propriety. The Prime Minister had shown himself partial to a communist cause in utter disregard of national interest. In the process, he had made himself utterly ridiculous as well. On the one hand he said again and again that the protesters against China were only a few people who represented no one except themselves. On the other hand he chose to spend so much breath and create the impression that the event was very important. His threat of action against the protesters, of course, was nothing short of criminal.

But the work of the Committee continued in spite his fretting and fuming. After sometime, it organised a Himalayan Border Conference to prepare Indian public opinion against Chinese designs towards India, which were becoming all too clear even at that early date. More than a thousand people marched through the streets of Delhi demanding vigilance on our northern borders. But the Nehru Government's attitude towards this patriotic effort became even more hostile, still and responsible officers of the External Affairs Ministry re-echoed only stories published in R.K. Karanjia's yellow sheet as well as the traitorous communist press.

A regional meeting of the Himalayan Borders Conference was held at Patiala. The then Chief Minister of PEPSU, Col. Raghubir Singh, had sympathised with the Conference from the very beginning. He made a hall and other facilities available for the meeting. But just on the eve of the meeting, he received the "right" instructions from the External Affairs Ministry at New Delhi. He had to cancel his permission for the use of the hall, and withdraw all other facilities. Privately he regretted this forced decision on his part and, while confessing that he could not publicly offend the Big Boss, he contributed several hundred rupees to the Conference fund.

Pandit Nehru has been seeing "American imperialism" in every patriotic effort to explode the myth of the Soviet and the Chinese paradise. On the other hand, he has allowed the Communist Party of India to flood the country with cheap communist literature, all sorts of communist fronts, and the so-called "cultural delegations" from every communist country. If the Praja Socialist Party or the Jana Sangh publishes a small pamphlet or opens an extra office, he starts smelling "foreign money". But the Communist Party of India is currently spending something like 30 to 40 crore rupees every year on its party apparatus, open and secret. The recent report of the Press Commission that the Communist Party of India is the biggest press-lord in the country is only an indication of the enormous amounts of money the Party has been receiving from the Soviet Slave Empire for training saboteurs on Indian's own soil and subverting India's hard-earned freedom. He has never bothered to look into communist finances and the channels through which the finances flow. The Intelligence Department is kept busy in harrassing "American agents" and "communal fanatics".

II

Why is the average U.S. scholar, scribe and politician so blind to reality? Why did he fail to see the truth in time in the case of China? Why can he not see the truth in India today? Why is it that the U.S. advisers everywhere have been the sappers and miners of Communism? The present writer put these questions to a contemplative friend of his a few years back. And the reply that the wise man gave is quoted below in his own words:

"It happened in a dream. But the dream was no Freudian wish fulfilment. On the contrary, it was a nightmarish interpretation of waking life.

"A bunch of Indian eggheads had gathered in a highbrow seminar to compile an inventory of US sins. The roll was quite formidable. Monopoly capitalism, dollar imperialism, H bomb militarism, MacCarthy fascism, negro-lynching racialism, alcoholism, crime fiction, horror comics, juvenile delinquency, jazz music, and coca cola. Dante's inferno stood erupted right in our midst.

"The young swami in saffron looked bored and unimpressed. His lips twirled in a gesture of contempt as he surveyed the august assembly. Then he stood up, and summarily dismissed the eggheads as denizens of darkness dishing out dirt and disease. The singular sin of the United States, he said, was Dialectical Materialism.

"The eggheads stabbed him with hostile stares which soon

exploded in angry outbursts. How did this swine of a swami steal into the company of sober scientists? It was suggested that his person be subjected to thorough search. Some crevice of his ridiculous robe was suspected of being loaded with dollar bills. But better counsels prevailed and the seminar dispersed hastily. The holy hoax was not worth an audience.

"I accosted the swami on the road outside. He certainly seemed to be a very interesting man. Absolutely convinced. And immovably calm in a world where convictions created convulsions of hatred and self-righteousness. Very soon, I was sitting before him on a lawn, trying to share his uncanny insight. He smiled indulgently and spoke in simple terms:

" 'The United States has an idea. Democracy. She has practised it for long, and has prospered on it. There is no doubt that she cherishes the idea with sincere devotion. Her one ambition is to share it with every other country. And she spends billions to spread and safeguard it in all parts of the world.

" 'What does she do? She proclaims that democracy can be distilled from the standard of living. So let every country improve its agriculture and industry, and develop schools, cinemas, railways, roads. Let there be taller and heavier bodies which last better and longer. Let everyone have fruit juice for breakfast, wear a silk hat, ride a mercedes, and giggle at Marylin Munroe. And democracy will develop to the detriment of all other ideas.

" 'The United States protests that democracy must perforce depend upon dictators who can push through plans for industrialization. She seeks out Nehrus Nassers, and Soekarnos who have power, prestige and a lot of pugnacity. She turns a deaf ear to the denunciations they daily hurl at her. Dip them with another darned good dose of dollars, and in due course they shall deliver democracy. That is the formula.

" 'The United States cannot bother about blighters who believe (!) in democracy, and who write and fight for it. After all, the miserable scribes have no power to persecute or protect. She cannot waste her august attention on inspired idiots and discredited do-nothings. She cannot afford to provoke people in power for a pack of funny friends, hated and hunted by their own people. No. She is practical. And she is precise.

" 'Now, all this is exactly what we know as Dialectical Materialism. In the universe presided over by this deity, consciousness oozes out of matter like oil from sunflower seeds, ideas are concomitants of material changes, and the human mind an effeminate evolute of the human body. It is a universe of objective and subjective necessities, in which there is no freedom and, therefore, no place for faith.'

"There was a pause. I gave him my reactions. I had suddenly become very optimistic about peaceful co-existence, now that I knew that both the Soviet Union and the United States shared the same creed. The Swami laughed aloud and said:

" 'Who told you the Soviet Union promotes Dialectical Materialism? That is a damned lie, as big as the other lie that the United States promotes Humanism. The Soviet Union only sells Dialectical Materialism to those she wants to defeat and destroy. As for herself, she stands for what in philosophy we call Idealism, a rigorous and uncompromising type of Idealism.

" 'The Soviet Union too has an idea. Totalitarianism. She has polished and perfected it over the years. She is passionately dedicated to it. She wants this idea to prevail permanently, for, without it, she sees no hope for humanity. And she also spends billions to spell and secure it in every corner of the world.

" 'What does she do? She propounds that the standard of living and much more follow from faith in totalitarianism. She elaborates the idea in an unending stream of books, pamphlets, posters, handbills, and films, produced in every language and suited to the lowest intelligence and the meanest pocket. She employs an army of men and women to retail this idea on a mass scale in order to convert or corrode as many people as possible, and to ultimately impose it with force of arms in true crusading fashion.

" 'The material conditions may differ from Czechoslovakia to Albania to Tibet. But they are all equally ripe for totalitarianism. The triumphal march of an idea does not and should not depend on any material preparation. The idea cannot and should not wait for slow and stupid material changes. What the idea needs is human minds, their craving for it. The minds can be captured and the craving created by means of books and the party apparatus.

" 'Nor does the Soviet Union seek for any credentials of power or prestige in choosing her friends. All she cares for is their convictions. Let the convinced ones be obscure and unknown. She makes them famous overnight by powerful publicity. Let the convinced ones be poor. She makes them prosperous by placing them in her paid hierarchy. Let the convinced ones be hated by their own people. She makes them loved by discovering in them virtues which no one ever suspected.

" 'If you can turn a phrase, you can be turned into a world famous author, without your ever bothering to write a line. People everywhere will be informed by the Soviet network that your wonderful works are under translation. Royalties on enormous editions will come pouring into your pocket. And so on, you can be a renowned scientist, or doctor, or lawyer, or musician, or poet, or priest, as it suits your taste, and go about as an honoured guest in every capital of the world. All you have to do is to believe in and seek for totalitarianism, and the rest in added unto you.

" 'This is not Dialectical Materialism. This is Idealism, according to which consciousness converses with consciousness as one lamp is lighted by another, ideas implement ideas, and one human mind meets another, directly without any material aid. In this universe, the ill-fed and ill-clad underdogs have as much capacity as their more privileged fellow-beings. For, this is the universe of freedom, and of faith.'

"There was another pause. I was too flabbergasted to offer any comment. After a while, the swami himself resumed:

" 'You were talking of peaceful co-existence. I do not know what that phrase really means. What I see before my eyes is a neat division of labour between the United States and the Soviet Union, at least in this part of the world. The United States is trying to take care of our bodies, our hearths, and our homes. The Soviet Union is taking care of our heads, and showing extreme concern for our mental, moral and spiritual needs.

" 'The United States builds schools and spreads literacy among the peasants. The Soviet Union provides them the newspapers they read. The United States erects factories in which the workers can earn a livelihood. The Soviet Union bands them into trade unions, trains their leaders, and gives them a cause to die for. The United States gives scholarships to promising students for studies abroad. The Soviet Union equips them with political glasses through which they can survey the world. The United States builds hospitals and furnishes them with soft beds and rare medical supplies. The Soviet Union indoctrinates the nurses who attend and attract the patients. The United States spends on library premises. The Soviet Union stocks the shelves within with her own choice of literature. The

United States pampers regime after regime with the paraphernalia for pomp. The Soviet Union creates an elite capable of possessing power in every land...'

" The swami looked at his watch, and stood up. He was now in a hurry. I accompanied him to the nearest bus stand, and shot my only question at him: 'Why do you think Dialectical Materialism is a sin?' He raised his eyebrows, looked grim, and whispered:

" 'I am a man of God. I have seen Him face to face, even as I see you. I know He is pure, unmixed Consciousness. Self-existing, All-sustaining and Blissful Consciousness.'

"And then suddenly pointing his well-shaped finger towards a heap of dirt, he roared: 'Dialectical Materialism says that Mahatma Gandhi and Albert Einstein evolved out of that filth. That is blasphemy. And a sin. A cardinal sin.'

"I woke up with a start. There was no swami, no bus stand, and no heap of dirt. Instead, I lay in a bed scattered with the writings of the Right Reverend Pandit Jawaharlal Nehru. Perhaps I had been bored to an early doze by his bad paraphrase of communist scriptures."[4]

Opposition to Communism has never been and shall never be a mechanical concomitant of any class, or social status, or nation, or creed, or interest. Every class, every social status, every nation, every creed, and every interest will become an opponent of Communism the moment it becomes conscious of certain moral and spiritual values which ought not to be sacrificed in exchange for any amount of material good or political benefit. And every class, every social status, every nation, every creed, and every interest has cooperated and will continue to cooperate with Communism so long as it takes resort to expediency for securing selfish gain, and is prepared to sacrifice moral and spiritual values in exchange for its own temporary survival or the destruction of its temporary enemies.

So far Communism has been opposed only by isolated individuals and groups who have done so mostly at the cost of their reputation in the communities to which they have belonged. A

---

[4] This was actually an article I wrote in 1956 for a conservative U.S. magazine which turned it down. But it found its way first into a paper submitted by a famous French scholar to the North Atlantic Treaty Organisation (NATO), then into a monthly magazine published from West Berlin by refugees from Stalin's Russia, and finally into the Congressional Record of the U.S.A. But it is doubtful if those who appreciated it were able to understand the message it conveyed.

history of these heroes and their endless endeavour has still to be written. The scholars of the so-called free world have no time to spare for such a study because they are more than busy in their studies of the Soviet Union, its Satellites, and its paid puppets all over the world. The libraries and reading rooms of the free world are loaded with surveys, statistics, specialised monographs, brochures and bulletins, all of them brooding over the least little detail regarding communist countries, communist conspiracies, and communist crimes. The "bourgeois" press reserves all its headlines for communist hooliganism in every walk of life, in all parts of the world. It pays no heed to efforts aimed at stopping that hooliganism. But if a study of anti-communist effort is ever undertaken, it will reveal unmistakably that the courage to oppose Communism has always been the concomitant of some moral and spiritual spark, and seldom a companion of man's craving for cash or creature comforts.

The spark will become a blazing fire at the touch of a spiritual world-view. And India is the land which has been specially chosen for such momentous missions all through human history. For, India is the home of *Sanātana Dharma,* a world-view which is at once eternal and universally valid. All other spiritual world-views have imprisoned themselves within the confines of a particular book, or a particular prophet, or a particular church. *Sanātana Dharma* alone rises above all sectarian semantics and sophistry, and takes us straight into that sunshine of the Supreme Spirit which has sanctioned the rise and spread of Communism, and which will sanction its death and destruction as well. Let us start that *dharmayuddha* in the *dharmakshetra* that is Bharatavarśa.

India is *Kurukshetra* too, the battle-field on which the moral and spiritual intuitions and imperatives of man's higher nature must manifest themselves into concrete and coherent action. Let the spirit of *Sanātana Dharma* re-awaken and spread once more in the land of its first though immemorial dawns. Let us look at Pandit Nehru and his hoodlums from the vantage point of that spirit. Then we shall see immediately as to who is the arch-villain in this dismal drama, and stop wasting our time and energy in weeping and whining against mere minions like Comrade Krishṅa Menon.

NINETEEN

CHOOSING BETWEEN USA AND USSR[1]

Communist China's aggression along our Himalayan frontier has once again posed before the nation the problem of finding friends against foes in a dangerous and divided world. The nation had faced this problem at first when Pakistan signed a military pact with the United States of America, and started talking tough in the context of her self-chosen controversy over Kashmir. During those days, at least, it was seriously apprehended by the Indian people at large that Pakistan might mount an aggression against India from a position of superior military strength. The same people now fear that a militarily mightier China may choose any day to convert isolated border incidents into an all-out war.

The Government of India had proclaimed in the midst of our first predicament that, in spite of everything that had happened in the meanwhile, India should and would continue to pursue her earlier policy of non-alighnment with any power bloc support of world peace, and friendship for all nations including Pakistan. But a vigilant and well-entrenched communist movement inside the country had used the opportunity to push our foreign policy in a definite direction till in every essential except verbiage it came quite close to Soviet foreign policy. Whatever might have been the intention of the Government of India, at least the man in the street had been led to believe that Russia was India's unfailing friend against an America conspiring for an armed conflict between India and Pakistan. The man in the street was supported in this belief by repeated statements from Government spokesmen that an armed conflict between India and Pakistan would very soon spread into a world-wide conflagration. The one clear impression that was thus conveyed was that both Russia and America were bound to collide in an effort to help their respective friends, India and Pakistan.

[1] This article was a comment on a bunch of "intellectuals" who held a seminar in October 1962, in New Delhi, and called upon the Government of India to plunge into immediate military action against China. A pamphlet, *Action Now*, issued at the end of the seminar pretended that the "intellectuals" were mature military strategists as well. Two of them who were the tallest of these "intellectuals" left India the very next day for taking jobs in U.S. universities, leaving it to me to translate their *Action Now* into Hindi. They had not thought it fit to invite me to the seminar. I was not supposed to be an "intellectual". It was out of regard for personal friendship that I did the translation. But it left a bad taste in the mouth.

In the present predicament also, the Government of India continues to proclaim the same policy of non-alignment, world peace, and friendship for all including China. Again, whatever may be the intention of the Government of India, at least the man in the street has already started looking towards America as India's inevitable friend in the event of a showdown with China. And once again, the Government is supporting the man in the street in this belief by repeated statements that a war between India and China will very soon engulf the whole world. The one clear impression that is thus being conveyed is that, in the event of China attacking India, America will surely rush to India's rescue and force Russia to side with her ally in the communist camp.

But with these similarities between the earlier and the present situation, there are certain clearly discernible differences as well.

First of all, there is no organised movement inside the country which may attempt to influence our foreign policy in favour of a pro-American orientation. Some isolated individuals may have occasionally advocated some sort of an alliance with America. But the political climate in the country as a whole has not evinced any marked enthusiasm for making such a commitment. India's foreign policy has, by and large, continued to grind in its old grooves, although shorn of much of its earlier aura of infallibility so far as the mass mind in the country is concerned. There has been no mass fervour in favour of a friendship with America such as was noticed earlier in favour of Russia, though the feeling of extreme hostility towards America has tended to decline except in pockets of communist dominated public opinion.

Secondly, there is a feeling among our intelligentsia at least that, in the final round, Russia and China may not turn out to be the friends we have assumed them to be. In fact, it is believed by an important section of the intelligentsia that China has held her hand and hesitated in pressing her initial advantage to the hilt due to some direct or indirect pressure from Russia. This section also entertains the hope that, sooner or later, there is going to be a big burst-up between the two communist countries, and that Russia will certainly contain China and force her to renounce her aggressive designs against India. If it is pointed out to these people that there is also an equal possibility of an eventual patch-up inside the communist camp, they maintain that, in that event, Russia will surely secure a peaceful settlement between India and China, provided India continues to cultivate her friendship with Russia in the meanwhile.

Whatever be the line of reasoning or absence of it, this much at least is obvious that, unlike in the earlier situation when practically every political party tried to outdo the others in denouncing Pakistan's ally in the arms pact, no section of Indian political opinion has so far stepped forward to foment a feeling of mass hostility towards China's ally in the international alignment of forces. The feelings of our people at large as well as the relations of our Government have till now continued to be more or less normal so far as Russia is concerned. No doubt, the extreme forms of enthusiasm expressed earlier have tended to decline over a period of time. But people who entertain any serious apprehensions about Russia are few and far between.

Small wonder, therefore, that the politically informed opinion inside the country should still be debating the question whether India should continue to cultivate friendship for Russia as a solution of her difficulties with China, one way or the other, or move decisively towards America as an insurance against an eventual showdown. The Government of India is, on the whole, still sticking to its previous policy of friendship for Russia, though its earlier enthusiasm for everything Russian has declined in a marked degree, while its impeccable hostility towards America has become increasingly diluted even in the face of American insolence. But there are persistent misgivings in the minds of many patriotic people that, having failed to enter into an alliance with America in the meanwhile, India may find herself friendless in the event of a war with China. It is felt by these people that Russia is surely not going to quarrel with China over the latter's quarrel with India, and that the timing of a burst-up between the two communist countries may not suit the strategy of India's defence.

The result of all this shilly-shallying has been a sense of confusion amounting to callousness which ill-behoves a nation standing face to face with a calamitous situation. In the absence of a clear vision and all that follows from it, India has not been able to give any positive shape either to her military preparations and dispositions or to her foreign policy pursuits, so that if a showdown is forced upon her in the near future she is sure to be caught napping. The Government of India has not been able to make progress beyond a series of protest notes and an intermittent show of strong language against the aggressor. And the public is not at all sure which way to shape and project its agitation for a suitable change in Government policy. The total scene is one of paralysis in which hopes and fears are inextricably mixed up in one prevailing national mood of doing nothing and waiting like weaklings till some decisions are dictated by the onrush of world events.

II

Now, the first thing that strikes a serious observer of the political scene in India at present is her hopeful though helpless dependence on international developments, none of which she is in a position to force or frustrate by throwing into the scales her own strength. There is a blind belief in India's political mind that India is too valuable for the forces of world democracy to be allowed to go down under the heels of a communist aggressor. There is also a cowardly calculation on the part of what passes for expert political opinion, particularly in circles close to the Government of India, that Russia is too jealous of China's growing strength to remain a silent spectator and permit her rival in the international communist camp to gobble up India all by herself. It hardly occurs to anyone in places of power and prestige and public responsibility that nothing can be more pathetic than a modern nation of four hundred million people staking her whole future on whatever little or great interest the Big Powers may be inclined to have at any time in the preservation of her independent identity.

That is not to say that India should shut her eyes towards international developments outside her borders, or that she should refuse to turn such developments to her own advantage. India should, on the contrary, be watchful of every turn and twist in the international situation, and profit from all available opportunities to improve her position vis-a-vis China. Self-preservation is the first law of life, and so long as India is not strong enough to protect herself against aggression, she has no moral right to transgress that law out of any consideration, idealistic or otherwise. But, at the same time, India has to realise that no amount of good fortune that may flow to her as a result of fortuitous developments abroad can ever be a substitute for her own positive strength to ward off or, if need be, deliver decisive blows in the domain of international diplomacy or mobilisation of military might. India will, go down in history as an imbecile nation if she stakes her future only on clever calculations about international developments, and fails to build up and maintain that minimum of military power without which no nation, big or small, has ever counted for anything on the chess-board of world politics.

In the absence of such a perspective, the entire controversy regarding a correct policy in the face of continued Chinese aggression has reached the limits of the ludicrous. On the one hand, we have a Government which denounces as warmongers all those who advise that this battle of protest notes should stop at some stage, and that India should seriously think of doing something which can register her strength of will in the mind of a determined adversary. On the other hand, we have some small groups, particularly in the opposition parties, who are currently agitating that our army should be permitted to drive out the Chinese intruders, and that India should straightaway reverse her present policy of taking no risk of a wider conflict. Both sides are equally blind to the realities and requirements of the situation.

The plea that our Government puts forth in defence of its policy of pouring out protest notes, is that we are still not strong enough to risk a trial of strength with a massively militarised enemy. And taken by itself, this plea cannot be easily brushed aside by anyone who has some acquaintance with the facts of our military position. China has not only a larger armed force as well as an initial advantage over us in so far as she started the build-up at a time when we were fast asleep under the soporiphic of *panchashil*; she also has in her possession a superior air force which can operate from a number of first class bases in Tibet and pulverise in no time the entire industrial heartland of India in the northern provinces. It would indeed be sheer folly on our part to risk a showdown with China so long as we have not matched her build-up with our own and, what is more important, before we are in a position not only to intercept Chinese bombers at our very borders but also to deliver blows that tell on China's own industrial network.

But that does not seem to be the reason why our Government has been holding up action all these days. Our present state of weakness seems to be, for our Government, only a cover for doing nothing beyond marking time till some chance turn in international events tips the scales against China and in our own favour. The Government has so far betrayed practically no intention of changing our state of weakness into a state of strength. It frittered away five years in a conspiracy of silence over what China had been doing since the middle of 1954. It admitted the truth only when it was forced to do so by the fast moving events after the sack of Tibet in 1959. And even after that, it has failed to take the nation into confidence about dimensions of the likely disaster and give a call to the people to get prepared for all eventualities. A tremendous lot could have been done during these three or four years to redress the military imbalance and discipline the nation to face and fight a fierce enemy if the worst came to the worst.

The small group which agitates for "action now" is sure that a show of strength will not lead to a general war between India and China. They suspect that, in all probability, China is playing a bluff and probing how weak-willed or determined India is at present. They advocate, therefore, that China's bluff should be called. In their estimation, that is the best way of avoiding a war now as well as in the long run. India should, they say, better take a chance of avoiding a war at present by a positive show of strength than make it inevitable in the long run as a result of unilateral appeasement. They add that if it does not turn out to be a bluff and becomes an all-out war, India should go ahead and fight it out before China gets further entrenched and is in a position to move armoured divisions into the arena. There is, they say, as much chance of India winning this war as of China winning it. Due to the peculiar nature of the Himalayan terrain, they argue, the over-all military imbalance between India and China is not of practical importance and if the issues are joined immediately China is not in a position to move into the arena more infantry divisions than India can do from her own side.

There may be some substance in this chain of arguments, but it is certainly mixed up with a lot of ill-informed enthusiasm. To start with, the entire argument hinges on an altogether unproved hunch that China may be bluffing and may quietly take a beating at isolated points where she has penetrated or is trying to probe into Indian territory. It is assumed without any fuller finding of facts that India today is quite capable of carrying out such an operation immediately and simultaneously at all points of her encounter with the adversary. All in all, we are asked to shut our eyes to the wider implications of a war with China. It is assumed arbitrarily that such a war will not involve the use of air force and remain confined to infantry action in the mountain fastnesses. India today is supposed to be capable of fighting and winning such a war though no grounds are given in support of such a supposition.

Apart from the inner inconsistencies and unwarranted assumptions contained in this reasoning as a whole, its perspective of India's long-term policy is more or less out of focus. The long-term intention of India's policy should not be to risk and wage a war successfully. On the contrary, India should do everything in her power to avoid a war and wait and work for peace in collaboration with whatever international effort in this direction may be afoot at any time. No doubt, India must be fully prepared to wage a war and win it in case it is thrust upon her in spite of her best efforts to preserve peace. But India should never take chances and provoke a war by miscalculation about the intentions of the enemy. It may sound very brave to talk of taking a war in our stride. But it is the limit of irresponsibility to miss the point that a war in our times is always likely to become a catastrophe beyond all human calculation.

III

This, then, is the proper perspective in which India's future policy has to be planned—preservation of peace with China so far as possible and preparedness to fight and finish successfully any war that may be forced on us. This is the perspective which must first emerge in the political mind of India before she takes into account any international developments. And the emergence of this perspective does not depend upon any outward circumstance, either in the international arena or in the political scene at home. Primarily, it has to be an effort of national will — an intellectual effort to walk out of the welter of sloganised sentimentalism and into the sunshine of a world vision which relates the highest type of idealism to the hardest of all realities; an emotional effort to look at ourselves not through the eyes of a national press pre-occupied with penegyrics but through the eyes of other nations, big and small, around and away from ourselves; and, above all, a moral effort to be able to stand for truth, justice, equity, friendship, loyalty, honour, and international rule of law instead of confusing all these values with the wishes or whims of Big Powers, as we have been doing hitherto.

Let us remember that India is not a small nation like Nepal or

Afghanistan or Switzerland to plead that no amount of strength she builds up out of her own resources will ever have much of a meaning in the world balance of military power. Let us remember that India is the second biggest country in terms of manpower and one of the four or five foremost nations in terms of industrial and military potential. If India looks into herself, her innermost soul, and senses the sources of her own intrinsic strength, she can become a formidable power capable of preserving not only her own independence and integrity but also of contributing to the cause of world peace. But if she fails to awaken to her own innate potentialities and persists in harbouring the illusion that her own frontiers as well as world peace will be preserved automatically by the competing interests of the Big Powers, she will surely fail and betray the trust which her hoary history has laid on her shoulders.

Meanwhile, we can analyse the international alignment of forces and find out for ourselves as to who between the USA and the USSR is likely to be our ally in the context of our quarrel with China. It is high time that we stopped this stock-taking of world politics in terms of professions made by the two Big Powers about their own policies and programmes, as we have been used to doing till today. It is high time that we took a close look at contemporary history and formed our own objective estimate of the goals which these Big Powers seem to have set for themselves, as also of the means and methods they employ for achieving those goals. The foreign policy of India, whatever be its own inspirations and aims, has to be projected on the canvass of world realities as they exist at present and are likely to be in future, rather than on wishful thinking about what those realities should be.

Ever since Comrade Zhdanov of Soviet Russia divided the world into two irreconcilably opposed camps—the camp of "socialism and peace" led by the Soviet Union, and the camp of "imperialism and war" led by the United States of America—in his Warsaw Speech in the Autumn of 1947, most of us have been inclined to take such a division for granted. Some of us may have changed the labels and described the USA as leader of the camp of "democracy and freedom", and the Soviet Union as leader of the camp of "totalitarianism and slavery". But the basic belief that the world has become divided into two camps between which an ideological strife is the primary inspiration for manoeuvres of international power politics, has sunk very deep into the minds of most of us.

And it is this basic belief which has been, consciously or unconsciously, colouring the greater part of our thinking about political issues including the foreign policy of India.

Now, it can be admitted that till very recently the Soviet claim that she is leader of the camp of international Communism has been quite true. There *has* existed, till recently, such a monolithic entity as the camp of international Communism and its head as well as heart has been located in the Kremlin at Moscow. The Soviet Union has been, in effect, in more or less complete control of nations that have been taken over by communist parties, no matter whether she exercised that control through ideological indoctrination, or through use of brute force, or through a combination of both devices. There has also been an international communist party line projecting a single world-view and a single world strategy, proclaimed and practised by every communist party of the world irrespective of the national situation in which the communist party concerned has had to exist and function.

But the same cannot be said about the other camp—the camp of "imperialism" or "democracy" or whatever else one may like to call it. The monolithic communist camp has all along been faced by a veritable mob of independent, semi-independent, and slave countries—some of them big or powerful and others small or powerless—amongst which there has not been anything in common except a cynical seeking of narrow national interests. Whenever a nation has been threatened by communist intervention from outside or a communist subversion from within, it has cried for help from non-communist nations, particularly America, and started seeing and advocating the need for an international anti-communist alliance which should strive to contain or conquer the communist camp. But whatever nations have remained free from such a threat, they have seen no harm in collaborating with Communism within its own borders as well as abroad, feeling all the time that it is too clever or too strong to be undermined in the process.

As regards the leadership of this so-called anti-communist camp, though the United States of America has all along laid claim to it, she has seldom lived upto her profession in practice. If we collect all relevant facts from the history of nations that have gone down in the face of communist onslaught, we can construct a pattern of American policy which has been fairly constant.

To start with, America encourages and sides with the communist movement inside a country and invariably uses her material resources as well as her propaganda power to strengthen and extend that movement. If there is any one thing which America hates from the bottom of her modern heart, it is the native nationalism of a country which alone is, in the last analysis, the armoury on which that nation can count in the face of the communist menace. America denounces that native nationalism by every method at her disposal and tries her utmost to see it defeated at the earliest, not only by propping up its communist enemy but also by pouring into the country concerned her own avalanche of an animal culture. America's hatred for whatever anti-communist movement may come up spontaneously from within a country, has to be known in order to be believed. The army of American scribes and spies let loose over the world lampoons and lambasts the native anti-communist of every sort, while enormous amounts of American money are spent in order to raise and maintain a motley crowd of mercernary "anti-communists" controlled and manoeuvred by the most unintelligent of all intelligence services — the Counter-Intelligence Agency (CIA) in Washington.

In the next stage, as soon as a country is caught in the communist flood and starts sliding towards the Iron Curtain, America uses its helplessness as an opportunity to reduce it to the status of a slave to be ordered about and abused and maligned according to every passing mood of her own massive but mad press at home. Finally, that country, mauled as it has been by the communist man-eater in the meanwhile, is sold over to the communist camp in the name of saving world peace or some other such excuse. The entire operation is given a finishing touch by a White Paper or a Senate Hearing in which chest-beating over her own mistakes is mixed up with self-congratulation for accepting the inevitable and extricating America out of a hopeless situation which no one could have helped.

That is the record of America from Eastern Europe to China to Korea to Viet Nam to Laos. It is the record of a nation sick with an incurable malady — treachery and foul play towards her friends, and a fawning and cringing fondness for her foes. If some nations in Europe and Asia have survived the plague of American friendship, it is simply because they had within them greater resources of inner strength than could be sapped by America. If America has failed to sell some of her friends in the international stock market of cowardice and cupidity, it is not because she had some scruples about it but simply because the nations concerned asserted themselves in time and saved themselves. It is, therefore, arrant nonsense to say that America is leader of any anti-communist camp in the arena of world politics.

It will be the most disastrous day in India's long history if she ever came to depend on America either due to a mistaken belief that America can be her friend in time of need, or due to an overt situation in which she is driven to the wall on account of her own lack of will and has no course left open except that of walking into the American trap. Let no one in India befool oneself with the hope that America will be willing or able to save her from calamity if she gets caught in one. American policy will be true to its pattern again, not because there is a conscious calculation behind it, but because there is the whole complex of American culture and thought and way of life as its ultimate source and support. Conscious calculation can be changed, but a culture cannot be cured except over a period of time which is irrelevant in the present context.

IV

But that is not to say that India should not seek and obtain America's assistance — moral, material, military, and diplomatic — whenever and in whatever degree such assistance is available. America is an arsenal of material strength from which India can pick up practically everything she needs for her short as well as long-term build-up. But that arsenal is accessible only to those who are capable of showing some strength of will and, above all, a sense of self-respect in their dealings with America. India will be able to avail herself of American might and material resources exactly in proportion to the strength she builds up from within, particularly the strength of a national character which knows no compromise on basic principles. That is the line which India should adopt in all her relations with America, present or future. While India should give up repeating, parrot-like, those slogans about America which she has borrowed from the communist camp—including the slogan that America is an inevitable ally of nations trying to counter Communism —she should learn from the experience of other nations, particularly Nationalist China, in their relations with America.

The one lesson which the experience of every nation that has gone down with the help of America is that India should never burn her boats with the Soviet Union. China would not have been what she is today if the Chinese Nationalists had not shown such consistent loyalty towards America which, consequently, felt free to sell them down the drain. Viet Nam and Laos would not have been in the plight in which they find themselves today if they had not shown such helpless dependence upon American aid and if they had bargained for an honourable settlement with the Soviet Union as well. India should take note and refuse to follow in the footsteps of these nations, whatever the shape and size of the emergency she encounters at present.

No doubt, it is very difficult to deal with the Soviet Union which has based its strategy so far on Lenin's famous dictum — "we support Mr. Henderson as the rope supports the hanged man". No doubt, the Soviet Union too has her own deadly designs and dirty methods to force nation after nation behind the Iron Curtain through the instrumentality of her communist parties. No doubt, a country should be extremely cautious in bargaining with the Soviet Union and in no case an extension of the communist network within its borders should be a part of that bargain. But, after all is said and done, the Soviet Union is still easier to deal with in terms of a consciously conceived policy because she herself has a consciously conceived strategy behind all her world operations. The Soviet Union at any time is managed by one mind with which a purposeful dialogue is possible, unlike in the case of America which thinks and moves like a mob all the time.

Fortunately for India, the Soviet world strategy at present is showing some cracks through which we can peep in and explore the possibility of a purposeful dialogue. It can be assumed in ali certainty that the international communist camp is no more the monolith it had been till recently, and that Russia and China are seriously at loggerheads over a number of issues including the issue of leadership inside the communist camp. Russia is, therefore, and for reasons of her own, not likely to look favourably on whatever steps the Chinese communists take to increase their power or prestige in the arena of world politics. On the contrary, Russia is more likely to try to frustrate such Chinese efforts till the Chinese surrender and fall in with the Russian Line. There can be no peace within the communist camp till the supremacy of the Kremlin over that camp is restored back to its earlier position.

But as it is inconceivable that China can be dealt with by Russia in the same way as Poland or Czechoslovakia or Hungary were dealt with, the chances are that the breach between the two will widen with the passing of each day. India should not hestitate to turn every such breach in the communist camp to her own advantage, including the offer of arms and ammunitions from Russia. In exchange, India can very well collaborate with Russia over those foreign policy issues where Russia happens to be following a line which is objectively consistent with India's own foreign policy purposes. But all the time, India should go on building up and augmenting her own strength so that she may not be outmanoeuvred by any sudden turn in Sino-Soviet relations.

One such likely turn can be an open breach between Russia and China and a consequent cold war which both of them may try to heat up on the peripheries by using such pawns as they can find. Russia will, in that event, like to push India into a war with China so that China may be weakened and India softened sufficiently for an eventual takeover by the Communist Party of India. The Party will, in that event, leap up with patriotic cries of an immediate showdown with China. We know that the giant communist machine in this country is quite capable of mobilising our public opinion for such a mad adventure. We should be consciously prepared for such an eventuality and refuse to pull any Soviet chestnuts out of the fire. While we should be prepared to fight a war if one is forced on us, we should refuse to be pawns in the political game of any Big Power. The best course will be to keep a careful watch on the communist movement within the country while we get ready for all emergencies. That will also enhance our own manoeuvring power and leave us free to shape and pursue a policy design of our own choosing.

INDEX